OTHER BOOKS BY HOWARD R. CROUCH

*Relic Hunter, The Field Account of Civil War
     Sites, Artifacts and Hunting*

*U.S. Small Arms of World War 2: A Guide for
     the Collector, Shooter and Historian*

*Virginia Militaria of the Civil War--Buttons,
     Buckles and Insignia*

The Author

CIVIL WAR ARTIFACTS

A Guide for the Historian

Howard R. Crouch

SCS Publications

ACKNOWLEDGEMENTS

The author is indebted to the many individuals who have allowed him to photograph their collections for this work. Foremost among these is Richard Hammond, whose collection of fine artifacts has added immeasurably to the scope of the book.

Special thanks to Bob Buttafuso, Steve Hall, Terry Heilman, Tom and Mike McLaughlin, Mike Singer and Chuck Thompson for allowing their collections to be photographed and for their steady input of relevant data.

The importance of the contributions of Michael J. O'Donnell of O'Donnell Publications has been invaluable. Many of the photographs used herein were taken by him at numerous shows across the country.

The bulk of the period photographs are courtesy of various archival sources of the U.S. Government.

Further, the author's deep appreciation goes to the following individuals for their generous assistance.

Kevin Ambrose
Benny Atkinson
Steve Baker
Bob Boden
Danny Boston
Butch Brown
Robert Brown
Charles Burnett
Ron Callahan
Raleigh Cassidy
Denny Chafin
Ed Cheslock
Robert Coli
Kenny Copelin
Dennis Cox
John Craig
Giles Cromwell
Richard Crouch
Sonny Crumpler
Bruce Daigle
Ray Davenport
Charles Ergman
Dave Garrett
Peter George
David Goodman
John Graham
Rod Graves
Paul Hammond
Charles Harris
Nick Harris
Donny Hayden

Bert Hayes
Jim Hemphill
Dan Hoffman
Kevin Hooper
Sarah Hill
The Horse Soldier
  of Gettysburg
Gary Indre
Dennis Irvin
Paul Irvin
John Jackson
Tim Jenkins
Steve Johnson
Chuck Jones
Joe Kadora
Mike Kehoe
Lon W. Keim, M.D.
Wendell Lang, Jr.
Lewis Leigh, Jr.
William Leigh
Randy Lewis
Jim Livesay
Ronnie Mantlo
John Marks
Andy Martin
Miles Micciotto
Ken Mooney, Jr.
Dave Morrow
Jim Moser
Steve Mullinax
Chris Nelson

Mark Olsen
Steve Pittman
Sanford Potts
Lloyd Pugh
Dalton Rector
Tim Ridge
George Sempeles
Ray Shaw
Joe Sorah
Doug Stein
Fred Stevens
Larry Swift
Steve Sylvia
James Thomas
Ken Turner
Barney Tyree
Harry Visger
The VMI Museum
Kevin Walls
Nancy Weber
Kenny West
Sam White
Gary Wilkinson
Jim Wilson
Gary Williams
Jim Williams
Kevin Williams
Tucker Williams
Oliver Wood

Additional thanks to: Annette Barr, Joe CanoleJr., Perry Cummings, Jim Livesay. Jim McNew, Bobby Payne and Lou Reid.

For My Family

INTRODUCTION

For four years the Civil War raged back and forth across the South, leaving much of the land ravaged and barren. Great battles had been fought across what once had been peaceful farm fields, leaving them covered with broken equipment, ordnance, gear and bloody discarded uniforms.

Huge forests had been turned into endless campgrounds with once stately oaks and pines turned into rough winter cabins or burned for warmth. Between the stumps the soldiers slogged through mud, churned to great depth by teams of mules and horses drawing supply wagons and artillery pieces. Here too would be left great amounts of cast- off, worn out clothing, cartridge boxes, belts and bullets. Into trash pits and dug out latrines would go bottles, crockery, lice infested uniforms, and garbage. Buttons, coins and personal items would be lost in the dirt- floored huts.

Routes of march, picket posts, temporary camps (often in farm house yards) would also become the repository for the endless variety of items lost in the backwash of the armies. With the end of the war in 1865 the survivors on both sides returned to their homes and nearly all of these sites returned to their peacetime appearance. The deep siege trenches and fortifications around such places as Petersburg, Richmond, and Vicksburg would exist well into the 20th century, as would hut-site excavations in the deep woods, all being leveled out with the passing of time.

On some of the battlefields, civilians would scour the brush and thickets for any relic that had been missed in the immediate post battle gleaning by the victorious army. Those sites within an easy carriage ride of town, such as Manassas and Gettysburg, saw an endless stream of these visitors. Many of them were veterans, now organized as the G.A.R. or U.C.V. Some of the sites were so large, thickly wooded and remote that even this was hardly done. A good example was the Wilderness Battlefield in Virginia, where only the farmer's cleared, plowed fields would turn up the spent bullet, shell or bayonet.

It seems though, that by the early 20th Century, with the First World War and the passing of the old veterans, what lay beneath the Civil War fields was almost forgotten. Only the aforementioned farmer, piling up the "junk" in field corners, or the poor who searched the fields for spent lead bullets to sell as scrap, had any concern for the relics at all. The 1930's and early 40's saw a small surge of interest in the recovery of artifacts, particularly in Virginia, where plowed fields could be walked for bullets and trenches could be shoveled out and sifted.

All of this was quickly changed after World War II with the availability of the Army mine detectors now available as surplus. They were heavy, clumsy and not particularly sensitive but they did work. The 1950's would see more sophisticated machines and the concurrent enormous rise in interest due to the approaching and well publicized Centennial.

Hunters, even in those early days, realized that the Federally owned battlefields, where hunting was prohibited, held only a fraction of the relics to be found. As we have pointed out before, the large camp and bivouac areas were well removed from the battlefields, and small skirmish sites were numerous. These were often well recorded as to location in the large number of reminiscences and regimental histories written by the old veterans themselves. Armed with the general location, a topographical map and a compass, the early hunters began finding scores of the old sites.

Although for a number of years the hobby was quite small, numerous finds were made, bringing to light specimens of bullets, buttons, shells, plates etc. that no then-living person could identify. The few books on Civil War material offered illustrations and data on only the most basic of equipment and nearly all of that was on the traditional US equipment.

By the late 60's and early 70's the hobby was growing more sophisticated, helped along by the new transistorized Metrotech detector, which was a giant step ahead of most earlier machines. Since that time well over one hundred reference books have been published by hunters and collectors on many specific fields of Civil War equipment. The author's first book, *Relic Hunter, The Field Account of Civil War Sites, Artifacts and Hunting*, (1978) was the first work to give a comprehensive overview of each site, from research to location, and an enumeration of artifacts found.

Since that time an enormous number of Civil War sites have been built over and probably nowhere more so than in Northern Virginia. The huge, first winter cabin camps and forts at Centreville are under asphalt parking lots and shopping centers. Nearby, most of the Ox Hill Battlefield is under town houses. As of this writing, Brandy Station, the site of the largest cavalry battle ever fought in this hemisphere, is slated for a large auto racetrack. The story is the same in every direction and indeed in every state.

The artifacts shown in this book come from the shores of the Atlantic to the trans-Mississippi states. They are the product of hundreds of thousands of hours in the field by many individuals. In some cases the location in which an artifact has been found will be noted; space permits only a few. However, most hunters do list all finds in carefully kept field books.

Artifact or relic hunting is a field which the general public knows little about, and this is what allows them to accept the bad press and often distorted picture that is painted of it. The story is often the same; because a few misguided individuals choose to break the law by hunting on off-limits Federal land and are caught, by inference other hunters are suspect.*

Far outweighing the above, the public is often not aware that across the country each year, many Civil War historical organizations hold large shows full of complex educational exhibits based on excavated artifacts--all widely advertised and open to the public. Additionally, well over one hundred books have been published by hunters and collectors, sharing with readers the knowledge they have gained in the field.

The search for these artifacts is at once a science and often a demanding work, for nearly always the best finds have belonged to those individuals who would do the endless research in the printed word, with the map, and then in the woods itself. Often the site is never found or it will have been developed long since. The site, in many cases, after the war, may have been plowed, covered with broken pieces of barbed wire fence, shotgun shells, modern foil, cans and the occasional fallen-off tractor part, then plowed again assuring a good mix.

It is quite unreasonable to assume that in this age of shrinking budgets any governmental agency is really going to send a $500-per-hour archaeological team into a situation like this to recover even more articles (all of them made during the machine age), in most cases on private land, when the publications of the relic hunters are already in most public libraries detailing and discussing their finds.

Further, adding to a small time window, unlike Indian arrowheads and pottery fragments, the thin brass Civil War plate or insignia or the pewter eating utensil that is still there undergoes an inexorable, steady degrade in condition, particularly under limed or fertilized fields.

The artifacts shown herein have been saved from that fate and they speak to us across time of a period in American history which is long gone but lastingly remembered.

* **NOTE:** IT IS STRICTLY ILLEGAL TO HUNT OR BE IN POSSESION OF A METAL DETECTOR ON NATIONAL BATTLEFIELD PARKS AND ALL OTHER FEDERAL AND STATE PROPERTY. Fines and penalties can be severe. It is the individual's legal responsibility to know the boundary lines and any other laws concerning the collecting of historical artifacts in a given situation. Much battle area and bivouac land is in private hands and may be searched with permission. When an artifact in this book has been attributed to a certain battle area it has come from such land.

FOREWORD

Webster's defines relic as "an object, custom, etc., that has survived wholly or partially, from the past; often something that has historical importance because of its age and associations with the past, or that serves as a keepsake or souvenir of the past."

Accurate yet broad, this definition merely hints at the emotions that cause people to keep relics. And it is these complex emotions that have resulted ultimately in the vast collections that fill our nation's museums. Visitors seldom realize that most of the artifacts they view on display were gathered painstakingly, often piece by piece, and donated to these repositories. Museums generally cannot afford to purchase items for display, nor can they afford to send archaeologists into the field to excavate artifacts for their collections. Instead, they must rely on donated or loaned relics for their exhibits. Each artifact was preserved, often by successive generations of private owners, as a reminder of an event that had instilled the jubilation of conquest, the sorrow of loss, or simply the celebration of survival.

It appears to be an element of human nature to keep and preserve relics whether they be family heirlooms or even otherwise insignificant items that remind them of important events. Archaeologists have uncovered proof that early man occasionally kept items that were not peculiar to his culture or day-to-day environment

Americans are no exception to this ancient custom, and in our culture there is no better example than artifacts of the American Civil War. Since the first day of battle in April 1861, Americans have preserved and revered souvenirs of the war, testifying to the significance of that devastating conflict. The soldiers and civilian witnesses to the war gathered relics by the thousands. From battle flags to bullets, nothing was too insignificant to keep as a memento of a great battle because the relic itself was not nearly as important as the event that it related to.

Unsurprisingly, the collecting of relics from the War Between the States continued after the war. Newspapers and magazine articles through the end of the 19th century testify to the efforts expended by aging veterans and battlefield visitors in their quest for relics on the old battlegrounds. Small museums blossomed at the few northern battlefields and throughout the war-torn south, established more often than not by veterans. The great early chroniclers of the war offered further testimony to the continuing practice well into this century.

With the 20th century development of the electronic metal detector, the search for relics buried beneath the soil began to flourish. Today, the battlefields and campsites of the Union and Confederate armies are disappearing rapidly as the relentless tentacles of progress reach further and further into the once remote areas occupied by these troops. Contemporary relic hunters are the last group who will be able to venture into the woods and fields in search of relics of those stalwart Americans who wore the blue and the grey. A few years hence, there will be few areas left to yield such artifacts.

In the pages that follow, Howard Crouch presents an exciting array of relics rescued from extinction by members of this hardy band of amateur archaeologists. The stories they tell recall those days of glory and valor, of pride and sacrifice, when our nation passed its final test of endurance.

Stephen W. Sylvia
Orange, Virginia
March 1995

TABLE OF CONTENTS

1 STORIES FROM THE SOIL

Above: Winter 1995. A scenario which could be duplicated almost anywhere in the southeastern US. A bulldozer has taken a hilltop off, next to a main Civil War era maneuver area and route of travel, in this case marked by the roadside power lines at left. Smeared into the hilltop among the exposed and twisted tree roots is a mix of metallic junk going back one hundred and fifty years. If there is a story here only the patient and hardworking hunter will find it -if- there is time before another five feet of earth is quickly taken off and the area is paved over. **The Find:** A lucky one for these days; a beat-up US boxplate amidst a bunch of period nails. No real story to be told; monetarily worth little, it is just one of many thousands of like specimens that once were plentiful. It simply shows "that they were here".

1

2

1. In June of 1861 the newly-formed Confederate forces under General Beauregard had massed behind Bull Run where they were attacked by Union troops under General McDowell. Both armies felt that this could be the decisive battle that could decide the war. Groups of civilians including members of Congress came out from Washington with picnic baskets to watch the battle from the high hills to the east. Shortly they were caught in the hurried retreat of the Union Army. Wagons and carriages were stampeded and overturned. This engraved tag to an unknown chest or box was found at the scene.

2. After the battle of Ball's Bluff many of the wounded were taken to an area off of the field. It is recorded that local civilians tended the wounded by candlelight. This 1830's period candlestick was found there.

"December 23, 1864
*   We finally got orders to go into winter camp and build cabins. We are on Dr. Harvey's farm about 4 miles back from the river and 3 miles from the Central Railroad. Short rations and not much firewood...."*

Above: A dozer clears a portion of a huge tract of woods for a golf course community in central Virginia. Shown below are two real prizes to the historian who has long searched for this site. **1.** The hunter notes the early, irregular brick, a good sign but not yet definitive. **2.** The next find would pass completely unnoticed by most, as nothing but a piece of scrap tin. The experienced hunter quickly notes the seamed edges and distinctive solder lines which identify it as part of a cartridge box tin, a good sign of one time military occupation.

Left and Above: The only remnants of an early home site in a woods near Gravelly Springs, Alabama, where some 25,000 Union cavalrymen wintered in 1864-65. Soldiers often visited nearby farms and this one was no exception. This is the bottom of a shoulder scale "pan" found close by. Cut-in are the initials of an unidentified trooper. Initials are occasionally seen on artifacts; in the days when no ID tags were issued this often could be a soldier's last chance for identification on the battlefield.

1. The hard-riding Confederate cavalry left much behind also. This is a CS two-piece sword belt buckle with remnants of its belt. **2.** A pair of CS spurs found in a trashpit. When unearthed almost all of the boots were there; note the heels and strap fragments. From Shelbyville, Tennessee.

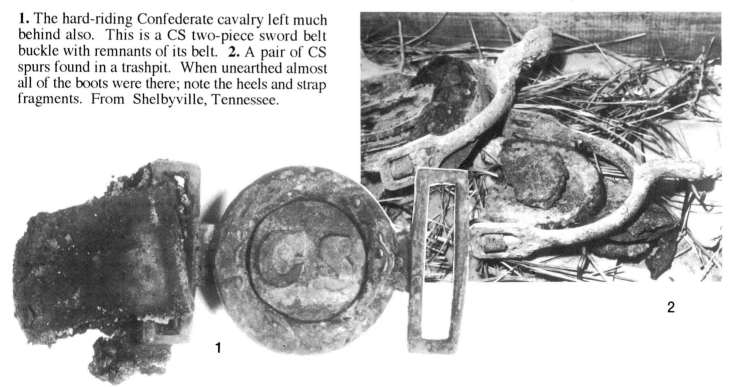

1

2

Above: A familiar sight on any newly cleared spot is northern Virginia, country blues singer John Jackson, an old time hunter. He is holding the "RG" plate he found and also shown at center. It came from an early-war site once occupied by the 1st Regt., Virginia Volunteers, one of whose companies was the Richmond Grays. Conclusive ID on the unique plate would come ten years later when this picture of the pre-war Grays came to light. The soldier at left clearly wears an identical one. **Below Right:** One of three bottles excavated from a pit, all filled with pistol bullets.

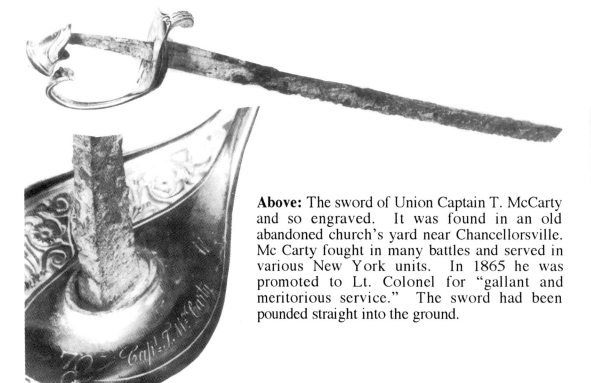

Above: The sword of Union Captain T. McCarty and so engraved. It was found in an old abandoned church's yard near Chancellorsville. Mc Carty fought in many battles and served in various New York units. In 1865 he was promoted to Lt. Colonel for "gallant and meritorious service." The sword had been pounded straight into the ground.

2 CAMP ITEMS

Above: Members of the "Clinch Rifles" a pre-war Georgia unit, in camp. Their folding chairs, camp chests, and other extra equipment would be left behind as the war progressed. **Inset:** Two iron rings, 2"wide, used to reinforce the tops of tent poles. They are common camp finds. **1.** Frame to a small travel clock. **2.** Portion of an iron stove about 14"x20", depicting a country scene of a child chopping wood with a cabin in the background.

1

2

Nos. 1&2. These two buckles were found on the same site, probably dating to the mid 1700's. No.1 is about 4" long and roughly made of iron. It was almost surely a piece of draft horse equipment. In contrast, the small apparel buckle No. 2 is made of silver plated pewter and only about 1&1/2" long. The site was located in the middle of a large Civil War camp. Most buckles of the Colonial period are of recognizable styles and are shown elsewhere in this book.

3. This row is composed of commonly found iron buckles, with and without rollers and shown actual size. Many of those found are from horse's harness simply because of the sheer number of them so used. Even if found on Civil War sites, a number of them were of course lost either before or after. Some, if found with a McClellan saddle, pack parts, the remains of a cartridge box etc., can be specifically identified.

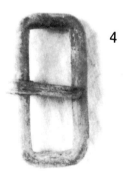    

Nos. 4 through 7. All shown actual size. 4. These solid brass buckles are most likely from rifle slings. 5. This is a silvered harness buckle with a distinct curve often found in CS sites. 6. These are well made brass specimens that have been identified as having been on some type of general issue waist belt. There is some indication they were used on imported British packs also. 7. A well made brass buckle of an often seen pattern which varies in size. These were used on the shoulder slings of many pre-war haversacks.

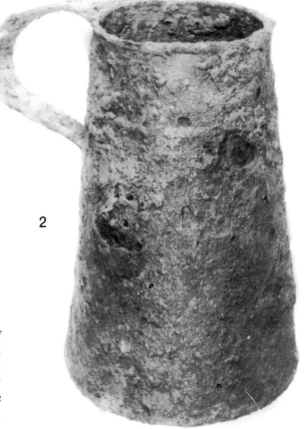

Coffee was of great importance to the soldier. Frequently the beans were issued green and had to be parched in a frying pan and then crushed. By mid-war it was rarely seen in the South. **Nos. 1&2.** Standard issue type pots or "boilers" as they were known to the troops. They average about 9" high and were usually made of sheet iron. **3.** A large tin cup turned into a pot by adding a heavy wire bail.

ELLSWORTH'S ZOUAVES

COOKING DINNER.

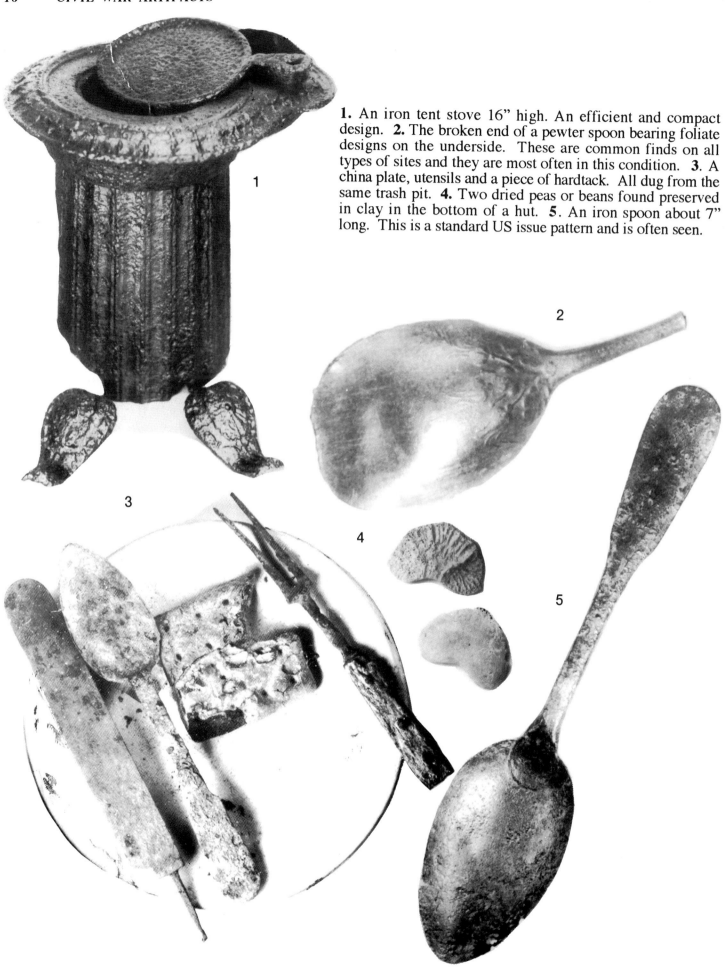

1. An iron tent stove 16" high. An efficient and compact design. **2.** The broken end of a pewter spoon bearing foliate designs on the underside. These are common finds on all types of sites and they are most often in this condition. **3.** A china plate, utensils and a piece of hardtack. All dug from the same trash pit. **4.** Two dried peas or beans found preserved in clay in the bottom of a hut. **5.** An iron spoon about 7" long. This is a standard US issue pattern and is often seen.

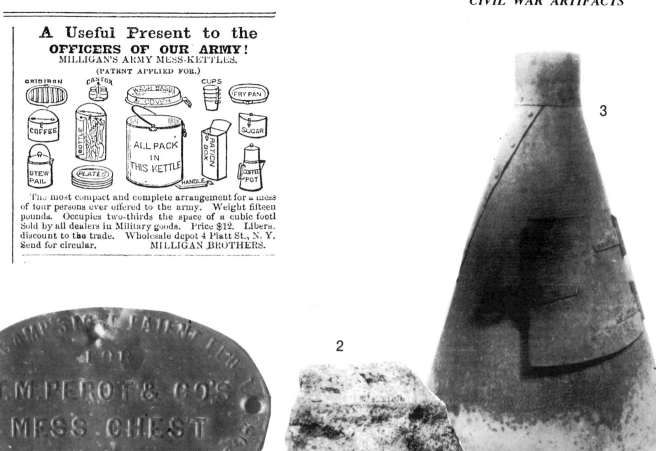

1. A commercial mess chest tag.   2. The ever present piece of broken iron pot; note the curvature and "rib".   3. The famous "Sibley" tent stove, made of sheet iron. Though obviously valuable to the troops, some are found in camps where they were probably left behind for want of transportation.   4. Various patent water purifiers, generally filled with powdered charcoal and attached to a rubber hose.   5. From a CS commissary site in Centreville, Va., this end of a large beef bone shows the butcher's saw marks.

1. A bone handled fork. **2.** A field-made fork. **Nos. 3,4&5.** Various issue type tin cups. **6.** A pewter tankard, engraved "WHM" found in the rocks around a spring between the lines at Chancellorsville in 1932. **Nos. 7&8.** Large butcher knives.

1. An iron mess plate and utensils from the same Union trench at Cold Harbor. **2**. A large iron cook's spoon about 14" long.

3. A silver teaspoon marked "Fauquier White Sulphur Springs", a resort of the Civil War period near Warrenton, Va. It was found in a Union campsite some thirty miles away and was probably "liberated" from the resort's hotel. Close-up shown above. **4.** Another silver teaspoon, this one from a CS camp. It was furnished by and marked "Mitchell and Tyler", a famous Richmond firm that supplied all types of military goods and other items.

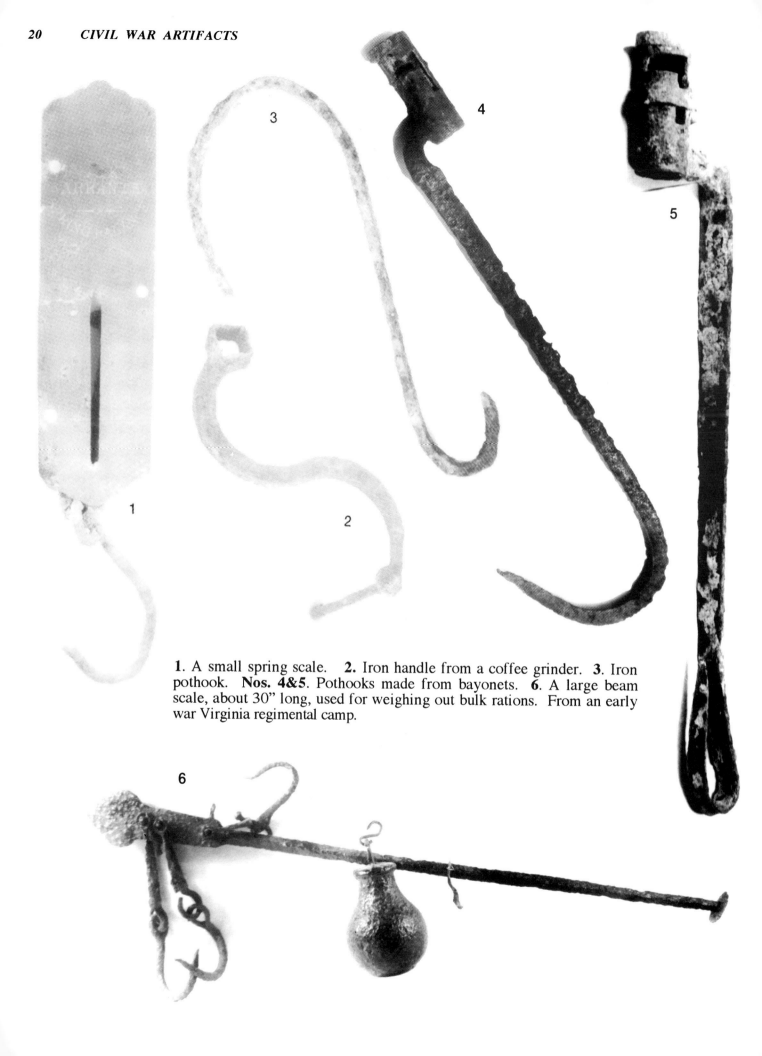

1. A small spring scale.   **2**. Iron handle from a coffee grinder.   **3**. Iron pothook.   **Nos. 4&5**. Pothooks made from bayonets.   **6**. A large beam scale, about 30" long, used for weighing out bulk rations.   From an early war Virginia regimental camp.

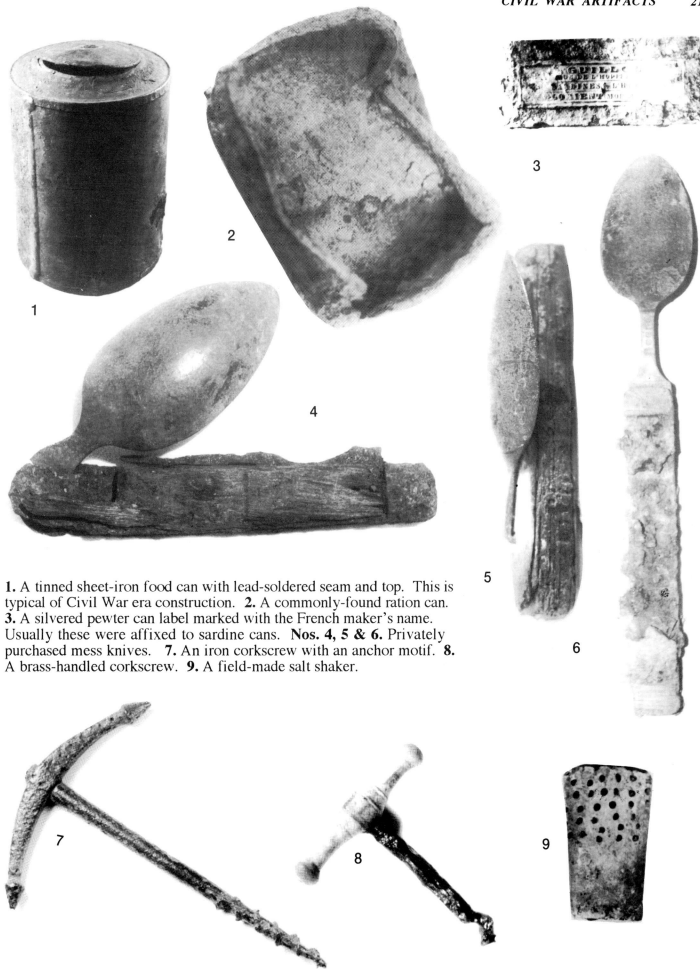

1. A tinned sheet-iron food can with lead-soldered seam and top. This is typical of Civil War era construction. **2.** A commonly-found ration can. **3.** A silvered pewter can label marked with the French maker's name. Usually these were affixed to sardine cans. **Nos. 4, 5 & 6.** Privately purchased mess knives. **7.** An iron corkscrew with an anchor motif. **8.** A brass-handled corkscrew. **9.** A field-made salt shaker.

1. A large sheet copper pot with rolled edges and riveted-on handles. 2. A heavy cast iron Dutch oven marked "STARKE 3". The "3" is its capacity in gallons. It was found in a Louisiana winter camp buried deeply upside down and had originally been wrapped in a poncho. The inside was coated with grease as a preservative. 3. A standard issue type steel frying pan about 12" in diameter.

1. Found in a Union trash pit near Culpeper, Va. this fine bottle is marked "Lediards-Wheat-Restorative". **2.** The typical Civil War whiskey with an obvious seam and applied lip. **Nos. 3&4**. An unusual whiskey with a glass screw cap. Marked "Weeks&Potter-Boston". Top is marked "Pat. Jan. 1861". **5.** One indicator of early glass of many types is typified by this inkwell. Note the broken off glass stub on the base called a "pontil mark". These were hand blown through a tube from a glob of molten glass, then a solid "pontil rod" was attached to the base while the lip was formed. When the rod was snapped off it left this mark. **6.** A "US Navy" marked food bottle. **Left:** Union officers at mess in the field. Note the bottles on the table.

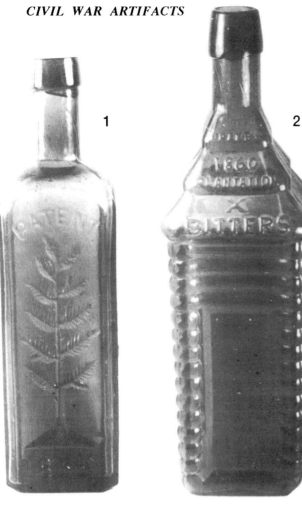

Bitters were popular Civil War products. Sold basically for their medicinal value, they contained a fairly high alcohol content. Since the manufacturers paid lower taxes on bitters versus liquor, they could sell them cheaper. **1.** A "Pine Tree Bitters" bottle, bearing a stylized embossed pine tree. **2.** The famous "S.T. Drake's / 1860 Plantation Bitters" made in a log cabin design. **3.** "Old Cabinet 1850 Rye" **4.** "Brown Stout" (beer). **5.** This pontil marked drinking glass is a rare find as they were normally not seen in the field. **Nos. 6&7.** Two white china cups, both dug in Union camps.

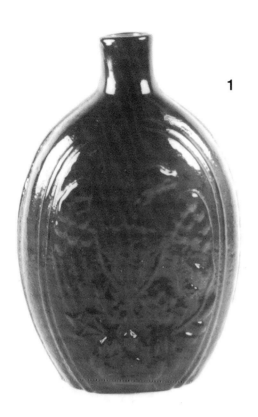

The flasks shown and others similar are among the most prized of American antiques. In most cases they were originally sold empty and were often used for carrying spirits. **Nos. 1&2**. These are classified as "pictorial" flasks and carry eagle motifs. **3.** This is a "historical" flask that shows a bust of Gen. Zachary Taylor, "Old Rough and Ready". **4.** One of a series of various size medicine bottles marked "U.S.A. Hosp. Dept.". Like most all bottles, the colors in these will also vary.

5. A small embossed pocket flask. Typically they carried the maker's name and address but were often blank. **6.** These four small, embossed bottles are of the type that was used for cosmetics, medicines etc.

1. A food jar with glass closure device. **Nos. 2,3 &4.** Various sizes of cathedral bottles used for pickles, honey, sauces etc. **5.** A "patent" metal jar top.

6. This fine barrel mustard was found near Manassas. Marked "N. W. Upperman Mustard Factory". This and many other sauces made the field butchered meat more palatable in camp. **Below:** From Harpers Weekly, a product of long lasting popularity.

LEA & PERRINS'
Worcestershire Sauce,
EXTRACT
of a Letter from a
MEDICAL GENTLEMAN
at Madras
TO HIS BROTHER
at Worcester,
May, 1850.

PRONOUNCED BY
CONNOISEURS
TO BE THE
Only Good Sauce
and applicable to
EVERY VARIETY
OF DISH.

"Tell LEA & PERRINS that their SAUCE is highly esteemed in India, and is, in my opinion, the most palatable, as well as the most wholesome SAUCE that is made."
JOHN DUNCAN & SONS,
Union Square and Fourteenth Street, Sole Agent.

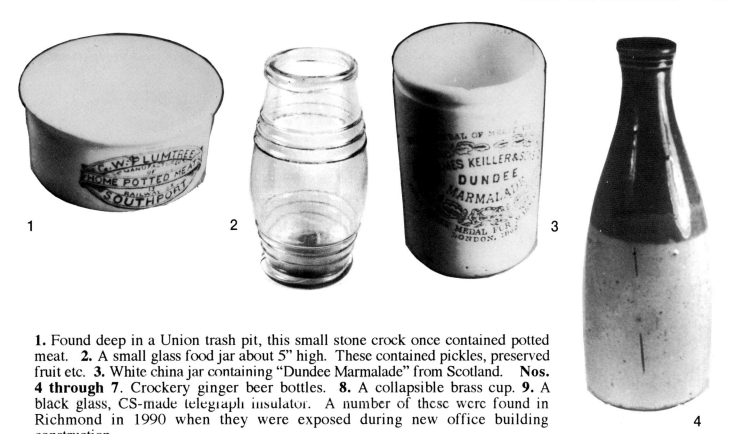

1. Found deep in a Union trash pit, this small stone crock once contained potted meat. **2.** A small glass food jar about 5" high. These contained pickles, preserved fruit etc. **3.** White china jar containing "Dundee Marmalade" from Scotland. **Nos. 4 through 7**. Crockery ginger beer bottles. **8.** A collapsible brass cup. **9.** A black glass, CS-made telegraph insulator. A number of these were found in Richmond in 1990 when they were exposed during new office building construction.

1

2

The stoneware shown here has been painstakingly reconstructed from pieces sifted out of CS hutsites near Manassas. The pieces were cleaned, sorted, then glued back together. **1.** A food jar, 8&1/2" high. Marked "Milburn-Alexandria, Va." **2.** A 1/2 gallon whiskey jug, marked "D.H.and Son, Lexington Courthouse, S.C." **Inset** shows the marking on another jug denoting a two gallon capacity.

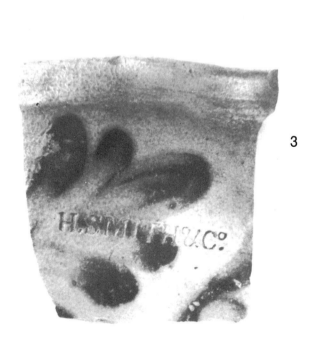

3

4

3. This piece of stoneware was found in the leaves in a CS camp. Marked "H.Smith & Co." This was probably an Alexandria, Va. maker. **4.** This milk pan measures 11" wide and was in only a few pieces.

Above: A silver fountain pen, excavated in a Union campsite and a small glass inkwell, which is still full of dirt as found. Despite the fact that they are quite fragile, "inks", as they are called, were once fairly common finds in Union camps. This is due to the large numbers that were used and left behind.

1. Eight-sided "umbrella " inkwell, the type most commonly found on Civil War period sites. Found in shades of blue, green, brown and most often in a light aqua; about 2" high. **Nos. 2&3.** Very small square and round inks. **4.** "Tea kettle ink". The spout would have taken a brass cap. **Nos. 5&6.** Hard rubber inks. **Nos. 7&8.** Cylindrical crockery inks, of brown clay with a glazed finish. **9.** Crude CS- made unglazed clay ink. Many of these show flaws and imperfections in manufacture.

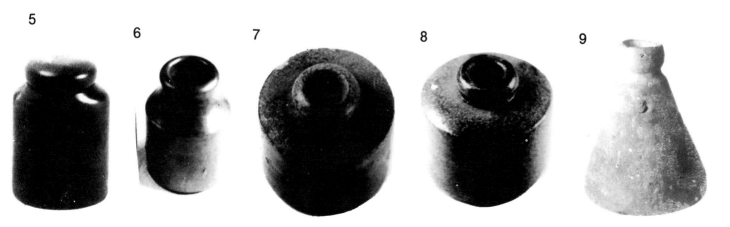

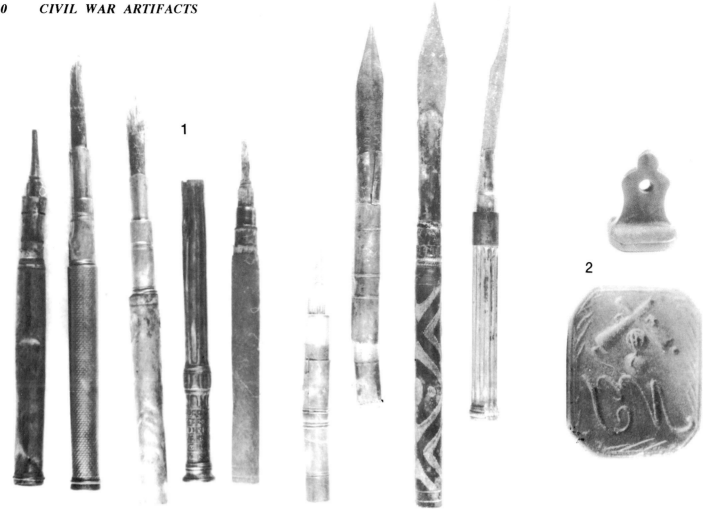

1. Many variations of collapsible mechanical pencils, inkpens and combinations of both. 2. A wax seal, used for sealing documents, letters, etc. Inset of face shows crossed cannons and the letters "N.J." 3. Pencil sharpeners of brass and pewter. 4. Brass case containing pen points. 5. Silver fountain pen, found in a soldier-carved wooden case on the mud flats at Belle Plain, Va., a large Union supply depot. 6. Portion of a writing slate inscribed with the initials "J.W."

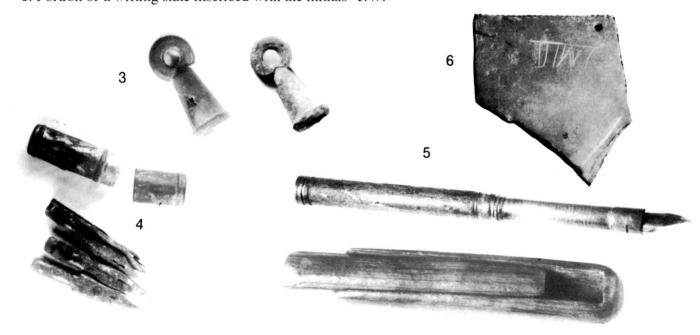

SUPPER AFTER A HARD MARCH.

1. Clay pipe bowl in the shape of a man's head wearing a turban. This type of pipe took a separate reed stem. 2. Carved soapstone pipe bowl from a CS camp at Union Mills, Va. 3. Decorated clay pipe bowl. 4. Two views of a rare white clay pipe showing patriotic designs and a banner reading "Washington via Baltimore". This specimen would date to the very opening days of the war. 5. This is obviously a sailor's pipe.

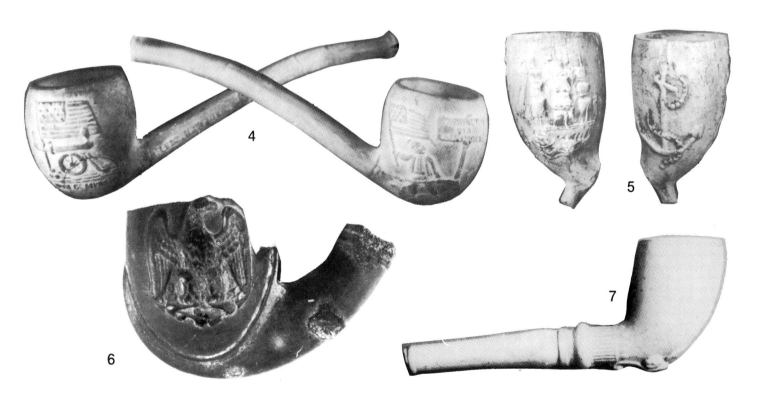

6. A rare hard rubber pipe with an eagle design. The wooden stem is missing. 7. A clay pipe with the typical broken stem. Being very fragile, few intact specimens are recovered.

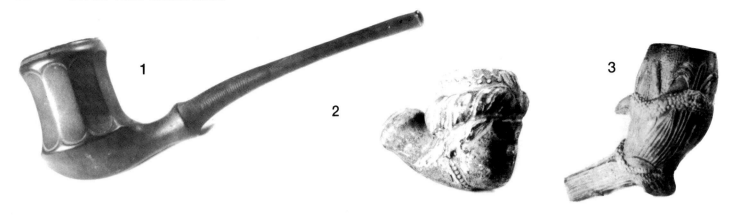

1. Hard rubber pipe, marked "Goodyear-1852".   **2.** Clay pipe, missing wooden stem, bearing a woman's face. **3.** Clay pipe, foliated design with encircling snake. **4.** Very large and rare pipe bowl formed of sheet brass lined with wood. The face is probably a representation of General G. B. McClellan. **5.** Unusual white china pipe bowl bearing three women's faces. **6.** Brass pipe bowl covers. The lower one is silver plated.

7. Brass match case engraved with eagle. Still carries original matches. **8.** Match safe of sterling silver. From a Union position on the Chancellorsville battlefield.

1. Crockery toothpaste container, dug in a camp trash pit. **2.** Remains of a toothbrush, typically made of bone. This one faintly stamped with maker's name. **3.** A similar item. **5.** Leather guard, used to slip over uniform button before polishing. Found in the mud at Harrison's Landing, Va., at low tide. **4.** Small pocket shaving mirror. **6.** Hard rubber comb. **Nos. 7&8.** Soldier-fabricated lead combs. **9.** Folding pocket comb of hard rubber.

Above: Soldiers' stencils belonging to men of the 126th Pennsylvania Volunteers, 36th Wisconsin, 32nd Maine, 123rd New York, 7th New York Volunteer Artillery and the 48th Pennsylvania Veteran Volunteers. In many cases, stencils are found cracked or broken. Most were made of thin sheet brass but a few are of pewter.

1

2

Top: Soldiers' stencils from the New York Heavy Artillery, the 32nd Maine Regiment and the 157th New York Volunteers. Stencils of this type are rather scarce finds and their use seems to have been limited to US troops. The author has never noted a CS unit marked stencil. **1.** Set of individual brass stencil strips. **2.** Small ink bottle and brush container as used with soldiers' stencils.

3

3. 3" x 3" brass stencil plates, used in the field for marking boxes, barrels, etc. Found at a Union supply depot in Tennessee. Part of a nearly complete set, some carry remaining traces of black paint.

1. Two straight razors found with honing stone, the latter often made from petrified hickory. **2.** Straight razor with hard rubber grip. **3.** No doubt the possession of an officer, this small collar iron is shown actual size.

4. A large pair of scissors, found with Louisiana buttons in a hutsite. **5.** Two brass thimbles, one silver plated. These are common to most every camp or housesite. **6.** Large steel pin. Often called a blanket pin.

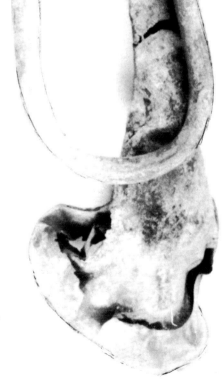

Above: Union musicians. **1.** A Union cavalry bugle, marked "Horstmann , Phila." on the bell. This die strike is so small as to almost pass unnoticed on an excavated item. From a US cavalry camp in Alexandria, Va. **2.** The crushed front portion of a US "regulation style" bugle; from the Seven Days battle area near Richmond. **3.** Turned brass mouthpiece to a horn or bugle.

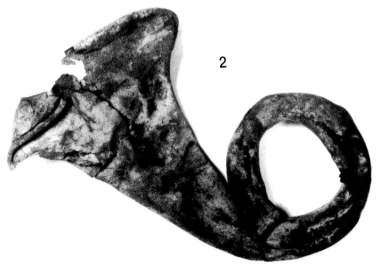

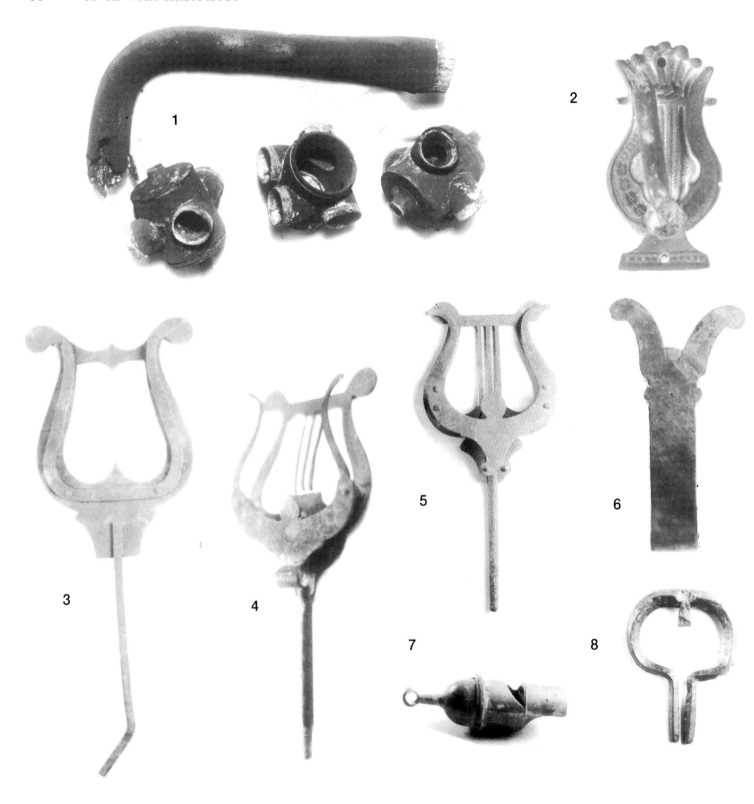

1. A piece of broken tubing from an unknown horn and three valves from the same instrument. **Nos. 2 through 6.** Music holders that attached to instruments. The workmanship and finish on some of these pieces must be seen to be appreciated. **7.** A small pewter whistle with a lanyard hole. These are occasionally called horse whistles and that is possible. More likely most of these are simply hunters' dog whistles lost over the years **8**. Jew's harp of brass.

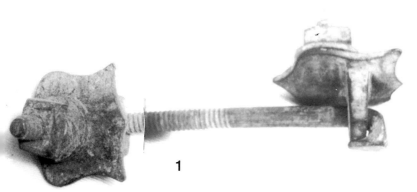

1. A brass drum head tensioning device, one of a number mounted around the drum. **Right:** Two Union infantrymen pose on either side of their unit's drummer.

Nos. 2&3. Intact brass harmonicas and unusual in that respect. Both of these are German imports. **No.2.** is marked "Gebr. Ludwig's Emmet Professional", so named for the famous Dan Emmet who popularized the song "Dixie". **4.** A heavy reed plate from a harmonica and made of pewter. **5.** Two brass reedplates. These are common finds on all types of sites of the Civil War period.

Various lead objects found in camps. **1.** A spike too soft to have served any practical purpose. **2.** 4" long cannon tube with bore and touchhole. **3.** Two lead sinkers; these are often seen items. **4.** Finished and unfinished figure fours. **5.** Snake and man representations. **6.** A very detailed claw hammer head about 1" long.

7. Poker chip from a South Carolina camp bearing a palmetto tree. **8.** Another, with a scratched-in tree. **9.** Bullet bearing the initials C.A.L. **10.** A ring or other object. **11.** A horseshoe. **12.** .69 cal. ball marked "Rebel". **13.** A Maltese cross or Union Fifth Corps badge. **14.** Counterfiet pewter 1853 quarter. **15.** An 1817 cent in mid conversion to a spur rowel. **16.** Brass hand-cut letter A. **17.** Head cut from a coin.

1. A brass lantern complete with glass from a CS fort in the South. 2. Pieces of oil lamps, very common campsite finds. Many will carry patent dates and maker's marks. **Nos. 3&4**. Folding iron keys. **5.** A large brass key with a roughly engraved tag. **6.**This brass candlestick was found in a Stafford Co.,Va. Union winter camp. **7.** These were popular among the troops and about the ultimate in portability for a candlestick. The point could be driven into the nearest log. **8.**This iron candlestick came from a hospital site at Cold Harbor.

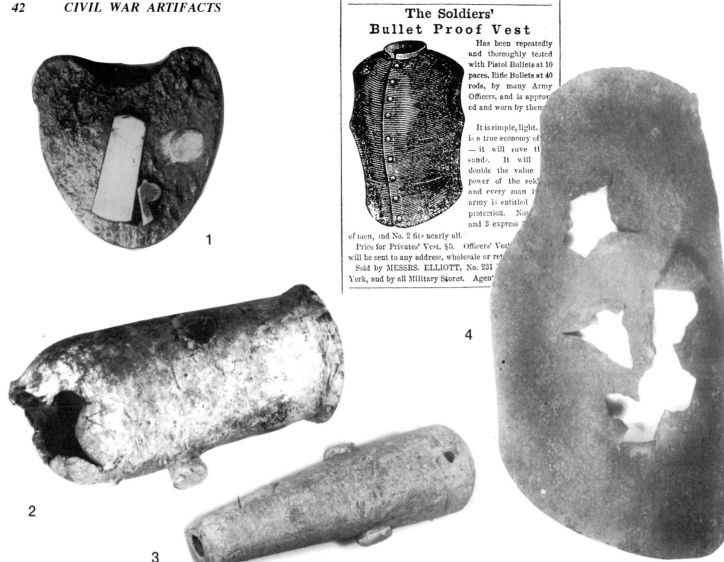

**The Soldiers'
Bullet Proof Vest**

Has been repeatedly
and thoroughly tested
with Pistol Bullets at 10
paces, Rifle Bullets at 40
rods, by many Army
Officers, and is approv-
ed and worn by them.

It is simple, light,
is a true economy of
— it will save th
sands. It will
double the value
power of the sold
and every man i
army is entitled
protection. Nos
and 3 express
of men, and No. 2 fits nearly all.
Price for Privates' Vest, $5. Officers' Vest
will be sent to any address, wholesale or ret
Sold by MESSRS. ELLIOTT, No. 231
York, and by all Military Stores. Agen'

1. Iron padlock, struck with .44 caliber pistol bullet, embedded to the right of the fly. **2.** Small field-made lead cannon with rear blown out. **3.** Similar lead cannon. **4.** One half of a set of iron body armor, purposely destroyed. These items are fairly rare as their use was not widespread. Note advertisement from "Harpers Weekly". **5.** Iron carpetbag frame with attached brass lockplate. Dug in a Virginia infantry camp near Fredericksburg. Engraved "Robert C. Randolph". Records indicate that he was later killed in the battle of Cedar Creek.

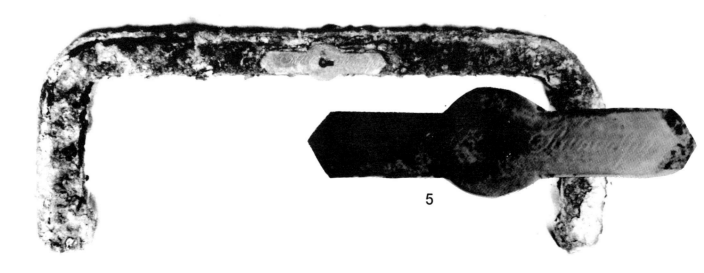

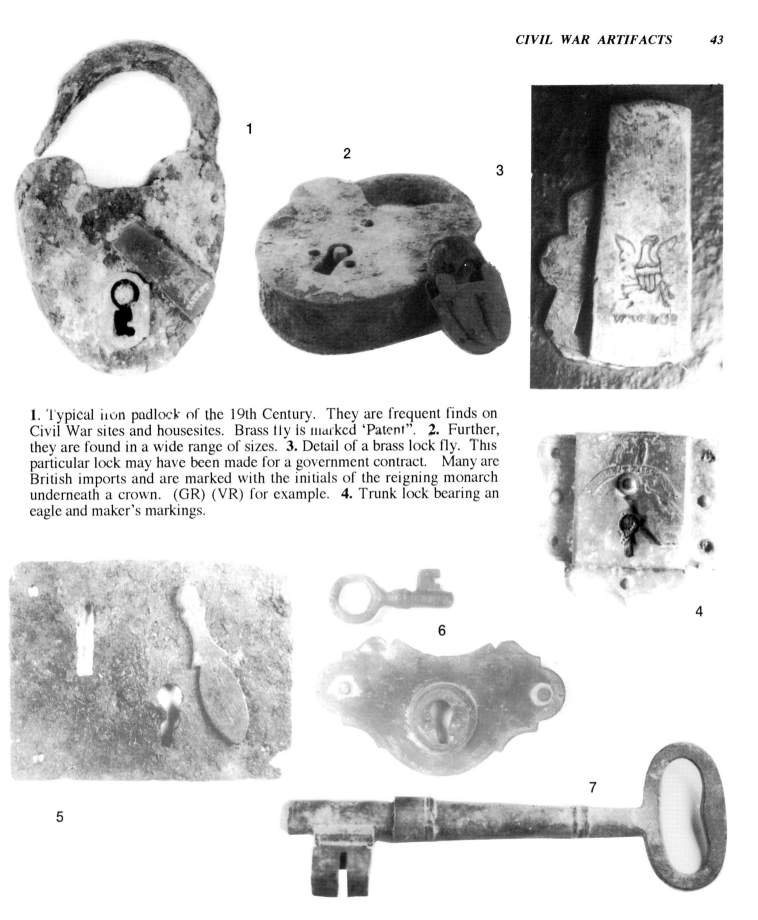

1. Typical iron padlock of the 19th Century. They are frequent finds on Civil War sites and housesites. Brass fly is marked 'Patent". **2.** Further, they are found in a wide range of sizes. **3.** Detail of a brass lock fly. This particular lock may have been made for a government contract. Many are British imports and are marked with the initials of the reigning monarch underneath a crown. (GR) (VR) for example. **4.** Trunk lock bearing an eagle and maker's markings.

5. The iron front plate to a door lock, with attached brass fly. **6.** Brass trunk lock and key found together in an Alabama infantry camp. **7.** Heavy brass key about 7" long. These were obviously souvenirs taken from houses.

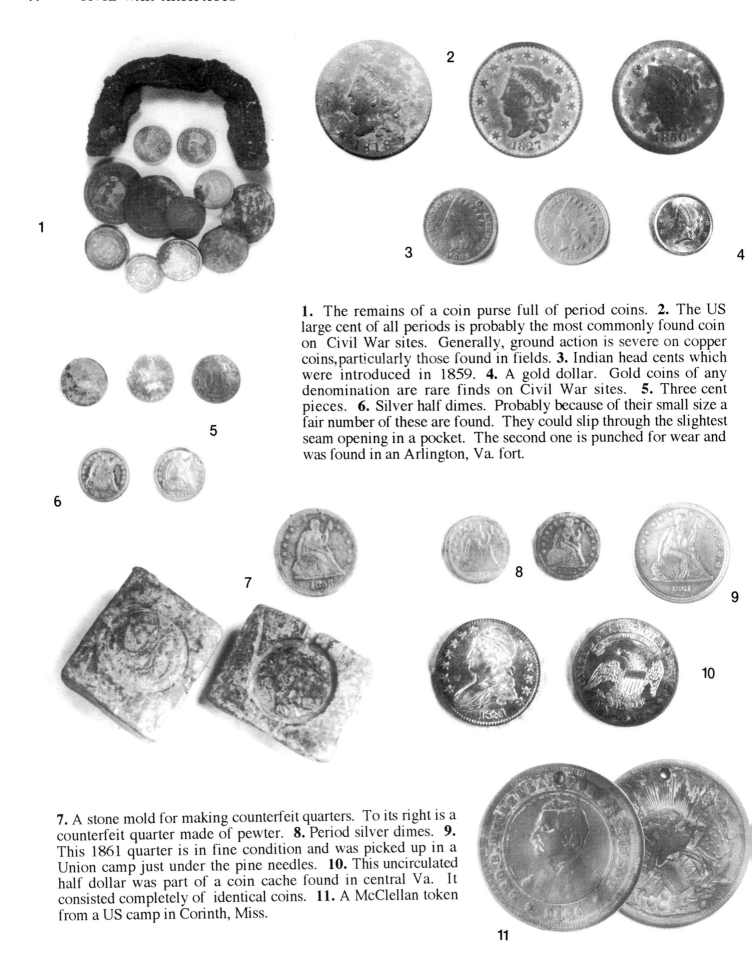

1. The remains of a coin purse full of period coins. 2. The US large cent of all periods is probably the most commonly found coin on Civil War sites. Generally, ground action is severe on copper coins, particularly those found in fields. 3. Indian head cents which were introduced in 1859. 4. A gold dollar. Gold coins of any denomination are rare finds on Civil War sites. 5. Three cent pieces. 6. Silver half dimes. Probably because of their small size a fair number of these are found. They could slip through the slightest seam opening in a pocket. The second one is punched for wear and was found in an Arlington, Va. fort.

7. A stone mold for making counterfeit quarters. To its right is a counterfeit quarter made of pewter. 8. Period silver dimes. 9. This 1861 quarter is in fine condition and was picked up in a Union camp just under the pine needles. 10. This uncirculated half dollar was part of a coin cache found in central Va. It consisted completely of identical coins. 11. A McClellan token from a US camp in Corinth, Miss.

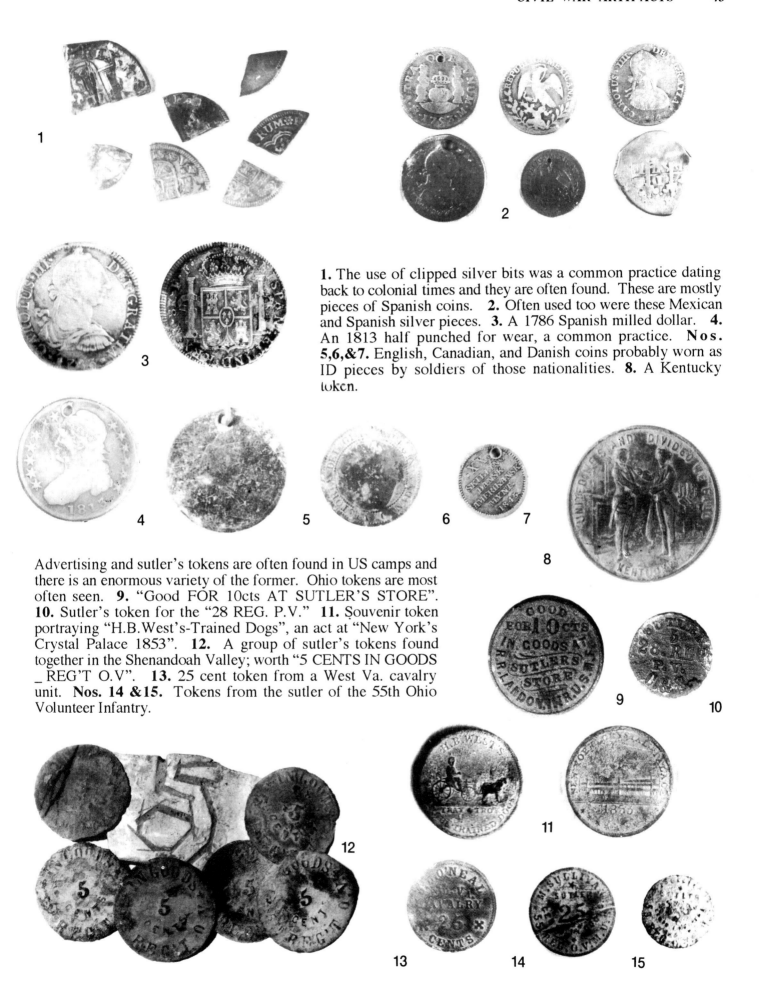

1. The use of clipped silver bits was a common practice dating back to colonial times and they are often found. These are mostly pieces of Spanish coins. **2.** Often used too were these Mexican and Spanish silver pieces. **3.** A 1786 Spanish milled dollar. **4.** An 1813 half punched for wear, a common practice. **Nos. 5,6,&7.** English, Canadian, and Danish coins probably worn as ID pieces by soldiers of those nationalities. **8.** A Kentucky token.

Advertising and sutler's tokens are often found in US camps and there is an enormous variety of the former. Ohio tokens are most often seen. **9.** "Good FOR 10cts AT SUTLER'S STORE". **10.** Sutler's token for the "28 REG. P.V." **11.** Souvenir token portraying "H.B.West's-Trained Dogs", an act at "New York's Crystal Palace 1853". **12.** A group of sutler's tokens found together in the Shenandoah Valley; worth "5 CENTS IN GOODS _ REG'T O.V". **13.** 25 cent token from a West Va. cavalry unit. **Nos. 14 &15.** Tokens from the sutler of the 55th Ohio Volunteer Infantry.

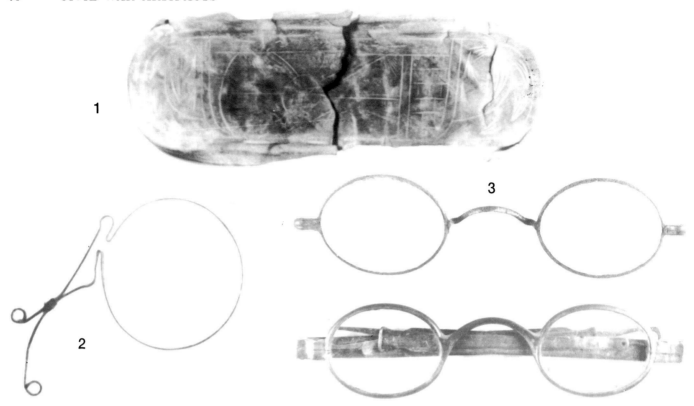

1. Eyeglasses case of thin brass with engraved ornamentation. 2. Monocle from a CS site in western Florida. This is the only excavated specimen noted by the author. 3. Two pairs of period eyeglasses, silver plated brass construction. These are also noted in solid coin silver.

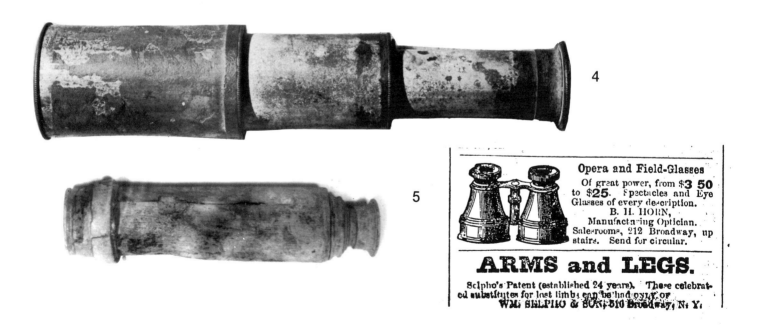

Opera and Field-Glasses
Of great power, from **$3 50**
to **$25**. Spectacles and Eye
Glasses of every description.
B. H. HORN,
Manufacturing Optician.
Sales-rooms, 212 Broadway, up
stairs. Send for circular.

ARMS and LEGS.

Selpho's Patent (established 24 years). These celebrated substitutes for lost limbs can be had only of
WM. SELPHO & SON, 516 Broadway, N. Y.

4. Large collapsible telescope, of the naval pattern, found near Ft. Blakely, Alabama. 5. Small field telescope, typically carried by officers. **Right:** While the officer could buy his field glasses from "Harpers Weekly" ads, the men on the opposite page would make better use of the second items advertised.

1. Large surgeon's bone saw, about 16" over all. **Nos. 2&3.** Steel friction tourniquets which worked with a woven cotton encircling band about 2" wide. **4.** Brass tourniquet device which was screw tightened. **5.** Portion of a brass tourniquet with maker's name and Hospital Dept. markings. Note that medical instruments of any kind are infrequent finds.

6. A brass plate once mounted on a surgeon's chest. Marked "U.S.A. Hosp. Dept". Found in the Wilderness. **Right**: Wounded soldiers, Fredericksburg, Va., May of 1864.

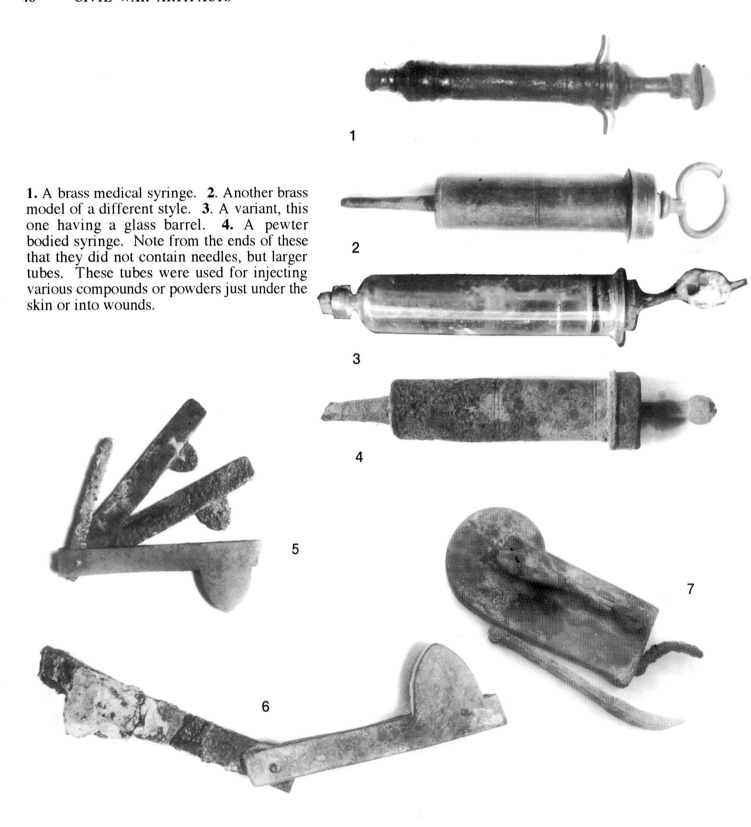

1. A brass medical syringe. 2. Another brass model of a different style. 3. A variant, this one having a glass barrel. 4. A pewter bodied syringe. Note from the ends of these that they did not contain needles, but larger tubes. These tubes were used for injecting various compounds or powders just under the skin or into wounds.

Nos. 5&6. Medical bleeders (or "fleams") of folding construction. The latter was dug near Ft. Pillow, Tenn. **7.** Bleeder with a spring loaded blade and triggering device. Supposedly this made the cutting operation less painful. The Civil War saw the last widespread usage of this dangerous and ineffective practice.

Right: A Union officer entertains a female visitor to camp. This is one explanation for the jewelry that is occasionally found on Civil War sites.

1. Gold gilt and cloisonne woman's dress belt clasp. This piece was undoubtedly made in Germany or Austria. Shown full size, the face exhibits multi-colored floral designs. Found in a Union cavalry bivouac, this may have been a memento from home or a piece from a local plantation. **2.** Sterling silver two-piece cape hook **3.** Locket **4.** Woman's belt clasp. **5.** Butterfly pin. **6.** Child's Ring.

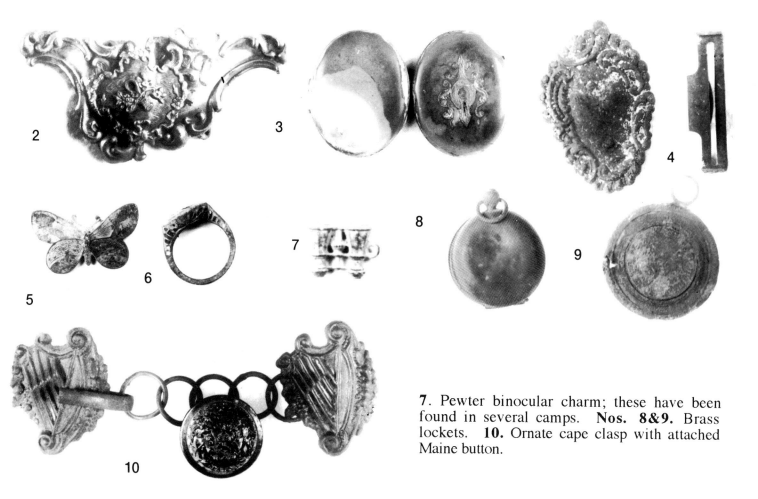

7. Pewter binocular charm; these have been found in several camps. **Nos. 8&9.** Brass lockets. **10.** Ornate cape clasp with attached Maine button.

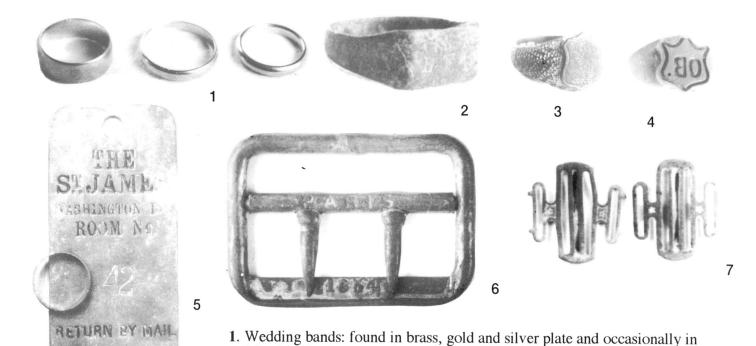

1. Wedding bands: found in brass, gold and silver plate and occasionally in solid gold. 2. Heavy cast brass ring of enormous size engraved on the face with two initials. 3. Ring engraved with a leaping kangaroo and presumably owned by an Australian. 4. Wax seal ring to impress the letters "O.B".

5. An untold story: Found together in a Confederate camp in Virginia - a room tag and ring. The ring is engraved "Darling". 6. A typical suspender buckle of the Civil War era. Actually 1" long, this specimen is gilted brass and marked "Paris" and "1854". 7. A pair of "Patent" suspender buckles and so marked.

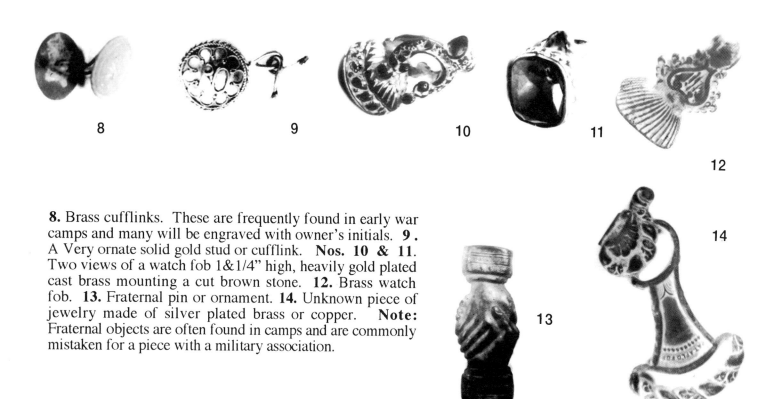

8. Brass cufflinks. These are frequently found in early war camps and many will be engraved with owner's initials. 9 . A Very ornate solid gold stud or cufflink. **Nos. 10 & 11.** Two views of a watch fob 1&1/4" high, heavily gold plated cast brass mounting a cut brown stone. 12. Brass watch fob. 13. Fraternal pin or ornament. 14. Unknown piece of jewelry made of silver plated brass or copper. **Note:** Fraternal objects are often found in camps and are commonly mistaken for a piece with a military association.

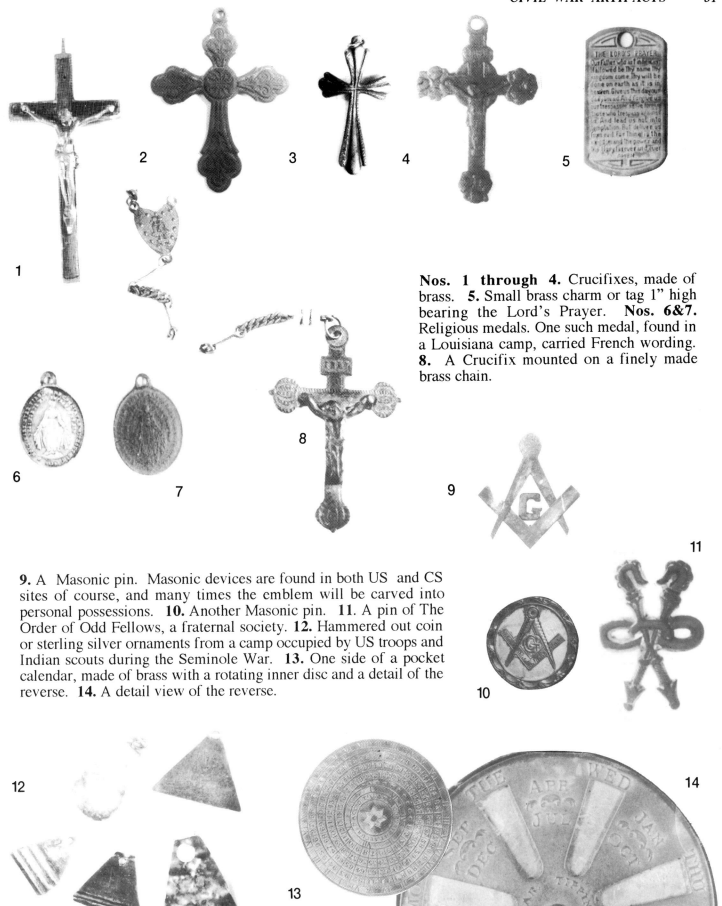

Nos. 1 through 4. Crucifixes, made of brass. **5.** Small brass charm or tag 1" high bearing the Lord's Prayer. **Nos. 6&7.** Religious medals. One such medal, found in a Louisiana camp, carried French wording. **8.** A Crucifix mounted on a finely made brass chain.

9. A Masonic pin. Masonic devices are found in both US and CS sites of course, and many times the emblem will be carved into personal possessions. **10.** Another Masonic pin. **11.** A pin of The Order of Odd Fellows, a fraternal society. **12.** Hammered out coin or sterling silver ornaments from a camp occupied by US troops and Indian scouts during the Seminole War. **13.** One side of a pocket calendar, made of brass with a rotating inner disc and a detail of the reverse. **14.** A detail view of the reverse.

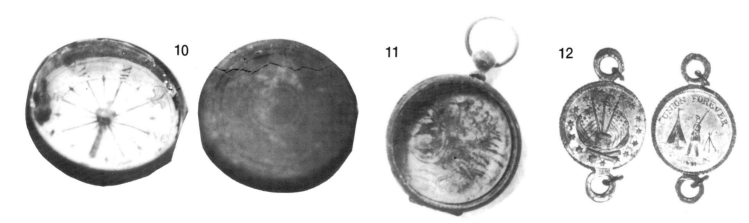

1. Locket bearing images of a man and woman, dug at Shiloh,Tenn. In most cases such dug images start a rapid degrade from the moment they come out of the ground. **2.** Pocket watch with hunting case made by "J. Tobias, Liverpool". **Nos. 3&4**. Watch cases. **5.** Watch key in the form of a musket. **6.** Fine quality, gold plated watch key with chain. **7.** Universal watch key of the type used by jewelers. **8.** Watch keys. **9.** Watch key bearing a coat of arms on one side and a squirrel on the other.

10. Brass pocket compass. **11.** Locket carrying pornographic etching of a soldier in uniform and a woman. **12.** Front and back of a finely made, gilted chain ornament showing flags, soldier and the motto "Union Forever".

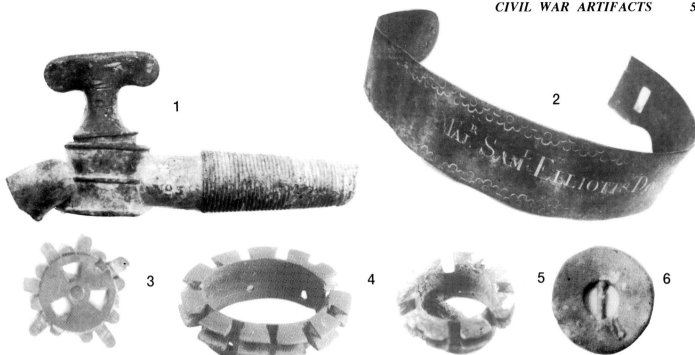

1. Pewter barrel tap. The scored tapered end fit into a matching hole at the bottom of the barrel. "No 3" is a size marking. **2.** Large brass dog collar for "MAJr SAMl ELLIOT'S DOG" and so marked. **3.** Brass "Patent" ventilator as sewn into the crown of hats. **Nos. 4&5.** Center portions of folding umbrellas, the use of which was common in the South for sun protection (among civilians). **6.** The commonly seen dress or coat hem weight; normally made of lead but very occasionally seen in brass. The design of these items was relatively unchanged for many years, and they are regular finds in Colonial to Civil War sites. In the latter Confederate areas they were probably used as buttons.

Nos. 7&8. Stamping dies that held and locked in lines of type. Used for marking equipment and clothing. **9.** Brass thimble from the end of a muzzle loading shotgun ramrod. **10.** Cast brass bell as occasionally used on civilian horse harness. **11.** Lead seal, made for sealing new bales of cloth and other goods. This one is marked 'Warrented-J.R.Taylor Co." and displays a square rigged ship. **12.** Tiny cast brass horse. Probably a child's toy and a memento from home. **13.** 1847 slave tag from Charleston, S.C. **14.** Fish hook made from a brass pack part.

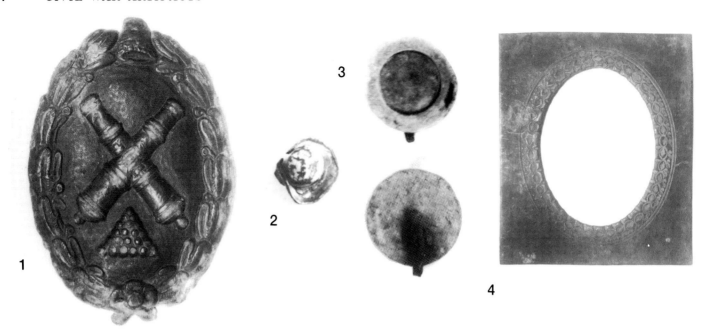

1. Bearing a military motif, the original use of this cast brass piece is unknown. **2.** Civil War period dime with embedded fired pistol bullet. **3.** Front and back of a stamped brass, lead filled, leather ornament with embedded attachment wire. Found in many sizes and designs, they were used on trunks, saddles, harness, etc. **4.** Gilted picture frame about 4" high.

5. A cast lead Louisiana buckle. A camp-made item, it carries no hooks. **6.** Lead poker chips with a penny shown for scale. **7.** Camp-made lead dice. **8.** A cast lead bar about 11" long marked "R.B.W. Co.D 11 VA". Also marked with a Masonic emblem.

1

2

Carved in stone: **Top**: This heavily moss covered rock was passed unnoticed for years - it has been brushed off and letters accented with chalk. Marked "Jas. Morrissey, Co. G, 123 N.Y.V." **1.** A carved soapstone "brick" bearing palmetto tree and soldier's initials from the camp of the 1st South Carolina at Manassas, Va. **2.** Tiny carved stone book, note penny for size. It may have been used as a whetstone.

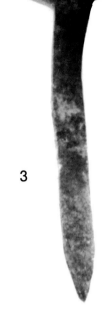

1. Brass keys to railroad padlocks. Many of those found will bear the markings of long defunct lines. **2.** Pewter token, given for fire wood supplied by citizens along the railroad. Marked "Eng. No 9 1/2 Cord". These were "chits" redeemable for cash or credit. **3.** Railroad spike. These are frequent finds in campsites near railroad lines where they were used as tent pegs or wood spikes. **4.** Engraved silver conductor's badge, a rare piece.

Above: Baggage tags found in camps. Early in the war much personal equipment and baggage was transported to troops in various positions. **5.** Marked "Through-Montgomery and Savannah". **6.** "C. R. R". **7.** "Richmond 3244 Lynchburg". **8.** "O.&A.R.R. Lynchburg 3240 Washington City". This was the famous Orange and Alexandria, which passed through much fought over territory. **Right**: An engine of the United States Military Railroad. The use of rail to transport supplies and troops was an important component of the war effort on both sides.

Above: Union soldiers aboard a troop train. **1**. Box car lock of brass with iron chain. Front marked "T. Blaigh-Agent" and rear marked "USMRR" (United States Military Rail Road). **2.** Car door seals of lead pressed around iron wire. Typically, they are marked "MRR" and the points of origin and destination. **3**. Railroad lock found at Manassas Junction. It was opened by CS troops without benefit of key, the body showing numerous hack marks. Stonewall Jackson's troops captured the Junction with its huge stocks of provisions on August 27, 1862. Records indicate that they broke into numbers of sidelined boxcars.

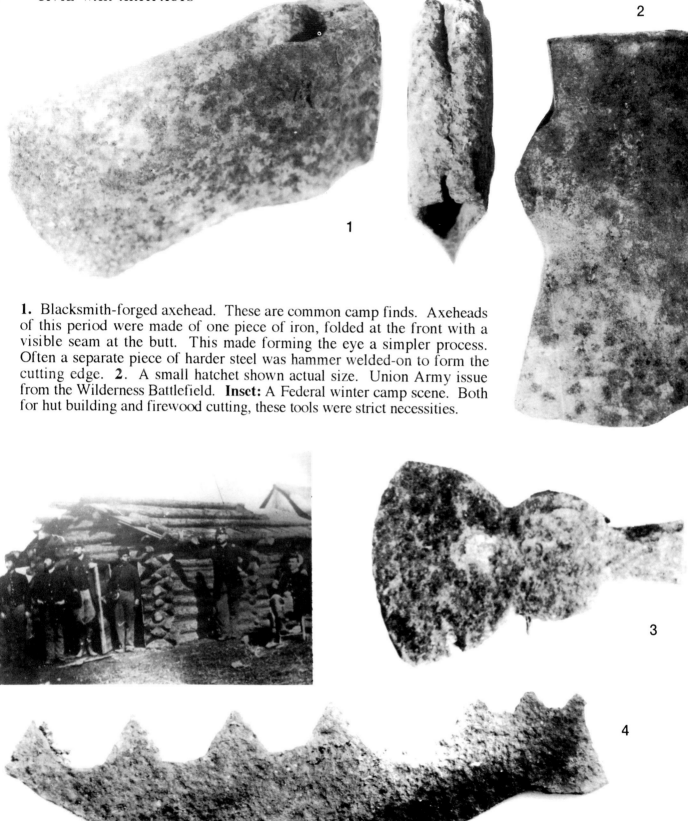

1. Blacksmith-forged axehead. These are common camp finds. Axeheads of this period were made of one piece of iron, folded at the front with a visible seam at the butt. This made forming the eye a simpler process. Often a separate piece of harder steel was hammer welded-on to form the cutting edge. 2. A small hatchet shown actual size. Union Army issue from the Wilderness Battlefield. **Inset:** A Federal winter camp scene. Both for hut building and firewood cutting, these tools were strict necessities.

3. Hatchet head 5" long. 4. Fragment of a large crosscut saw for working logs. This specimen was used in the construction of the CS winter huts at Manassas, Va. in the fall of 1861. Because it was the only portion found, it is possible the rest of the blade, along with the handle, was retained for use.

1. A 12" wide iron hoe head.   These are common camp finds in various sizes. **2**. Square nails of the period. **3**. Iron spikes 6" and 8" long, hand forged. **4**. Two iron or steel pick heads from a Virginia quarry site that was occupied by elements of the 123rd New York. They are both stamped with the quarry owner's name. **5**. Steel froe head, used for splitting out wooden shingles. **6**. Adze blade used for hewing logs.

1. Small brass frame for folding ruler. Wooden blades have rotted away. 2. Hammer head as used for working metal. 3. Iron plumb bob. 4. Brass socket from a carpenters brace. Right end took the base of a drill bit and the small hole took a set-screw. 5. Cobbler's or leather worker's hammer. 6. Brass rule and dividers set found in a CS camp. 7. Frequently seen brass discs, originally set in saw handles. Many times these will have an eagle motif and are mistaken for military items. 8. Heavy iron or steel bit to bore a 2" hole. 9. Steel gouge 10" long. It will be noted that Engineer and Pioneer troops carried such tools and many more. The contents of their company tool boxes were specified by Regulation.

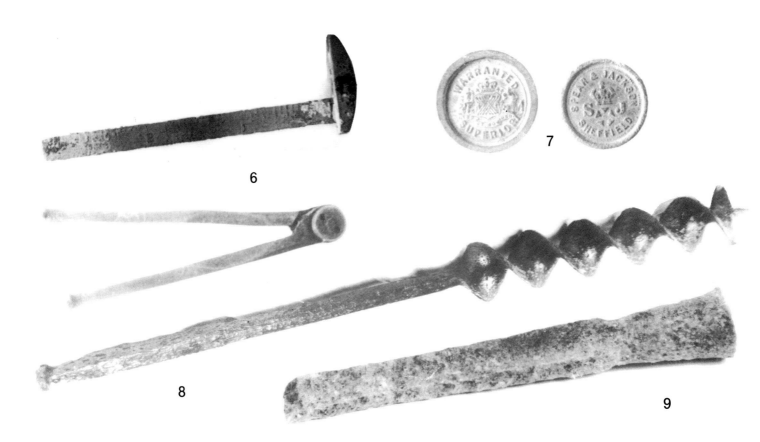

1. Typical iron shovel head of the period 9" wide. Such finds are not uncommon on Civil War sites, possibly indicating that tools with broken handles were simply cast aside during active campaigning. 2. A heavy iron wheel hub washer 4" in diameter. 3. Heavy iron wrench about 12" long. 4. Hand-forged iron tow hook. 5. Trace chain from a wagon, found in the stable area of the 6th North Carolina camp at Dumfries, Va. 6. One of a pair of hook assemblies that went on each end of a single tree. 7. Hand-forged wrench for a 2" nut.

Above: Sherman's men destroying railroad tracks by heating over a fire and bending. **1.** This iron device locked over the rail and a heavy pole was inserted to twist the rail as above. About 16" high. It should be noted that most rails of the period were smaller and thinner than modern ones and such destruction was easily done. **2.** A transit-like surveying instrument shown bottom and top. Precision made of brass bearing English markings.

3 WEAPONS & EQUIPMENT

1. A very rare and unique relic of the war. This is the triangular bladed lance head, 11" long, used by Rush's Lancers, the 6th Pennsylvania Cavalry. It tipped the end of a 9' wooden lance. 2. A detail of the lance socket showing the "US" markings. 3. A Confederate pike head as made during the opening months of the war. This one has a side hook or "bridle cutter". The uselessness of such weapons was realized early on. 4. This pike head of steel was found near Dumfries, Va., an area that once contained many CS camps. It is thought though that this piece dates to the war of 1812. 5. Brass butt cap as used on flagstaffs.

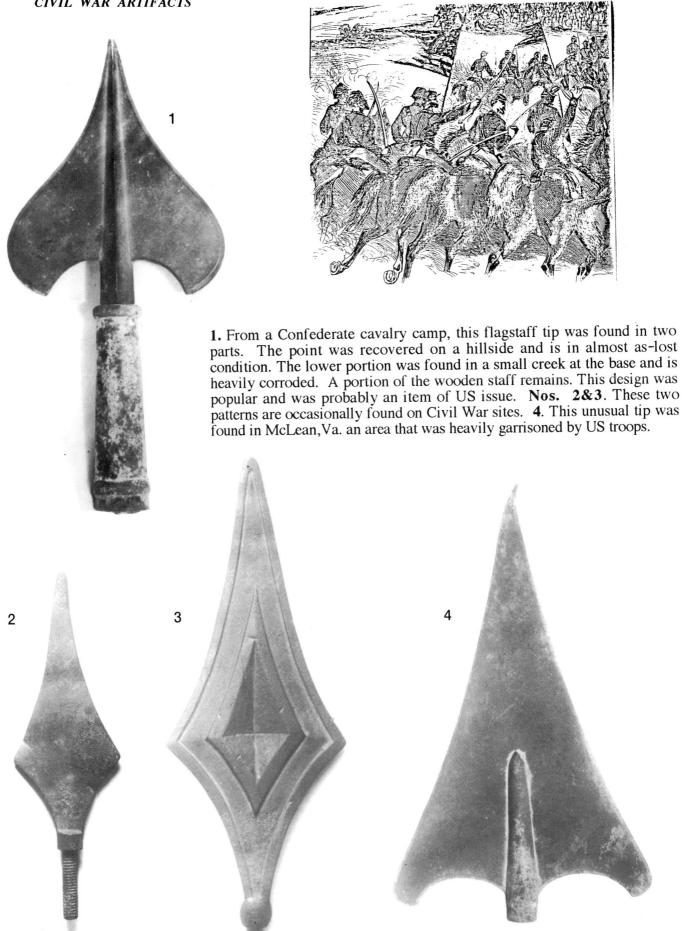

1. From a Confederate cavalry camp, this flagstaff tip was found in two parts. The point was recovered on a hillside and is in almost as-lost condition. The lower portion was found in a small creek at the base and is heavily corroded. A portion of the wooden staff remains. This design was popular and was probably an item of US issue. **Nos. 2&3**. These two patterns are occasionally found on Civil War sites. **4.** This unusual tip was found in McLean, Va. an area that was heavily garrisoned by US troops.

Nos.1,2&3. Large folding pocket knives of probable American manufacture, found in CS sites; all these carried bone handles. **Nos. 4 through 10** are shown actual size. **4.** Note horse head pommel. **5.** Carries silver plated mounts with foliate designs. **Nos. 6,7&8** carry patriotic motifs. **9.** Brass handled specimen marked "Union Knife Co. Naugatuck" (Mass.). **10.** A high quality product with rosewood grip panels and silver plated mounts.

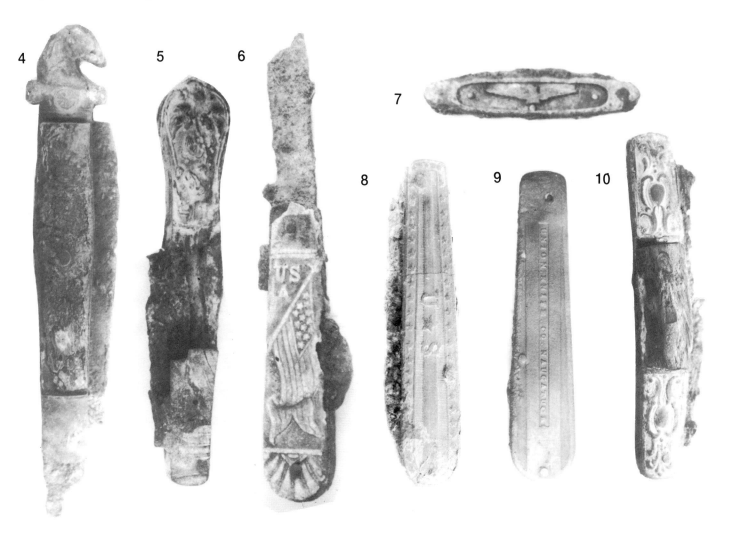

1. An arsenal-made D-guard with a 13" blade, plowed up in the Wilderness in the 1930's. **2**. A spear point D-guard. Note tin encircling ring to keep the wooden handle from splitting. **3.** A large Bowie with integrally forged guard, a most unusual design. Equally rare is the seamed tin scabbard, in itself the product of a real artisan. From a North Carolina camp.

1. A strongly made and massive side knife with a 13&1/2" blade from a North Carolina camp. Another identical specimen with a broken blade was found nearby. **2.** A well made dagger from a battery guarded by the 30th Va. Infantry on the Potomac River. The scabbard was made from one salvaged from a Union NCO sword. **3.** A thick brass side knife guard. **Below:** A Michigan soldier carries an impressive Bowie shoved into his belt.

Note : The knives shown here are are all of CS usage and are most likely of early war manufacture. The CS government referred to these weapon as "side knives". Collectors call the ones with a full knuckle bow "D-guards". **1**. Large spear point knife with a small turned brass finial. From a Georgia camp at Manassas. It has a 10" blade. **2.** D-guard found in housesite trash pit and obviously well used until it was discarded. **Nos. 3&4** Large, heavy side knives. **3.** Mounts a brass guard. Most CS-made knives are strictly iron mounted.

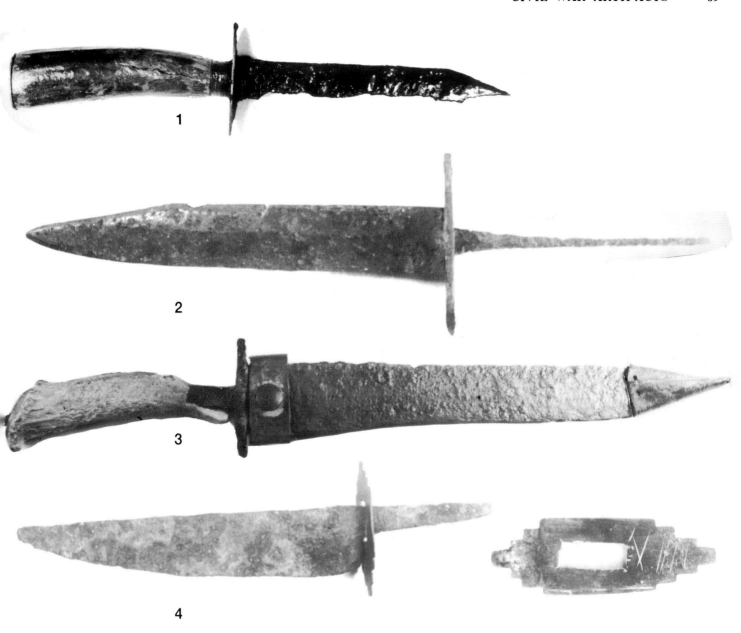

1. A finely made Bowie mounted in brass with antler handle, 5" blade. 2. Sturdy, blacksmith-made knife with iron guard. 3. Classic American Bowie of the 1840's or 50's. It is iron mounted with antler grip and brass scabbard mounts intact, 10" blade. 4. A small "rifleman's" knife probably dating to the colonial period. Note the crude brass guard with engraved decoration. 5. A large, heavy spear point Bowie with brass mounts, found at Cold Harbor.

More examples of commercially produced Bowies. **Nos. 1&2** have highly ornamented guards and pommels. Typically, they were sold in thin leather scabbards with brass mounts which were not suitable for extended field use. It should be noted that these knives were manufactured with almost no change in design well into the post-war era. Many dug specimens were no doubt simply lost by hunters.

A group of factory-made Bowie knives. Primarily from Sheffield, although by the 1850's there was some American mass production of this type knife. Blades varied in length from six to twelve inches on most. **Nos. 1 through 4** carried brass guards and stag or bone handles. **5.** An Italian or Spanish dagger that was part of the famous CS officer's cache at Port Hudson. Knives of this type were a rarity in the US.

1. A cast brass handled Bowie knife with lanyard loop. These distinctive pattern knives are attributed to the maker W. J. McElroy of Macon, Ga. The Bowie type (or clip pointed) blade originally measured about 11&1/2". The cut-in Roman numerals are standard for this item. McElroy originally owned a tin shop but began making weapons when the war began.

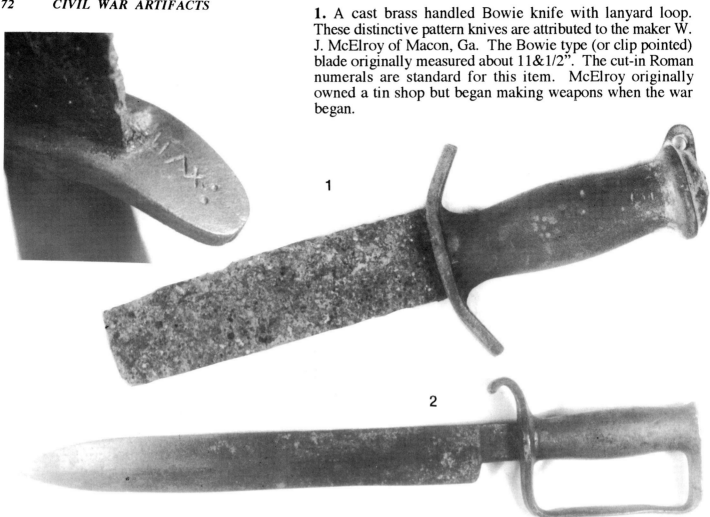

2. A D-guard Bowie with a cast-on brass grip and guard assembly, found at New Hope Church, Ga. Finely made products such as this must date to early in the war and are seldom seen. Casting of this type (around steel) was time consuming and exacting, further, the use of this much brass (a critical material) was unusual. **Below:** From an 1861 Harpers Weekly- "Mississippians practicing with Bowie knives."

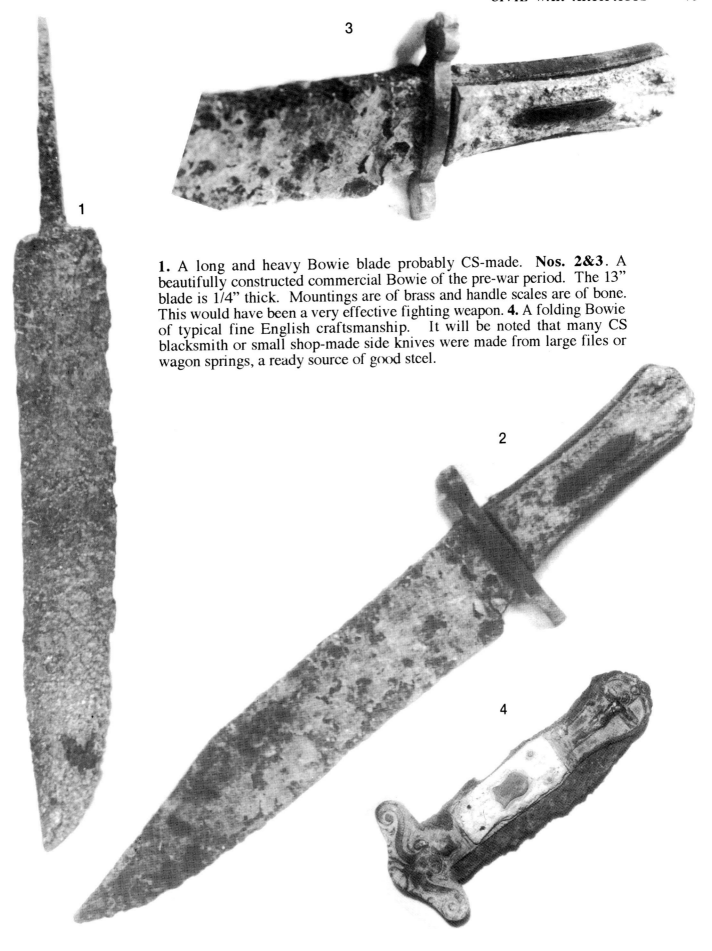

1. A long and heavy Bowie blade probably CS-made. **Nos. 2&3**. A beautifully constructed commercial Bowie of the pre-war period. The 13" blade is 1/4" thick. Mountings are of brass and handle scales are of bone. This would have been a very effective fighting weapon. **4.** A folding Bowie of typical fine English craftsmanship. It will be noted that many CS blacksmith or small shop-made side knives were made from large files or wagon springs, a ready source of good steel.

1

2

3

4

Below: A Union private holds his rifle and the Model 1855 sabre bayonet. Being shorter than the rifle musket with its angular bayonet, the rifles were issued with the longer sabre bayonet. Nearly all had cast brass handles. **1.** The Model 1855, probably the most widely issued. **2.** For the Enfield pattern '53 artillery rifle. These were of all steel construction with leather grip plates. **3.** For the Model 1862 Remington or the "Zouave". **4.** The angular or socket bayonet did most of the fighting as the heavier and more cumbersome sabre bayonet was often not carried by rifle armed troops. This is a CS-made specimen.

Nos. 1&2. The typical throat and drag to a sabre bayonet scabbard. They were worn on a leather frog.
3. Unknown bayonet scabbard tip. **Nos. 4&5.** Boyle, Gamble and MacFee bayonet adapter that allowed a sabre bayonet to be mounted on the rifle. This was a Richmond firm. **6.** The same company made this bayonet, probably for the Mississippi rifle. **7.** Unknown bayonet, probably Confederate. **8.** Bayonet made at Fayettevile, N.C. for the rifle of the same name. The grip has a distinctive eagle feather pattern.

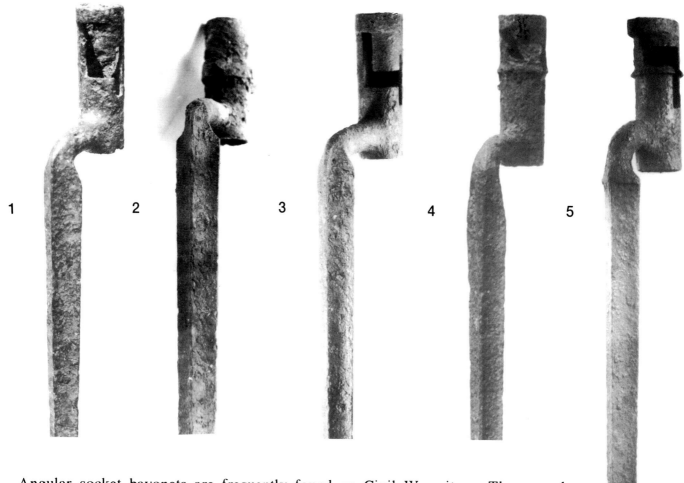

Angular socket bayonets are frequently found on Civil War sites. They can be differentiated by blade and socket length, locking cut pattern, bore size, and blade shape. On some, traces of markings can still be found. When a new longarm was introduced a bayonet would accompany it bearing the same designation. **1.** The US Model 1816. **2.** US Model 1842. **3.** Model 1819 Hall. **4.** This specimen is for the Model 1855 series of weapons and is commonly seen. Note the streamlined blade shape. **5.** Fitting the Enfield Model '53; these too are frequently seen. **6.** From a CS camp along the Rappahanock river, this specimen was cut down into a dagger. **7.** Another Enfield with a well preserved leather scabbard. **8.** Top and bottom mounts to an Enfield scabbard.

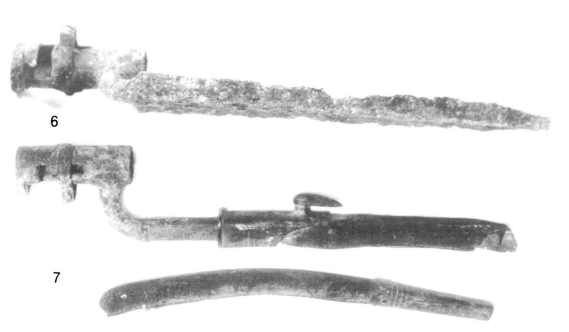

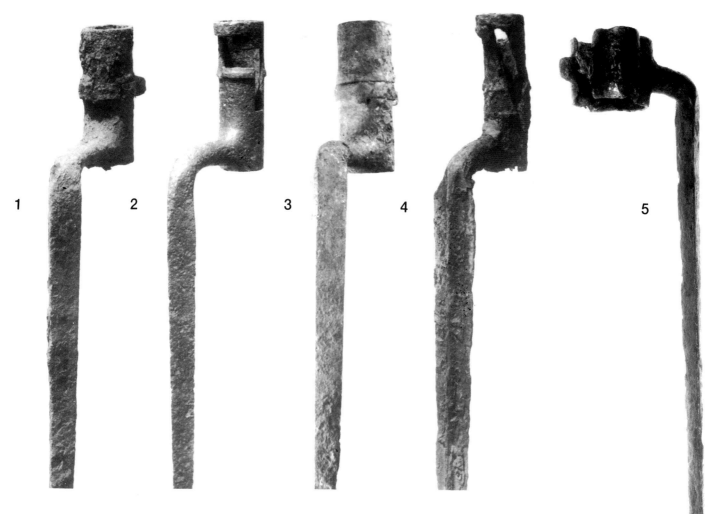

Nos. 1,2&3. These are all Confederate-made bayonets and they are uncommon. They are made like the US but the fullers were not milled-in. This was a manufacturing short cut. **1** and **2** were made for .58 cal. weapons while **3** is for a .69. These were once called "Tredegars" (Richmond), but there is documentation that they were made elsewhere on contract. The true "Richmond" government-made article was almost like the US, as they possessed the machinery taken from Harper's Ferry. The blade was slightly shorter than the US article. **4.** The four sided Austrian for use on imported muskets. **5.** A very rare double barreled shotgun bayonet. **6.** A bayonet locking ring. **7.** A CS bayonet made into a hook.

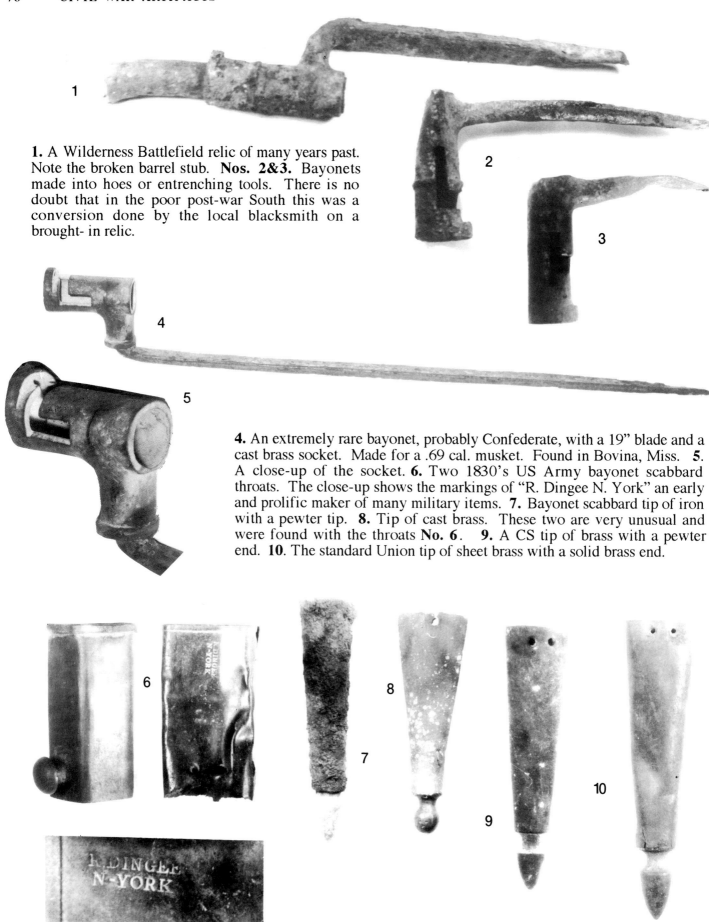

1. A Wilderness Battlefield relic of many years past. Note the broken barrel stub. **Nos. 2&3.** Bayonets made into hoes or entrenching tools. There is no doubt that in the poor post-war South this was a conversion done by the local blacksmith on a brought- in relic.

4. An extremely rare bayonet, probably Confederate, with a 19" blade and a cast brass socket. Made for a .69 cal. musket. Found in Bovina, Miss.   **5.** A close-up of the socket. **6.** Two 1830's US Army bayonet scabbard throats. The close-up shows the markings of "R. Dingee N. York" an early and prolific maker of many military items. **7.** Bayonet scabbard tip of iron with a pewter tip. **8.** Tip of cast brass. These two are very unusual and were found with the throats **No. 6**.   **9.** A CS tip of brass with a pewter end. **10.** The standard Union tip of sheet brass with a solid brass end.

Above left: US Cavalry trooper with the Model 1840 dragoon sabre. **Right**: A Confederate cavalryman carrying the same model. Despite the appearance of a lighter and more effective US sabre in 1860, the 1840 was the workhorse of the war and many thousands were produced during this period both North and South. **Nos. 1&2**. The model 1840 (nicknamed "Old Wristbreaker"). Note the stopped blade fuller. **3**. A destroyed guard that has been hacked apart. Note that on careful examination it is not unusual to occasionally find scratched-in owner's initials on sword guards.

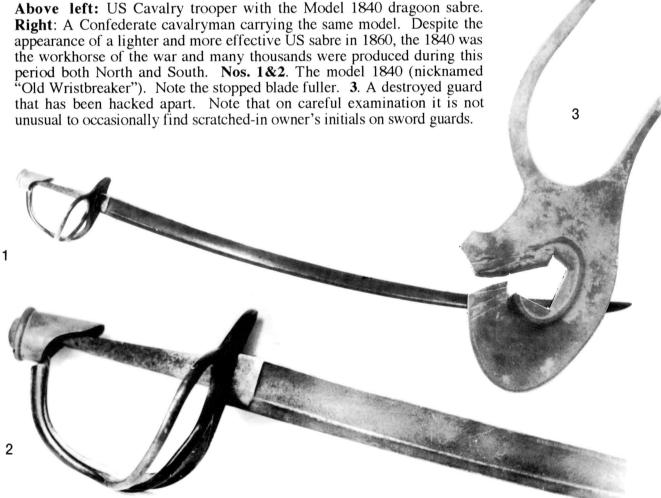

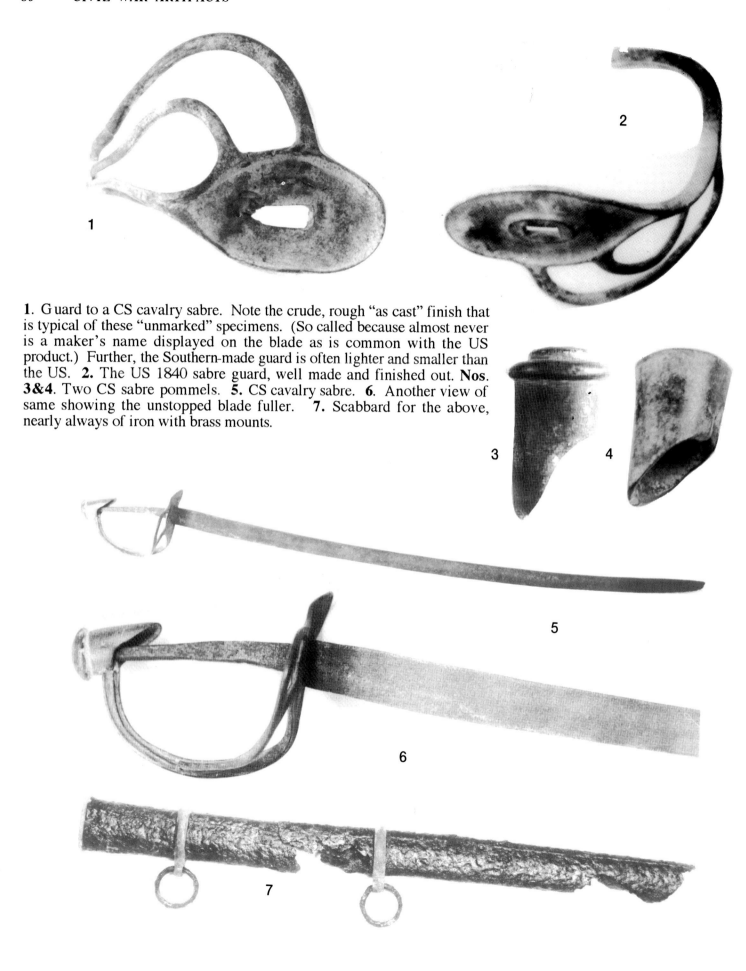

1. Guard to a CS cavalry sabre. Note the crude, rough "as cast" finish that is typical of these "unmarked" specimens. (So called because almost never is a maker's name displayed on the blade as is common with the US product.) Further, the Southern-made guard is often lighter and smaller than the US. **2.** The US 1840 sabre guard, well made and finished out. **Nos. 3&4**. Two CS sabre pommels. **5.** CS cavalry sabre. **6.** Another view of same showing the unstopped blade fuller.   **7.** Scabbard for the above, nearly always of iron with brass mounts.

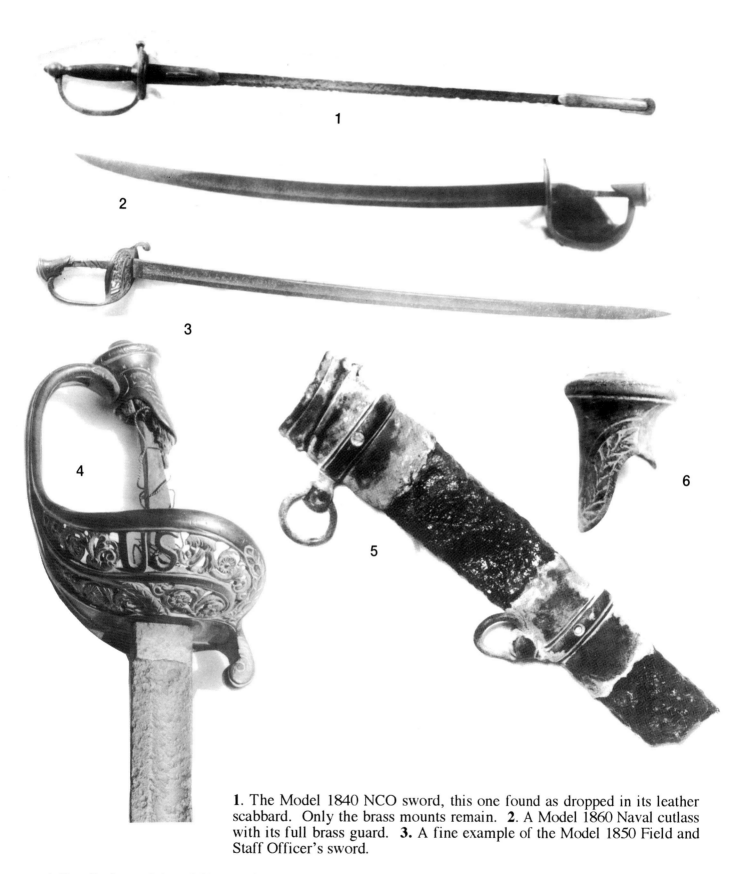

1. The Model 1840 NCO sword, this one found as dropped in its leather scabbard. Only the brass mounts remain. **2**. A Model 1860 Naval cutlass with its full brass guard. **3.** A fine example of the Model 1850 Field and Staff Officer's sword.

4. Detail view of the 1850 sword. These were privately purchased and most were of high quality with gilted brass fittings and engraved blades. **5.** The two upper mounts to an 1850 iron scabbard. There are many variants. **6.** The pommel to same with cast-in foliate designs.

1. US Model 1833 Dragoon sabre. These were made by N.P. Ames of Chicopee, Mass. Inspector's marks will be found on the guard and scabbard drag. **2.** Memphis Novelty Works sword found at San Jacinto, Miss. **3.** Portion of the hilt of a CS naval cutlass, made of heavy cast brass. **4.** US Foot Artillery sword Model 1832, cast brass hilt and 19" blade. Rather than being used as a defensive weapon these swords mostly performed the important task of clearing away brush from in front of the gun when it was put into a new field position. **5.** A CS version of the same. These were made in a number of variations.

6. Broken portion of an early colonial sword hilt. **7.** Another piece of broken hilt, this one from a foot officer's sword.

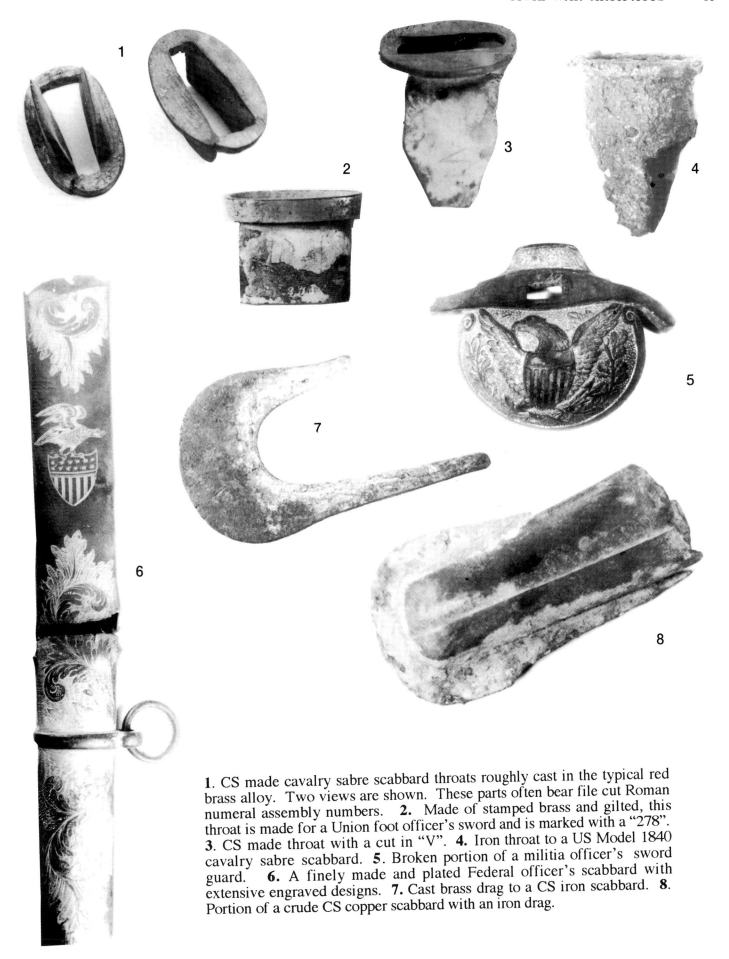

1. CS made cavalry sabre scabbard throats roughly cast in the typical red brass alloy. Two views are shown. These parts often bear file cut Roman numeral assembly numbers. 2. Made of stamped brass and gilted, this throat is made for a Union foot officer's sword and is marked with a "278". 3. CS made throat with a cut in "V". 4. Iron throat to a US Model 1840 cavalry sabre scabbard. 5. Broken portion of a militia officer's sword guard. 6. A finely made and plated Federal officer's scabbard with extensive engraved designs. 7. Cast brass drag to a CS iron scabbard. 8. Portion of a crude CS copper scabbard with an iron drag.

Right: The Northern soldier who fought to preserve the Union. He carries the Model 1861 Rifle Musket with its cartridge box, cap box, and a fixed bayonet. They fired the .58 cal. Minie ball. These were accurate, powerful, well made arms. **1.** A CS manufactured Richmond musketoon, made on machinery captured at Harper's Ferry. **Nos. 2&3.** A sight, lock, barrel band, nose cap and band springs from an 1861 Model. This model eliminated the complicated Maynard priming device. **Note:** Weapons parts are frequent finds on nearly all types of sites. This is the result of canabilization for repair or the destruction of outmoded or surplus captured materiel.

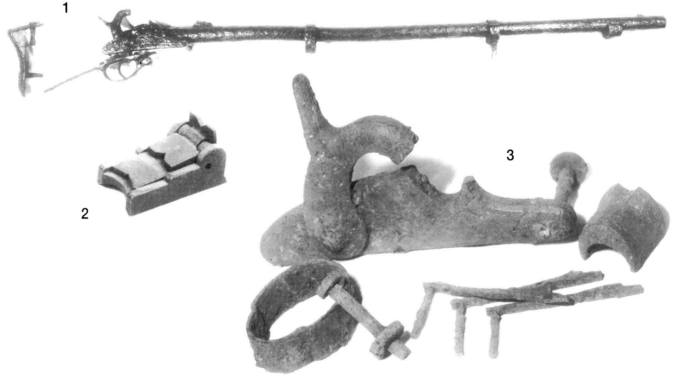

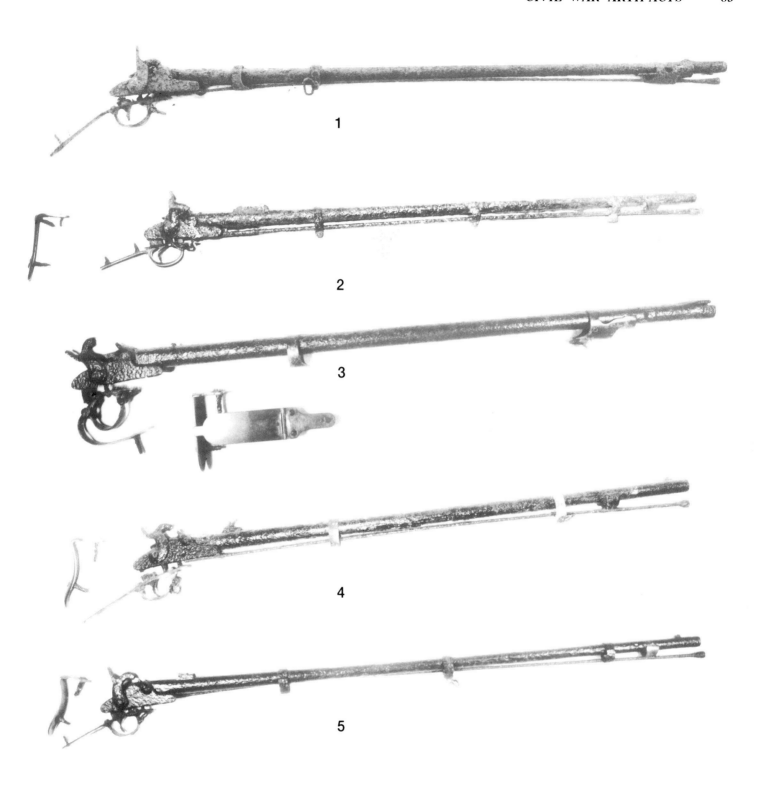

1. The Model 1842 musket. Though these weapons were obsolescent by 1861, many saw use in the war. They fired the often found .69 cal. round ball or the same combined with buckshot. **2.** The Pattern 1853 Enfield, a very popular weapon on both sides; cal. .577. **3.** The Model 1841 rifle (Mississippi rifle) originally firing the patched .54 cal. round ball. In the war they more frequently used a .54 minie ball. **4.** A CS Fayettville rifle. This was a modified copy of the US Model 1855. This one was found at Gaines Mill, Va. **5.** The Richmond rifle musket . This was a strong and reliable weapon and was the backbone of CS infantry armament. Note: In 1861 when the Southern forces siezed Harper's Ferry, the rifle making tooling was sent to Fayetteville, NC. while the rifle musket tooling went to Richmond.

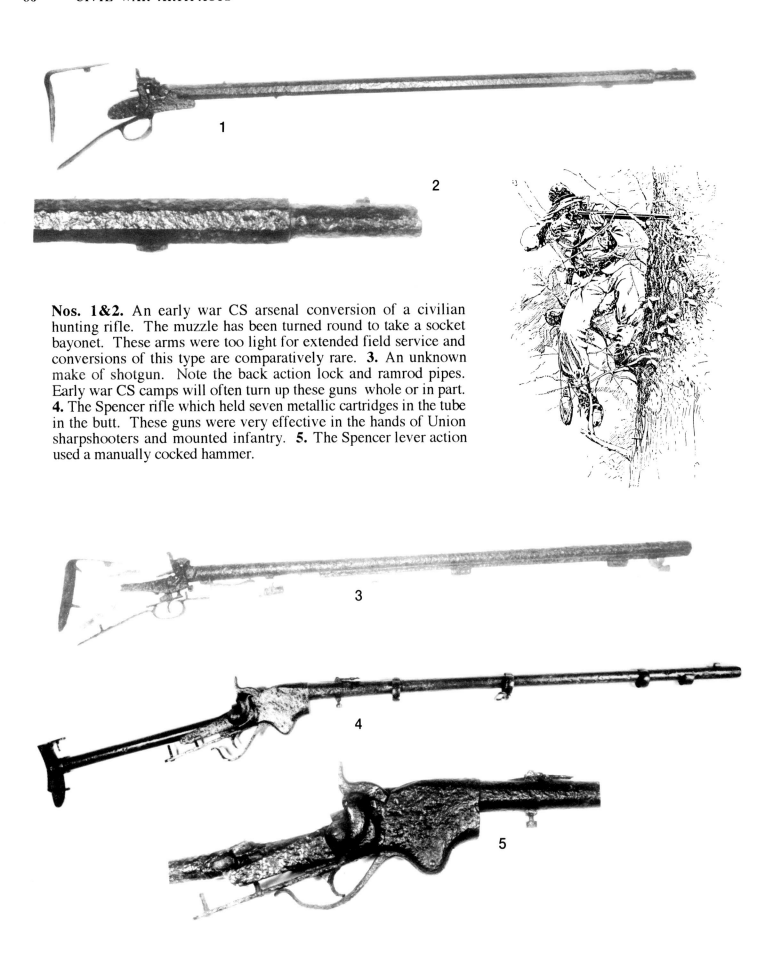

Nos. 1&2. An early war CS arsenal conversion of a civilian hunting rifle. The muzzle has been turned round to take a socket bayonet. These arms were too light for extended field service and conversions of this type are comparatively rare. **3.** An unknown make of shotgun. Note the back action lock and ramrod pipes. Early war CS camps will often turn up these guns whole or in part. **4.** The Spencer rifle which held seven metallic cartridges in the tube in the butt. These guns were very effective in the hands of Union sharpshooters and mounted infantry. **5.** The Spencer lever action used a manually cocked hammer.

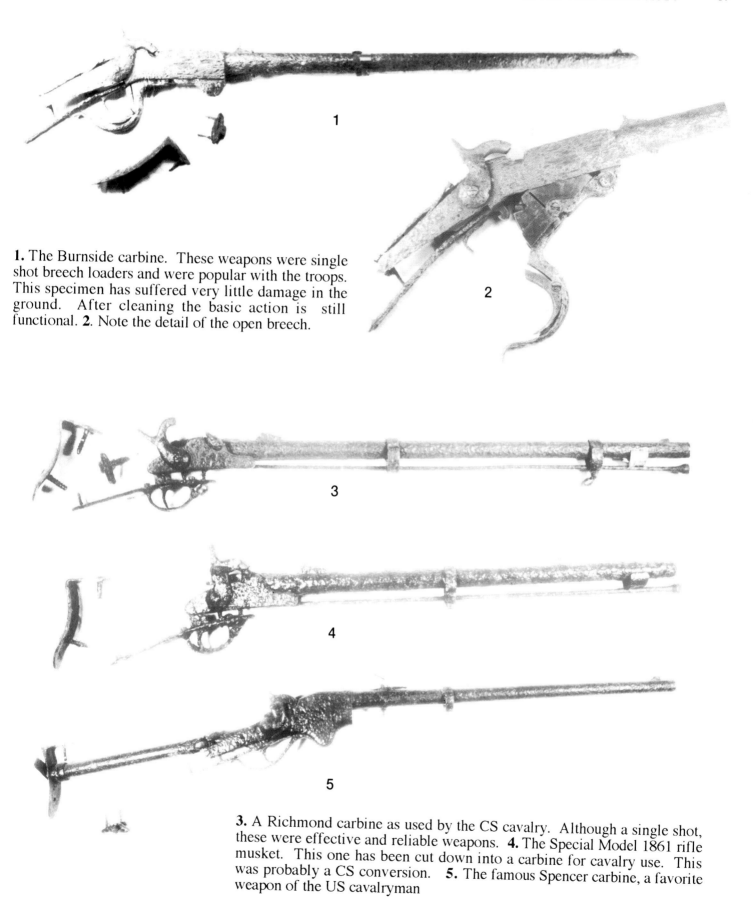

1. The Burnside carbine. These weapons were single shot breech loaders and were popular with the troops. This specimen has suffered very little damage in the ground. After cleaning the basic action is still functional. 2. Note the detail of the open breech.

3. A Richmond carbine as used by the CS cavalry. Although a single shot, these were effective and reliable weapons. 4. The Special Model 1861 rifle musket. This one has been cut down into a carbine for cavalry use. This was probably a CS conversion. 5. The famous Spencer carbine, a favorite weapon of the US cavalryman

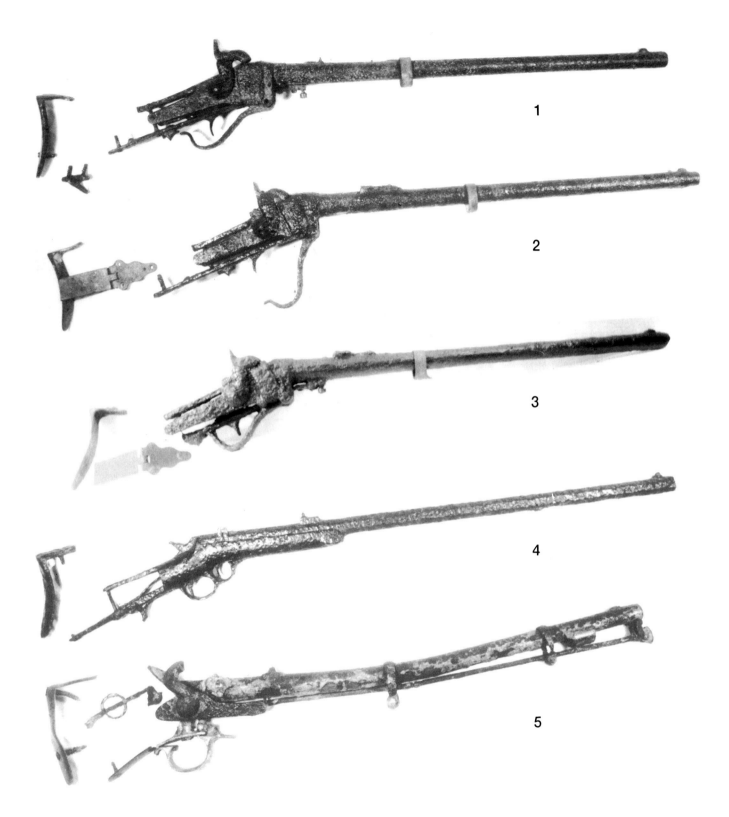

1. The Richmond Armory-made copy of the Sharp's carbine. These weapons were never as satisfactory as the original.   **2.** The Model 1853 "John Brown" Sharp's carbine. All of the various Sharp's carbines were extensively used by the cavalry of both sides.   **3.** Another Model '53, with typical brass patchbox and bands. This one was excavated in a yard in Harper's Ferry.   **4.** A civilian model .44 cal. Wesson carbine found in a North Carolina cavalry camp.   **5.** An Enfield cavalry carbine in .577 cal. from Jeb Stuart's cavalry camp south of Fredericksburg. Note the stock mounted bar and ring that the shoulder sling swivel snapped onto.

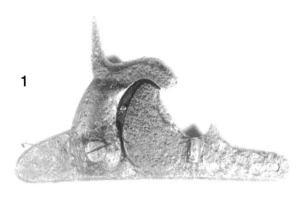

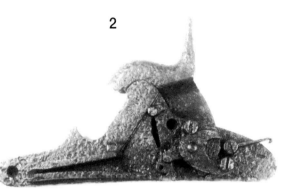

Nos. 1&2. Front and rear of a Model 1855 lock. Though heavily pitted it was cleaned by electrolysis to the point that it is functional. **3.** "Cook and Brother" lock; a CS maker in New Orleans and later Athens, Ga. Marked with the Confederate flag. **4.** Virginia Manufactory lock. **5.** '53 British Enfield lock. **6.** Model 1842 musket lock clearly marked "Springfield 1849". When recovered in this condition there is a theory that they might have been well greased or oiled when lost or discarded. **7.** Early model US musket lock converted from flint to percussion.

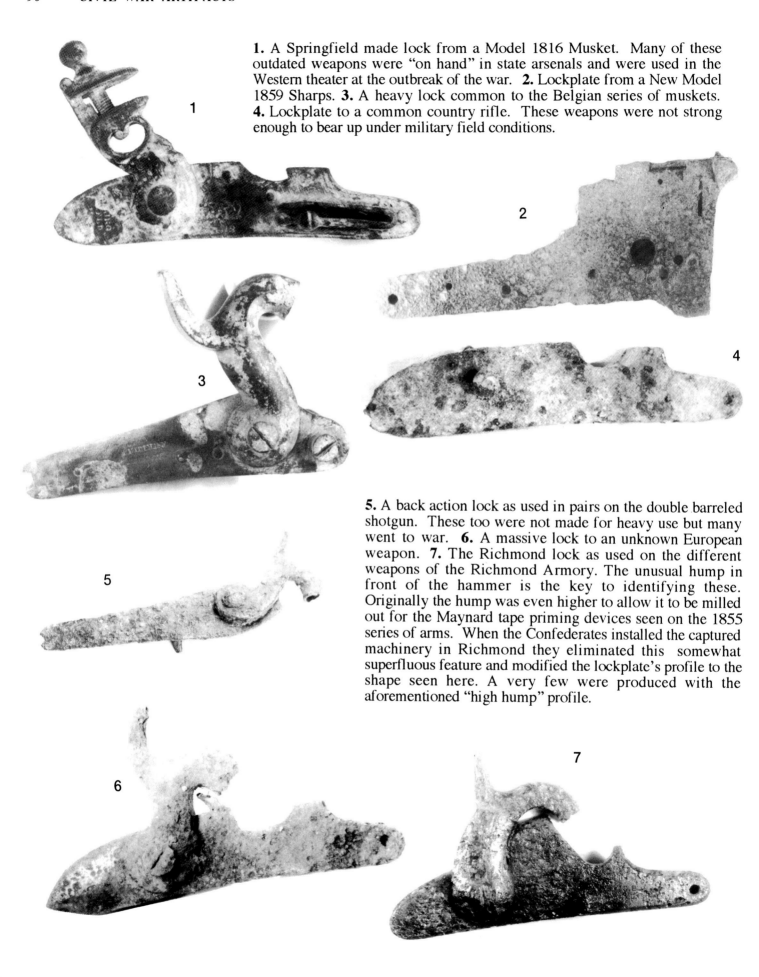

1. A Springfield made lock from a Model 1816 Musket. Many of these outdated weapons were "on hand" in state arsenals and were used in the Western theater at the outbreak of the war. **2.** Lockplate from a New Model 1859 Sharps. **3.** A heavy lock common to the Belgian series of muskets. **4.** Lockplate to a common country rifle. These weapons were not strong enough to bear up under military field conditions.

5. A back action lock as used in pairs on the double barreled shotgun. These too were not made for heavy use but many went to war. **6.** A massive lock to an unknown European weapon. **7.** The Richmond lock as used on the different weapons of the Richmond Armory. The unusual hump in front of the hammer is the key to identifying these. Originally the hump was even higher to allow it to be milled out for the Maynard tape priming devices seen on the 1855 series of arms. When the Confederates installed the captured machinery in Richmond they eliminated this somewhat superfluous feature and modified the lockplate's profile to the shape seen here. A very few were produced with the aforementioned "high hump" profile.

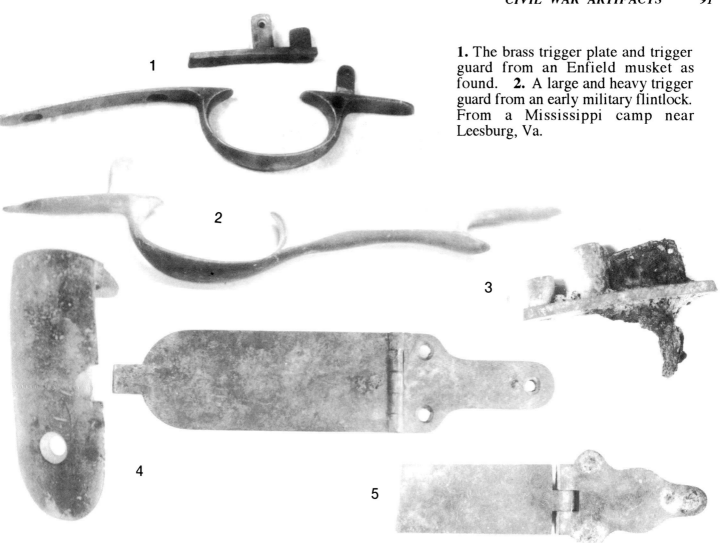

1. The brass trigger plate and trigger guard from an Enfield musket as found. **2.** A large and heavy trigger guard from an early military flintlock. From a Mississippi camp near Leesburg, Va.

3. An iron trigger with its brass mount from an Enfield musket. **4.** Buttplate to the Model 1841 rifle with its distinctive large patchbox door, both of brass. **5.** A Sharp's carbine patchbox door of brass. Identical ones of iron are also found. **6.** Iron buttplate to the US Model 1855 series of weapons. **7.** The Enfield buttplate of iron. **8.** A US Model 1842 musket buttplate with screws. **9.** Stamped "CSA" just ahead of the top screw, this is the Fayetteville buttplate of cast brass.

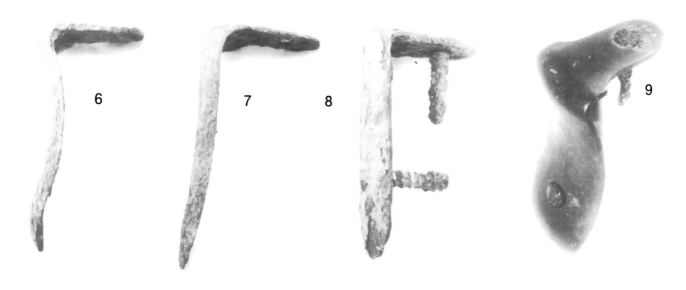

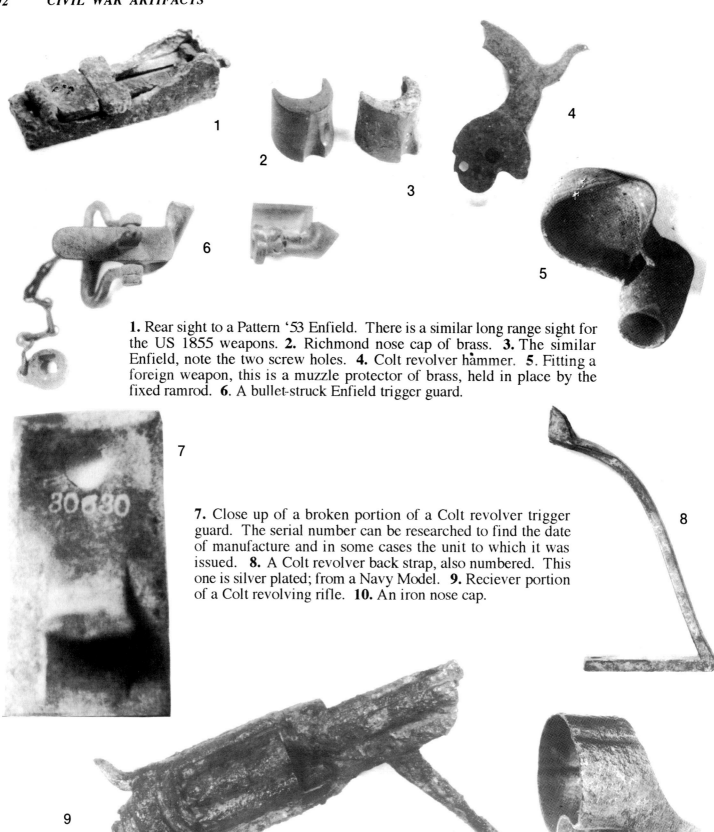

1. Rear sight to a Pattern '53 Enfield. There is a similar long range sight for the US 1855 weapons. 2. Richmond nose cap of brass. 3. The similar Enfield, note the two screw holes. 4. Colt revolver hammer. 5. Fitting a foreign weapon, this is a muzzle protector of brass, held in place by the fixed ramrod. 6. A bullet-struck Enfield trigger guard.

7. Close up of a broken portion of a Colt revolver trigger guard. The serial number can be researched to find the date of manufacture and in some cases the unit to which it was issued. 8. A Colt revolver back strap, also numbered. This one is silver plated; from a Navy Model. 9. Reciever portion of a Colt revolving rifle. 10. An iron nose cap.

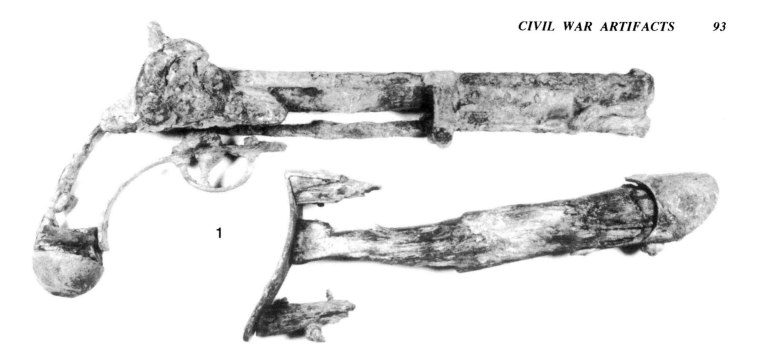

1. The Model 1855 pistol carbine with detachable stock and Maynard tape priming device. These were unpopular and clumsy weapons coming in at a time when dependable revolvers were in use. It was thought that with the stock affixed they could serve as a carbine. This one was found at Port Hudson.

2. A Hall's percussion rifle breech. These came completely out of the weapon for cleaning. In occupation duty after the Mexican War it has been recorded that these would be carried loaded and capped when out for a drink at the local cantina. It would be hoped that the load was a reduced one. **3.** The Colt .36 cal. Navy Model, a very popular weapon with troops of both sides. **Right:** A tough looking Yankee cavalryman carries a Colt revolver stuck in his belt.

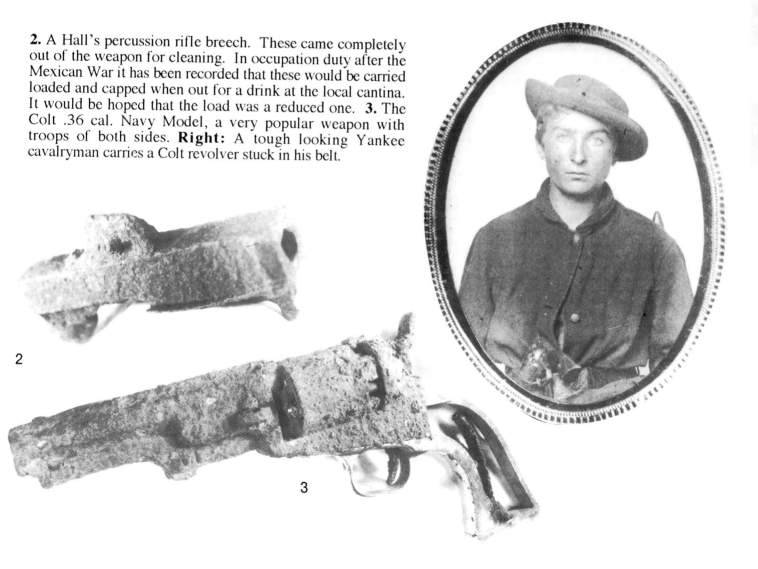

1. The Remington .44 cal. Army and Navy revolver. These were well designed pistols and were felt to be superior to the Colt by virtue of their solid top strap. This one was found in one of Sheridan's cavalry camps in Virginia. **Right:** An ad from "Harpers Weekly".

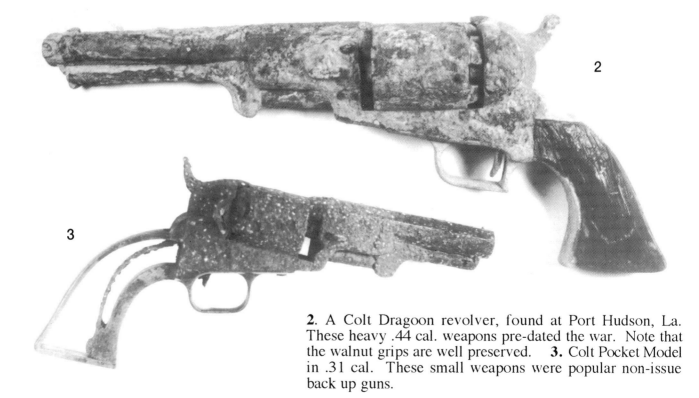

2. A Colt Dragoon revolver, found at Port Hudson, La. These heavy .44 cal. weapons pre-dated the war. Note that the walnut grips are well preserved.   **3.** Colt Pocket Model in .31 cal. These small weapons were popular non-issue back up guns.

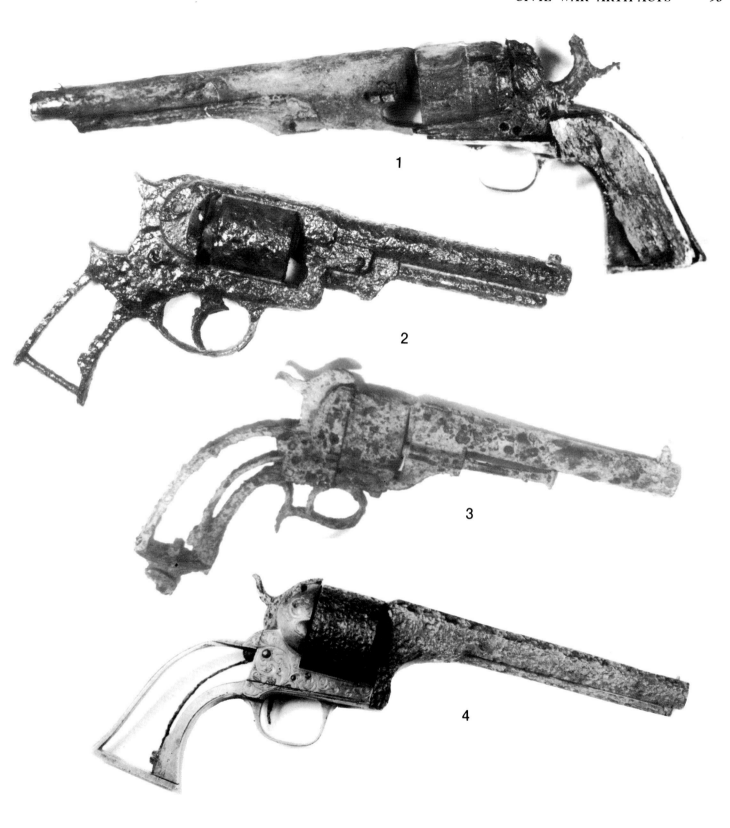

1. The famous Colt Model 1860 Army revolver. The Army specified a .44 cal. cartridge versus the Navy's .36. This weapon was well liked and effective. Many pistols are found loaded and cocked as this one, dropped in the confusion of mounted combat. **2.** The Starr Army Revolver in .44 cal., another popular pistol. **3.** The French Lefaucheux revolver, using a pinfire cartridge. These were issued to some Union troops. **4.** A Moore Revolver, found in Virginia . These were .32 cal. 7 shot guns. Not an issue item, they were carried by some Union officers.

1. The Model 1861 US Navy signal pistol, brass framed with US Navy Yard markings. There is a similar Army model.   **2.** The Model 1862 brass framed signal (or flare) pistol, this one made for the US Army and so marked. Any of the signal pistols are rarely found. **3.** A bar hammer percussion pocket pistol. These are generally .31 cal.

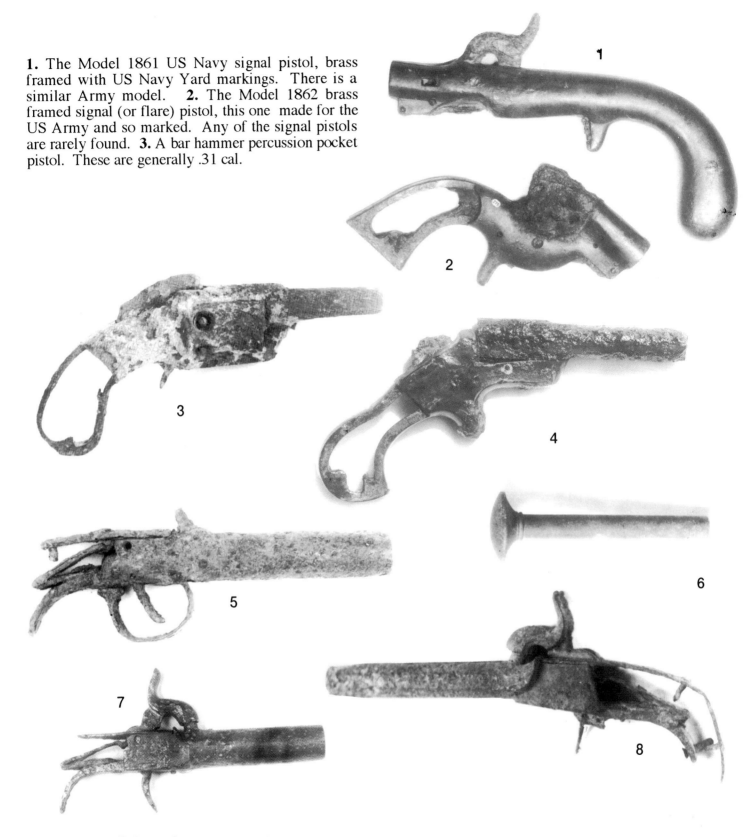

4. A small, brass framed, spur trigger, cartridge pistol of the type that became very popular in the early 1860's. **5.** An earlier percussion pistol of small size. These were the original "Saturday Night Specials" which in reality were the last ditch defense arms of many poor householders, travelers etc. When the war came many went along, and in this context they became known as "boot pistols". **6.** A solid brass ramrod, probably made for a high quality Deringer type pistol. **7.** A very small percussion boot pistol. **8.** This one is a double barrel model which is not seen as often as the single.

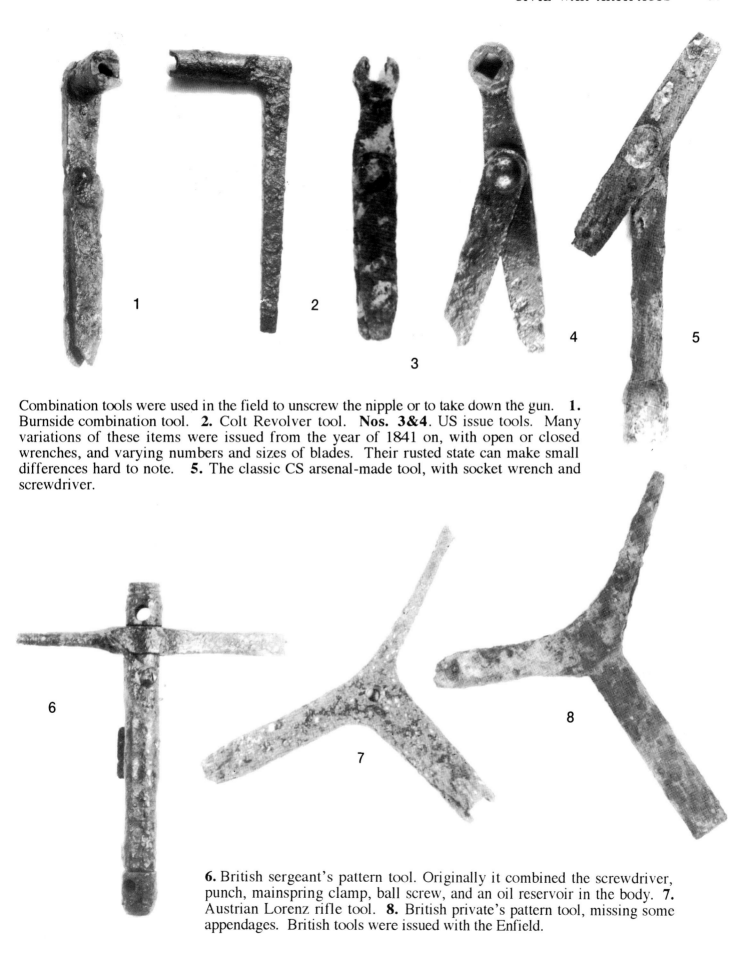

Combination tools were used in the field to unscrew the nipple or to take down the gun. **1.** Burnside combination tool. **2.** Colt Revolver tool. **Nos. 3&4**. US issue tools. Many variations of these items were issued from the year of 1841 on, with open or closed wrenches, and varying numbers and sizes of blades. Their rusted state can make small differences hard to note. **5.** The classic CS arsenal-made tool, with socket wrench and screwdriver.

6. British sergeant's pattern tool. Originally it combined the screwdriver, punch, mainspring clamp, ball screw, and an oil reservoir in the body. **7.** Austrian Lorenz rifle tool. **8.** British private's pattern tool, missing some appendages. British tools were issued with the Enfield.

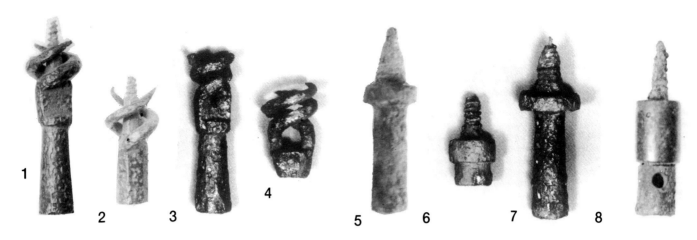

Nos. 1&2. These are combination ball pullers and wipers. Like all the tools of this type they threaded onto the end of the ramrod. **Nos. 3&4.** These are wipers, designed to hold a rag. **Nos. 5 through 8.** Ball pullers which screwed into the end of the bullet allowing it to be withdrawn. Other than firing it there was no other way to unload a muzzle loading weapon. **Nos. 9&10.** Cleaning jags.

11. This small can of grease and remains of a brush were found in a Union camp. **12.** Cone protector and chain issued with the Enfield. **13.** Brass cone protectors. **14.** The same but field-made of lead. **15.** Issue brass tompions that fit in the gun muzzle on the march. **16.** Brass tompion with a wartime patent date.

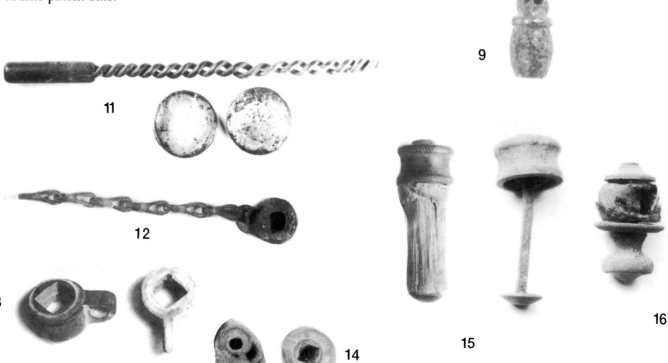

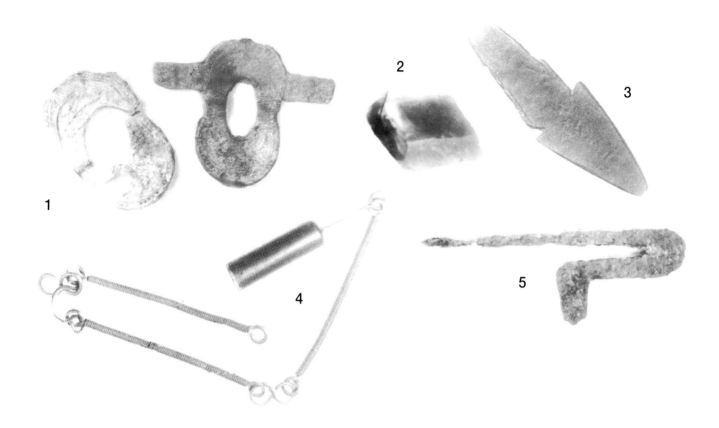

All of the above items were found in the same Civil War period camp in Florida. Records indicate that it had been previously occupied during the Seminole War. These items date from that earlier period. **1.** These pieces of sheet lead were folded around the gunflint before it was tightened in the hammer. **2.** Gunflint, one of a number found. **3.** A sheet brass arrowhead. **4.** The remains of an issue brush and pick set, used with flintlock muskets. **5.** This iron combination tool is thought to be for the Hall series of weapons. **6.** The commonly found blob of lead and melted bullet. In nearly every case these are not the results of field bullet casting. **7.** A mainspring vise containing a compressed mainspring. **8.** Musket wiper used to pull a bullet.

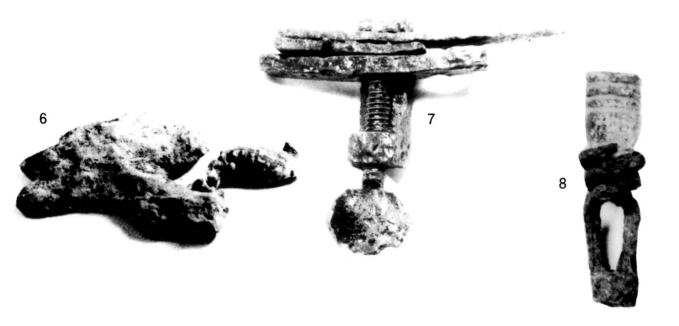

1. A Federal cartridge box with three ring bullets as found at Spotsylvania.
2. The standard US cartridge box tin. A pair of these went into the box.
Each contained twenty rounds for a total of forty. 3. A pewter version of the
same but CS-made. 4. A one piece tin of the US 1855 rifle box type. For
ease of manufacture the Confederates often copied this style. 5. A group of
finials from cap pouches and cartridge boxes. The US ones are of brass and
the CS generally of pewter or lead.

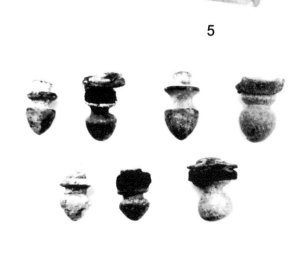

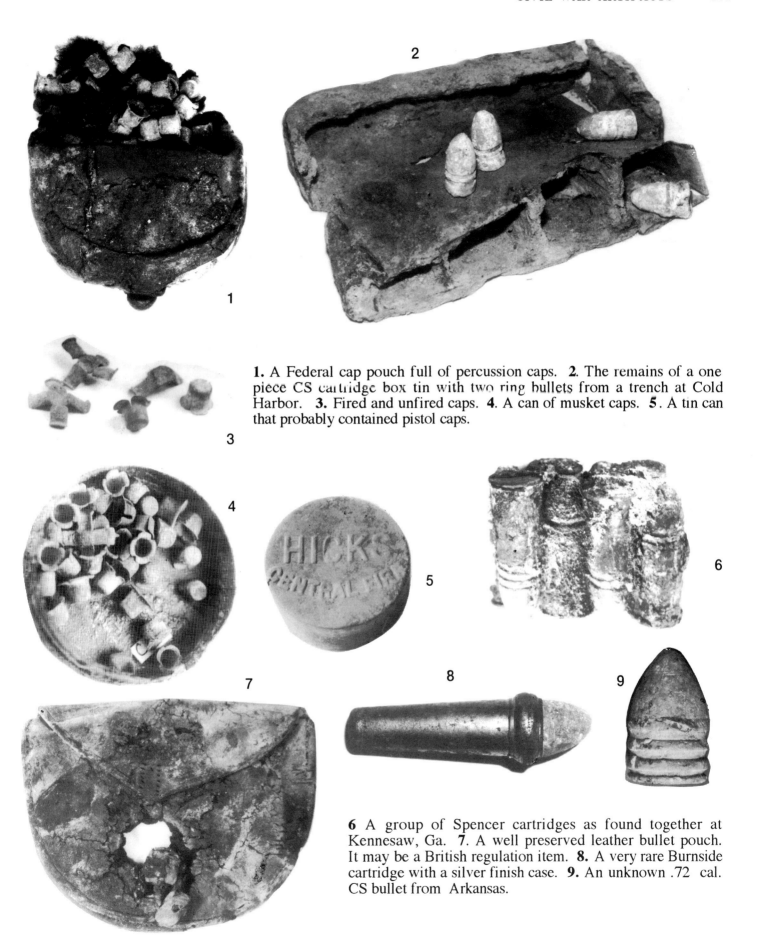

1. A Federal cap pouch full of percussion caps. **2.** The remains of a one piece CS cartridge box tin with two ring bullets from a trench at Cold Harbor. **3.** Fired and unfired caps. **4.** A can of musket caps. **5.** A tin can that probably contained pistol caps.

6 A group of Spencer cartridges as found together at Kennesaw, Ga. **7.** A well preserved leather bullet pouch. It may be a British regulation item. **8.** A very rare Burnside cartridge with a silver finish case. **9.** An unknown .72 cal. CS bullet from Arkansas.

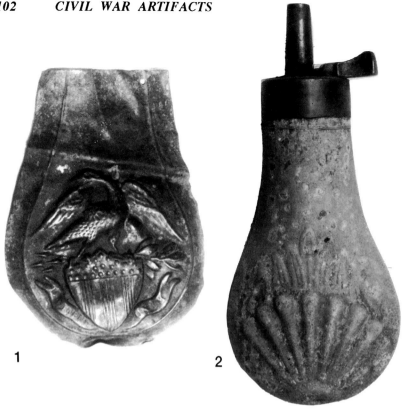

1. One side of a small brass powder flask. 2. An unusual pewter civilian flask with brass fittings.   3. A large rifle flask, US issue with rifle equipments. They were made by N. P. Ames and this model was called the "Peace Flask". 4. An adjustable powder flask spout marked in drams. 5. An unusually ornate flask marked "US".

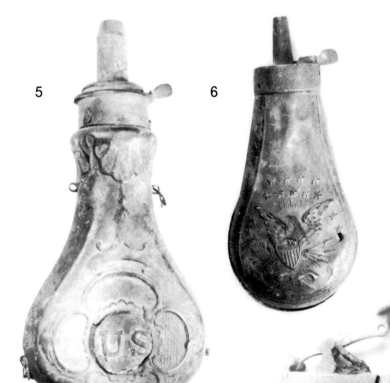

6. A small pistol flask. These were often cased with a revolver. There are many design and size variations in powder flasks. Nos. 7&8. These are adjustable mouthpieces to civilian leather shot pouches or flasks.

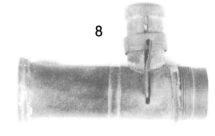

1. A lead "pig" weighing 149 lbs. This was typically the way lead was shipped from the smelter. Found on a Union supply ship which had sunk off of the North Carolina coast. 2. Another, produced in Boston. 3. A large gang mold capable of casting six .44 cal "Army" bullets at a time. It was probably made by Colt. 4. The brass ferrule carries a serial number.

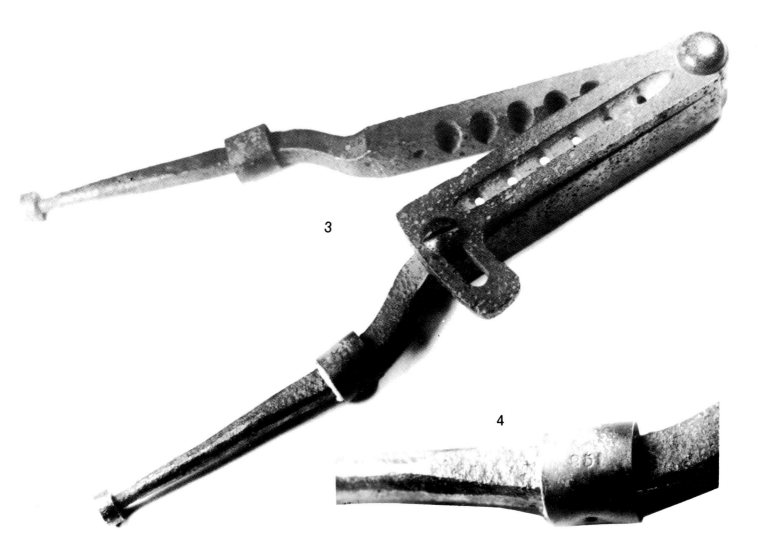

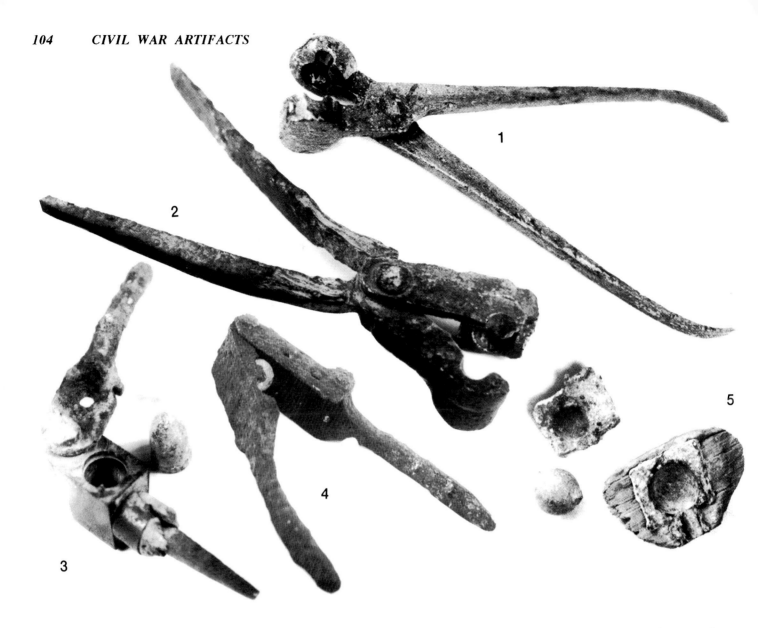

By the time of the Civil War, the military usage of bullet molds was slight. Stamping presses in armories could swage a denser bullet than by molding at the rate of hundreds of thousands per day. **1.** Round ball mold as normally used with civilian rifles, **2.** Pre-war military .54 cal. iron ball mold, with a movable sprue cutter. **3.** A very rare Starr carbine mold with bullet. The body is made of brass. **4.** The often seen Colt type pistol mold for casting a round ball and conical bullet. Seen in .36 and .44. **5.** An odd field-made mold of white metal surrounded by wood, casting a .54 ball. **6.** Heavy, well made model for the Sharp's carbine. The front part is an end cutter for clipping the sprue. **7.** Brass pistol mold for ball and conical.

Bullets: Bullets are the most commonly found relic of the Civil War and exist in many variations. A great variety of firearms were used both military and civilian, many taking their own specific bullet. Further, in most cases, there were many variants of each of these. Even the common three ring Minie was made by the different arsenals both North and South in a number of different patterns. Add to all of this the large number of imported patterns utilized and one can appreciate the huge variety and quantities used.

Types: In general all of these can be divided into four different types. **1.** The round balls, most often in .69 and less frequently in .54 and other sizes. **2.** Minie type bullets, .54, .57, .58 and .69. **3.** Breech loading carbine bullets, mostly .52 and .54. **4.** Pistol bullets from .22 up with the .36 and .44 the most common. Note that there are others outside of even these broad categories.

Specific identification: Bullets can be classified by general shape, caliber, type of base, number of raised rings or grooves and other factors. Anyone making a serious study of bullets should use a set of micrometer calipers for measurement. An excellent and comprehensive guide to the subject is the book *Civil War Projectiles II, Small Arms & Field Artillery With Supplement* by W. Reid McKee and M.E.Mason, Jr. Herein is detailed a concise system of identifying any of the bullets of the period along with photos of most.

Usage: While many patterns are specifically US or CS, the latter used large numbers of captured cartridges. In both theaters of war the .69 round ball is found often on early war sites and occasionally with the buckshot that was often used with it. The US .58 "three ringer" is found on nearly all types of sites, with the .58 two ring CS Gardner showing up in the field in 1862. Both of these will be found also in .54, indicating that quantities of the Model 1841 rifle were still being used. Further note that the .577 Enfield was extensively used, both in that gun and in .58 weapons. The various carbine bullets are almost always associated with the cavalry and the Sharps bullet is most often seen. Among the pistol bullets the .44 Colt shows up most frequently.

Rarity: Note that there are many rare and specific patterns, some issued to a particular group of troops, and often when found can trace that unit's movements or pin down their occupation of a specific point. In the early-war Northern Virginia campaign area only the famous Sixth North Carolina Infantry used the odd .69 Italian Carcano and it is a sure sign of their picket posts and camps. Note that in the Western theater of war the CS forces used many odd and seldom seen bullet types.

L to R: The standard US projectiles. .69 Minie, .69 round ball, two buckshot often used with the .69 ball, .58 Minie, .54 round ball (used with a patch) and a US paper cartridge containing powder and a .58 Minie. This type of loading is the reason why enormous numbers of cartridges were discarded in the field. On the march, many became loose, broken or wet. Note that as the war progressed, the .58 Minie became more and more the standard issue.

Right: US three ring bullets are found in many configurations. Shown are three .58s and two .54s. Base cavities vary . A star marked base is often seen while the "US" marking is scarce. One French import has a triangular cavity.

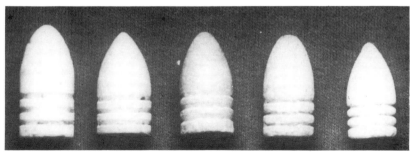

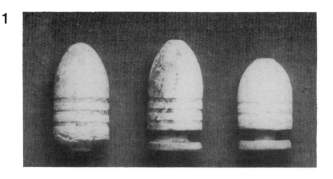

1. L to R: Williams cleaner bullets, types 1, 2 and 3. These bullets had a zinc disc on the base to scrape powder residue from the barrel when fired. One of these bullets was to be issued with each pack of twenty standard bullets. They were widely used. **2.** Two .577 Enfield bullets and a rare .69. Predominantly of CS usage, there are many variants and base markings. Some are found with a wooden base plug.

3. The US-used .58 Shaler patent bullet. It was intended that the parts would disperse, increasing the chances of a hit. They saw little field use. To the right are the two piece and three piece types.

4. F.J. Gardner was a CS Arsenal employee in Richmond who invented a machine that crimped the bullet base around the rolled paper cartridge sleeve. While this enabled a fast production it weakened the paper at the attachment point, causing many to be discarded in the field. Hundreds of thousands were made at various points and their use was widespread. **L to R:** The rare .69, two .58s, a .54, the unusual one ring type and a non-dug specimen.

5. The CS military used many three ring designs. Most are somewhat cruder than the US arsenal three ringers. **L to R**: .58 six ring, ..58 nose cast,.58 Georgia teat base.

Imports: Nearly all of these were of CS usage. Some were cast in the South with imported molds. All are scarce in comparison with US made bullets.

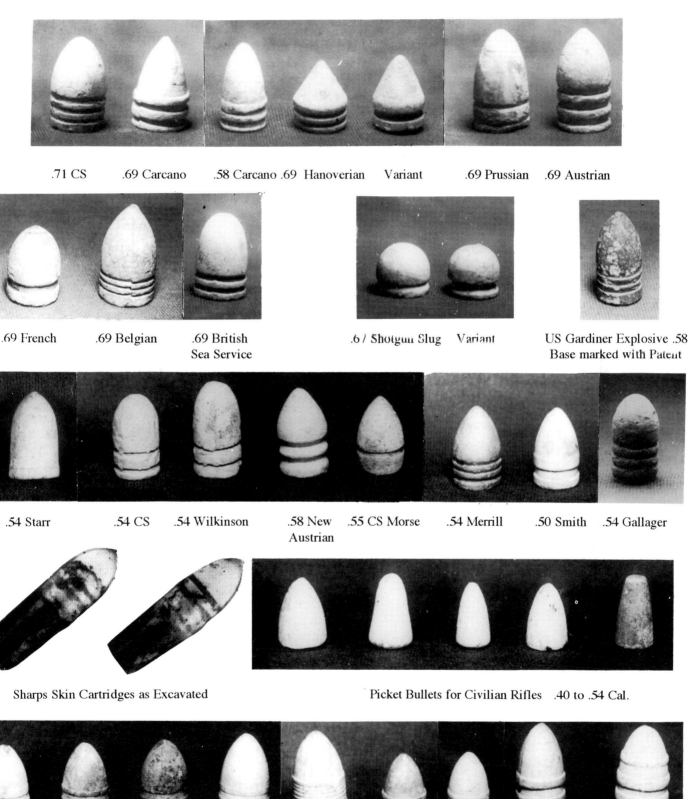

.71 CS .69 Carcano .58 Carcano .69 Hanoverian Variant .69 Prussian .69 Austrian

.69 French .69 Belgian .69 British Sea Service .6 / Shotgun Slug Variant US Gardiner Explosive .58 Base marked with Patent

.54 Starr .54 CS .54 Wilkinson .58 New Austrian .55 CS Morse .54 Merrill .50 Smith .54 Gallager

Sharps Skin Cartridges as Excavated

Picket Bullets for Civilian Rifles .40 to .54 Cal.

.54 Sharps .54 Richmond Lab. Sharps .54 Richmond Variant .58 Sharps .54 Sharps .44 Sharps Slant-Breech Variant .54 Sharps Ringtail .54 Four Ring Variant

.28 Rev.   .31 Rev.   .28 Rev.   .31 Rev.   .32 S&W   Bar   .31 Volcanic .41 Volcanic .39 Tranter .40 Tranter   Variant
Shot   British Rev.

.36 Prescott   .36 Colt .36 Water-   .36 Savage   .31 Colt   .36 Ball   .36 Starr .36 CS Rev.
vliet Arsenal

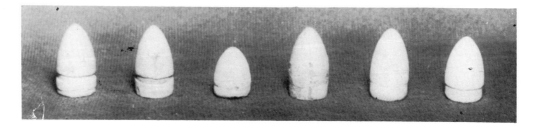

.44 Bartholow   Variant   .44 Rev.   .44 Colt   .44 Watervliet   .44 Colt

.44 Remington   .44 Sage   Variant   .44 Rev.   .44 Adams   .44 Johnson
& Dow

.36 & .50 Maynard- Cases & Bullets

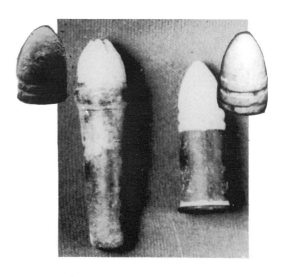

.54 Burnside & .54 Spencer- Cartridges & Bullets

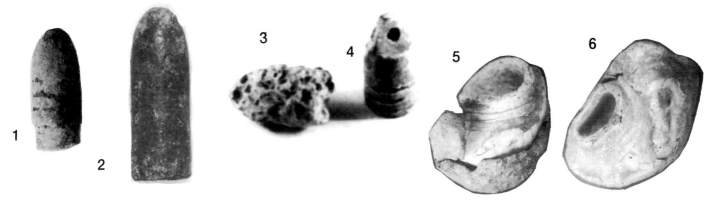

1. The von Lenk's gun cotton-.58 cal. bullet. **2.** Whitworth .45 cal. bullet. **3.** The famous "chewed bullet", which in most cases has been in a gravely roadbed, or has been gnawed on by squirrels. **4.** Lead sinker or watch fob. **Nos. 5&6.** Two mid-air bullet collisions. These are rare.

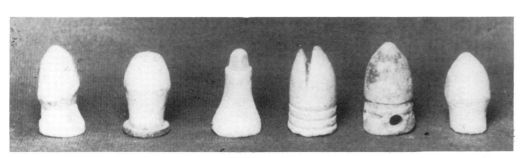

Above: These bullets have been carved or altered by the soldier. This activity was prevalent on both sides to pass long hours in camp. In some cases they are specific, like the pine tree on the right. Occasionally chess men are noted. **Right:** Bullets in wood. Although the rest of the tree has rotted away, The lead's chemical reaction has preserved the surrounding wood.

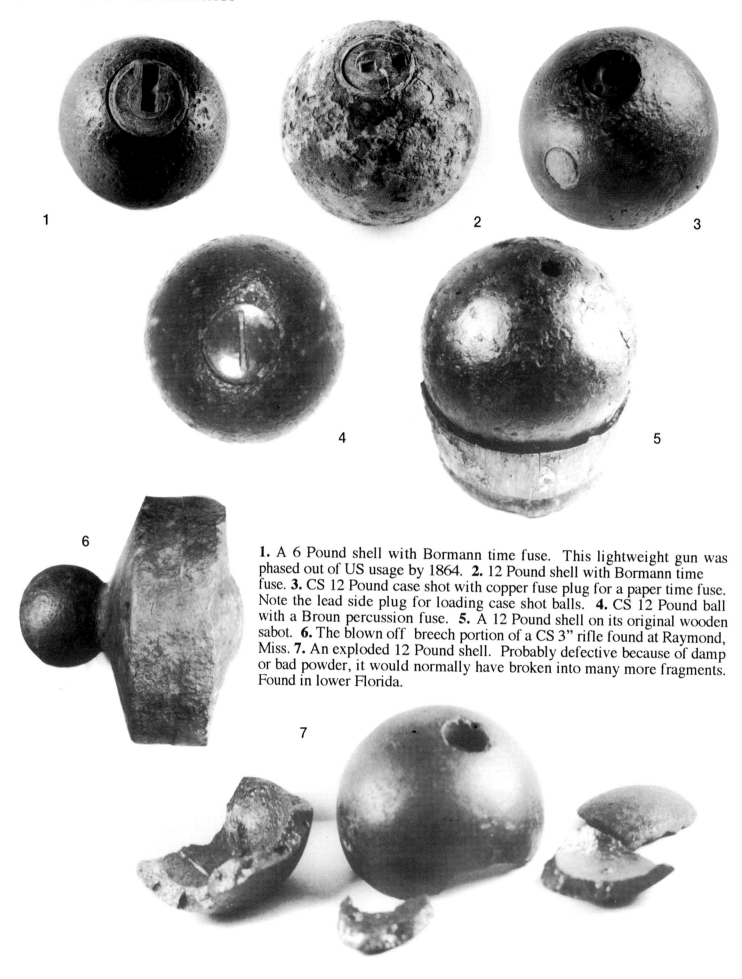

1. A 6 Pound shell with Bormann time fuse. This lightweight gun was phased out of US usage by 1864. 2. 12 Pound shell with Bormann time fuse. 3. CS 12 Pound case shot with copper fuse plug for a paper time fuse. Note the lead side plug for loading case shot balls. 4. CS 12 Pound ball with a Broun percussion fuse. 5. A 12 Pound shell on its original wooden sabot. 6. The blown off breech portion of a CS 3" rifle found at Raymond, Miss. 7. An exploded 12 Pound shell. Probably defective because of damp or bad powder, it would normally have broken into many more fragments. Found in lower Florida.

1. CS Parrott for a 3" gun. Note the "C" stamped at the top, a Tredegar coding. 2. The US 3" Schenkl case shot with combination fuse. This one has its original papier-mache sabot, a system that worked well. Many of these shells were manufactured during the war. 3. Schenkl shell as commonly found without sabot. 4. US 3" Parrott for a 10 Pounder Parrott rifle. 5. US 3" Hotchkiss, fuse missing with lead sabot. 6. CS Archer bolt, 3" with lead sabot. 7. 2.56" Hotchkiss with percussion fuse for the US 6 Pound Wiard rifle. 8. US 3.8" James with percussion fuse. Missing its tin and lead sabot which was covered with linen. Note: Nearly all shell types were made in different calibers, fusing, and many other variations. Further, many of the designs were used by both sides.

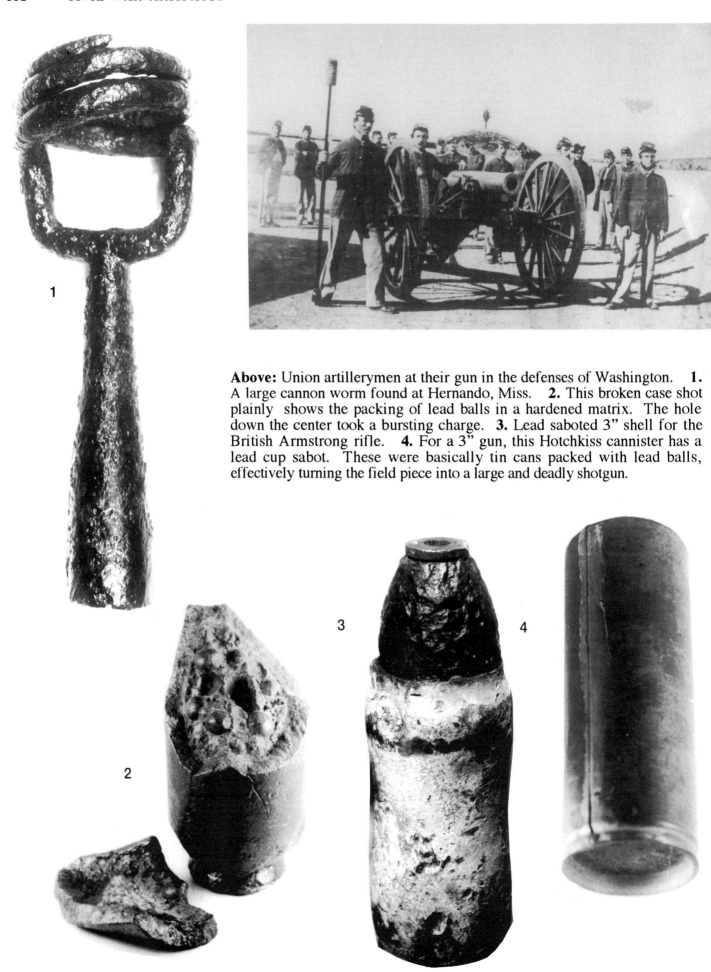

Above: Union artillerymen at their gun in the defenses of Washington.   **1.** A large cannon worm found at Hernando, Miss.   **2.** This broken case shot plainly shows the packing of lead balls in a hardened matrix. The hole down the center took a bursting charge.   **3.** Lead saboted 3" shell for the British Armstrong rifle.   **4.** For a 3" gun, this Hotchkiss cannister has a lead cup sabot. These were basically tin cans packed with lead balls, effectively turning the field piece into a large and deadly shotgun.

The shells shown on the top row are all CS Reads and were based on the original patent of Dr. John B. Read of Tuscaloosa, Ala. They are found in many variations and were widely used. These are all for a 3" rifle and have copper sabots. **1.** A case shot; note the lead filler plug on the left. It used a wooden adapter for a paper time fuse. **2.** A shell with a copper fuse plug for a paper time fuse. **3.** A bolt or "shot". These were solid projectiles for use against other batteries, fortifications and armor. **4.** This is a "common shell" often called a CS Parrott. Note the lead side load plug.

Left: Whitworth projectiles for the famous British breechloading rifle. These were superbly accurate long range weapons which saw limited but valuable use in the Confederacy. These are both 2.75" specimens. **5.** A shell. **6.** A more common bolt. Many Whitworths were brought in through the blockade but the South produced them also and most of these display an obvious mold seam.

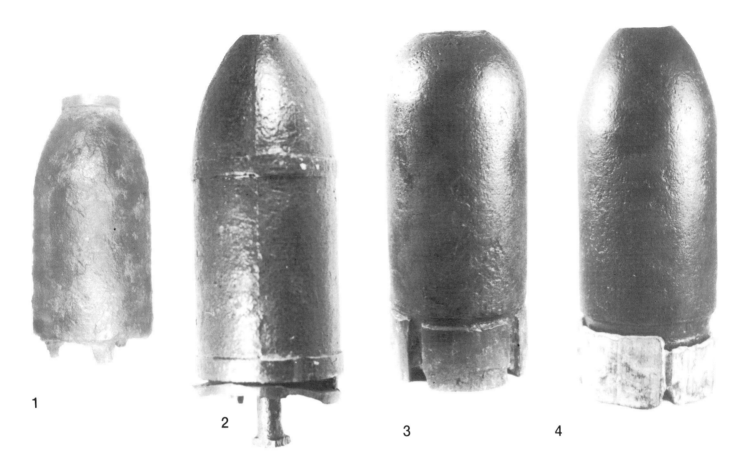

1   2   3   4

5

1. This is a rare 2.25" Mullane shell for the CS Mountain Rifle. It weighs only two pounds, eight ounces. **2.** 3" Mullane shell that used a wooden fuse plug for a paper time fuse. These shells used a copper disc on the base that expanded to take the rifling and are also called the "Tennessee Sabot" shell. **3.** The CS 3" Burton shell, with lead sabot. The obvious flame grooves in the sabot allowed the fire of ignition to ignite the paper time fuse. **4.** The US Dyer 3" shell. **5.** A stand of grape shot for a 32 Pound gun. These were primarily used in coastal batteries. On firing, the iron balls and plates would break apart.

1. A CS 6.4" Read, used in coastal defense guns. This one came from Alabama. 2. The late-war-developed CS Broun projectile for the 3" rifle. This one took a wood adapter for a paper time fuse. 3. A 3.67", rare finned Archer common shell missing its lead-band sabot. This was an early CS shell for rifled 6 Pounders. 4. Projectile for the British-designed, 3.5", 12 Pound Blakely rifle used in the CS service. Has lead cup sabot. 5. The CS Brooke shell for a 20 Pound rifle. This one was found in the Atlanta defense lines. The "G" stamped in the copper sabot identifies it as being made at the Selma Arsenal. This facility produced much ordnance for the Army of Tennessee.

WARNING: Shells and case shot of this period must still be considered armed and dangerous unless known otherwise. Black powder, even though in an excavated state, can ignite and explode. Disarming a shell is a job for the professional.

1. Weighing several hundred pounds, this CS spar torpedo was mounted ahead of the ship. It went off when its ship rammed another. **2.** The Ketchum 5 lb. hand grenade. These were originally equipped with a wooden tail with paper fins. **3.** Iron case shot as typically found in CS projectiles. **4.** A portion of a cannister round. **5.** An exploded CS land mine. **6.** The 2.25" Hale Rocket. These saw some field use at the battle of Seven Pines, Va.

As with the shells, many types and variations exist with regard to fuses. Further, many failed to function. **1.** US Parrott percussion fuse. These exploded on impact. **2.** Standard CS copper fuse plug for a ball. These took a paper time fuse cut for proper burning time to the target. They were ignited when the gun fired. Holes are for spanner wrench. **3.** Same but longer for a shell. **4.** Same type but US-made in zinc for the Parrott. **5.** Schenkl percussion fuse with name and patent date. **6.** CS watercap naval fuse. By interior design, this feature allowed the projectile to explode even in contact with water. **7.** CS percussion fuse; found only at Vicksburg and Port Hudson. **8.** Rare CS percussion model with interior sliding anvil.

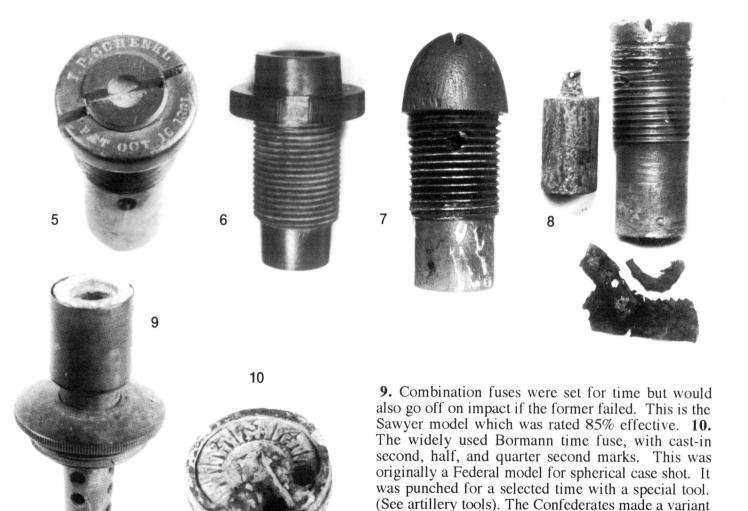

9. Combination fuses were set for time but would also go off on impact if the former failed. This is the Sawyer model which was rated 85% effective. **10.** The widely used Bormann time fuse, with cast-in second, half, and quarter second marks. This was originally a Federal model for spherical case shot. It was punched for a selected time with a special tool. (See artillery tools). The Confederates made a variant shown here.

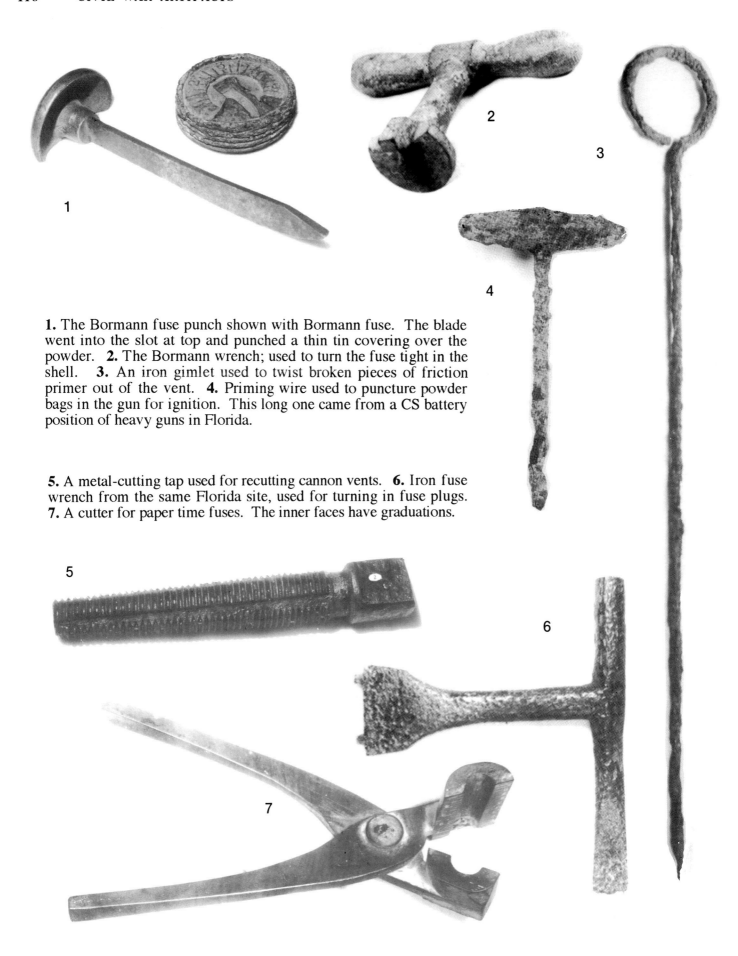

1. The Bormann fuse punch shown with Bormann fuse. The blade went into the slot at top and punched a thin tin covering over the powder.   2. The Bormann wrench; used to turn the fuse tight in the shell.   3. An iron gimlet used to twist broken pieces of friction primer out of the vent.   4. Priming wire used to puncture powder bags in the gun for ignition. This long one came from a CS battery position of heavy guns in Florida.

5. A metal-cutting tap used for recutting cannon vents.   6. Iron fuse wrench from the same Florida site, used for turning in fuse plugs.   7. A cutter for paper time fuses. The inner faces have graduations.

1. An artillery sponge bucket, made of iron. These carried water to swab the bore between shots. **2.** A brass tangent cannon sight. Each step is marked for range. **3.** A solid iron hammer as used by artillerymen. **4.** Artillery friction primers. **5.** This solid iron hatchet was found in a CS gun position outside of Richmond. **6.** A multi-purpose set of gunner's pincers from a camp of Virginia Artillery.

1. A cannon sight of cast brass. **Above**: Note the usage of this sight on the bow gun of the CS gunboat *Teaser*, captured on the James River by US forces. 2. The pendulum-hausse, actually a free swinging sight that mounted on a seat affixed to the barrel. 3. Made by Selma Arsenal and so marked, this brass gunner's level was placed on the barrel to determine the placement of the rear sight. 4. Brass cannon sight with a sliding bar for range.

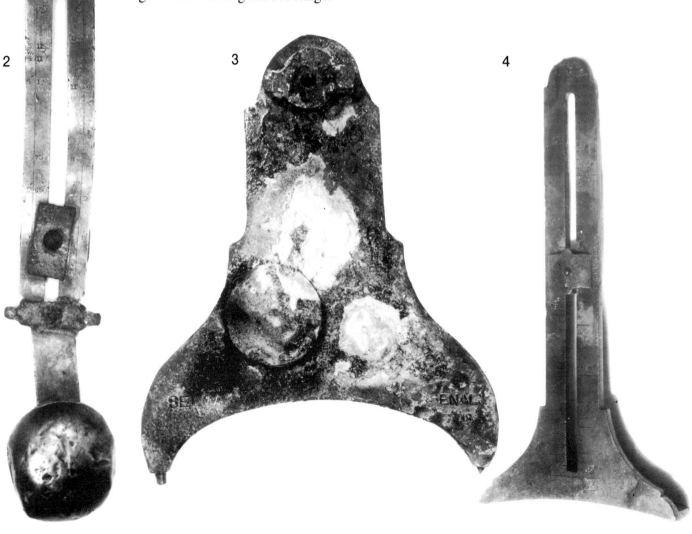

1. The standard US spur of the wartime era as worn by enlisted troops. These were of a sturdy design and were made in great quantities. Two sizes were made; #1 and #2. The #2 was only slightly smaller in width and length. Most are unmarked and some will bear an inner groove around the inside. These spurs continued to serve the US for years and many are found in the West. This example still retains its iron rowel. **Nos. 2&3.** Allegheny Arsenal made the only marked and inspected version of these spurs. Note that this is a size 2.

4. The standard US officer's spur of the Civil War period. They were a copy of the enlisted men's version embellished with cast-in foliate designs. Unlike other officer purchased items, some of these may have been arsenal produced. They are much rarer than the enlisted version.

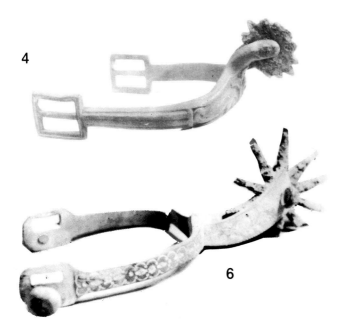

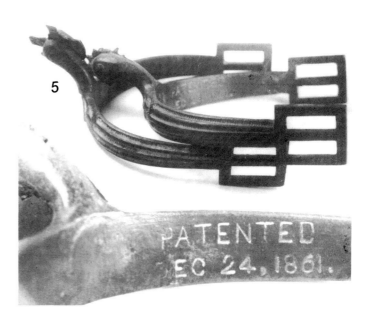

5. A pair of private purchase officer's spurs bearing patent markings on the inside. **6.** Gilted Mexican spur, possibly dating back to that earlier war. **7.** Worked down on a grindstone, this US officer's spur was converted to a screwed-to-the-boot type. This type of conversion will be noted occasionally.

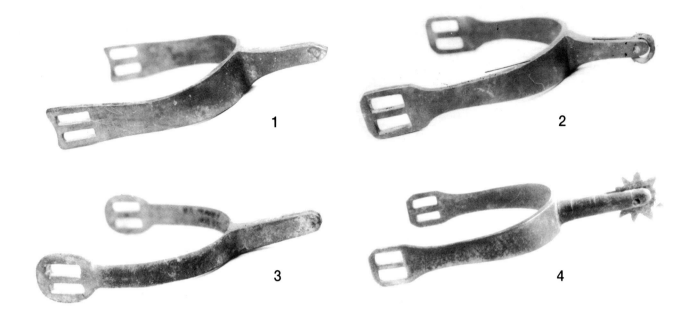

1. The standard issue "Richmond" spurs probably made at the Richmond Armory. These are large, heavy and sturdy and are characteristically made from a bronze-brass alloy. Variations exist in size and finish. 2. A seldom seen variation from North Georgia. 3. Called the "Mississippi" spur from their appearance in a Mississippi cavalry camp at Manassas, these specimens are fairly common. They are probably CS Government contract items. 4. The so-called "Brandy Station" spur. These specimens were widely issued from mid to late war.

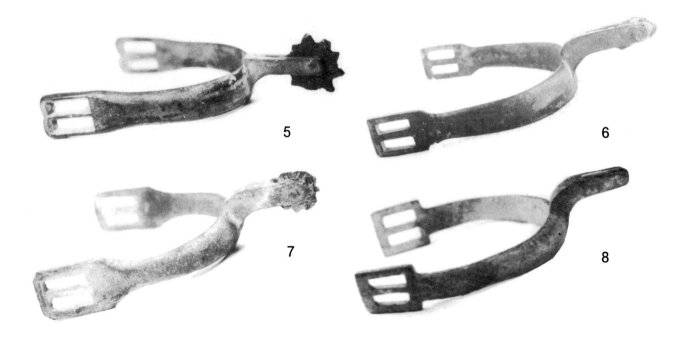

5. A rare western theater spur, having a straight neck. 6. A rare specimen, large and heavy, these are occasionally seen in the Virginia theater. 7. Probably the largest and heaviest of CS spurs. These items seem to have been designed to be unbreakable. 8. The only one noted of their type, this rare variation couples a CS style neck with a heavy US issue body.

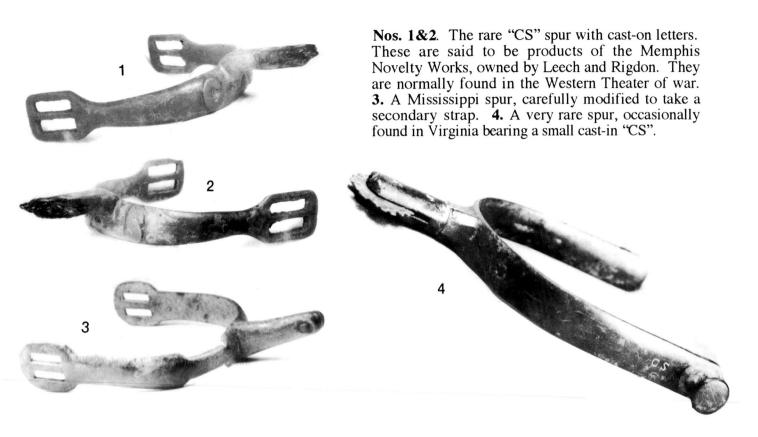

Nos. 1&2. The rare "CS" spur with cast-on letters. These are said to be products of the Memphis Novelty Works, owned by Leech and Rigdon. They are normally found in the Western Theater of war. **3.** A Mississippi spur, carefully modified to take a secondary strap. **4.** A very rare spur, occasionally found in Virginia bearing a small cast-in "CS".

Below: A grouping of civilian spurs as used during the Civil War period. **5.** A small screw-on model for a horse that apparently needed only a light touch. **6.** A small, lightly constructed spur that could have been used by a woman. **7.** A variant of the Mexican pattern with prominent rowel. **Nos. 8&9.** Two well made and strong spurs of fairly large size. **No. 8.** is made with an upswept design which is rarely seen. **10.** Made of iron, this spur is quite utilitarian in design.

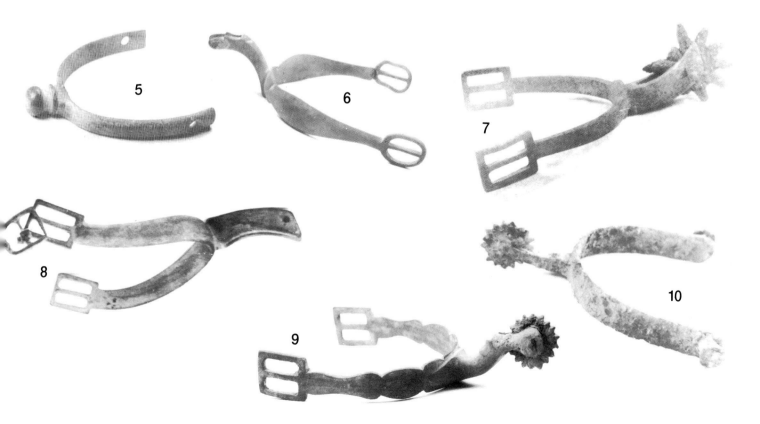

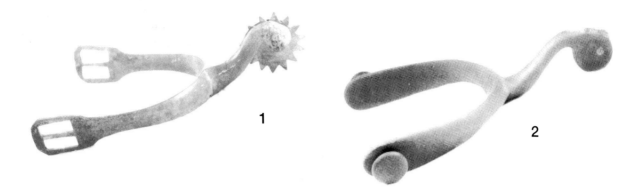

1. Probably a CS issue, this somewhat light and crude spur is fairly common. 2. Finely made pre-war civilian spur. 3. Well made iron spur which locked into a recess in the boot heel. 4. Large well made specimen that still carries portion of the leather boot strap. 5. Another "patent" spur device which locked into a projection fixed to the boot heel. 6. A rare pair of iron Mexican type spurs with horizontal rowels. Dug together in a Texas camp. 7. A finely made spring locking device spur bearing patent dates, the housing screwed to the boot heel.

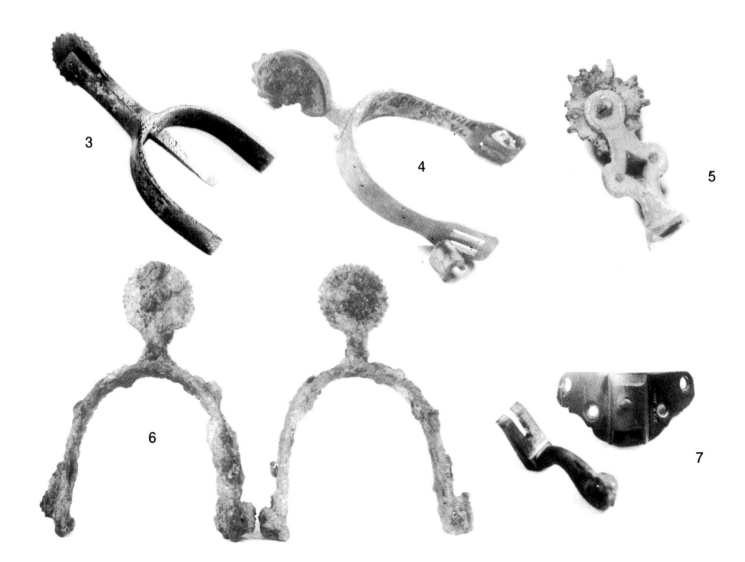

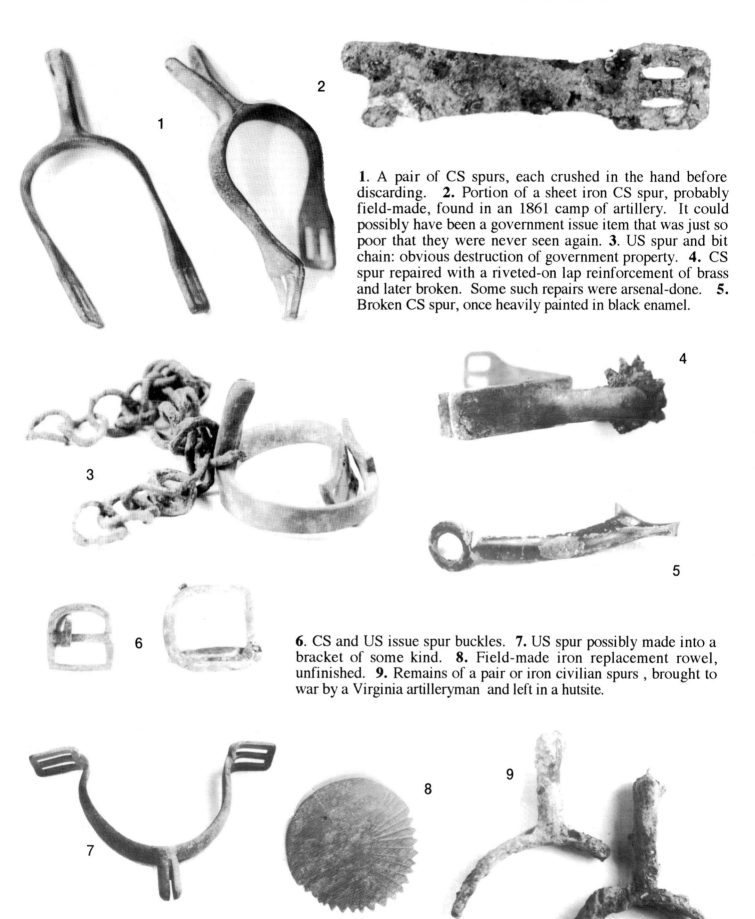

1. A pair of CS spurs, each crushed in the hand before discarding.   2. Portion of a sheet iron CS spur, probably field-made, found in an 1861 camp of artillery. It could possibly have been a government issue item that was just so poor that they were never seen again. 3. US spur and bit chain: obvious destruction of government property. 4. CS spur repaired with a riveted-on lap reinforcement of brass and later broken. Some such repairs were arsenal-done. 5. Broken CS spur, once heavily painted in black enamel.

6. CS and US issue spur buckles. 7. US spur possibly made into a bracket of some kind. 8. Field-made iron replacement rowel, unfinished. 9. Remains of a pair or iron civilian spurs , brought to war by a Virginia artilleryman and left in a hutsite.

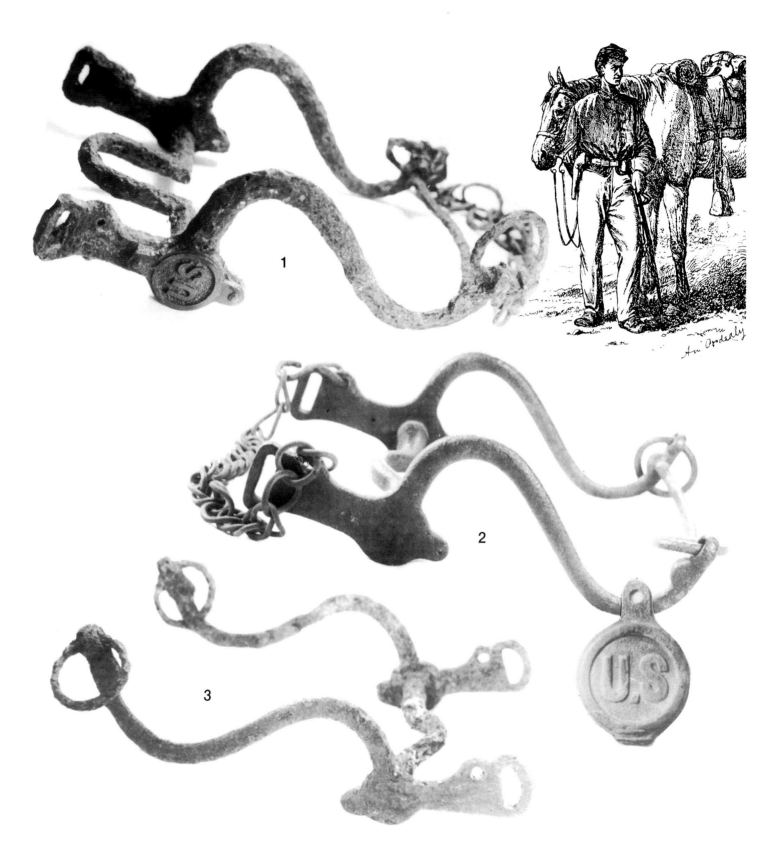

1. A complete standard issue Model 1863 US Cavalry bit with the high #4 port (upper cross bar). **2.** Another, with the more common (and less harsh on the horse) #2 port. These bits were furnished in four port sizes. Likely serving the CS, this bit has had the bosses removed (inset shows a hacked-off boss). **3.** A rare, flimsily made copy of the US bit. The sides are of flat iron. It may be a CS item or an earlier militia pattern. At top is a sketch by Civil War artist Edwin Forbes.

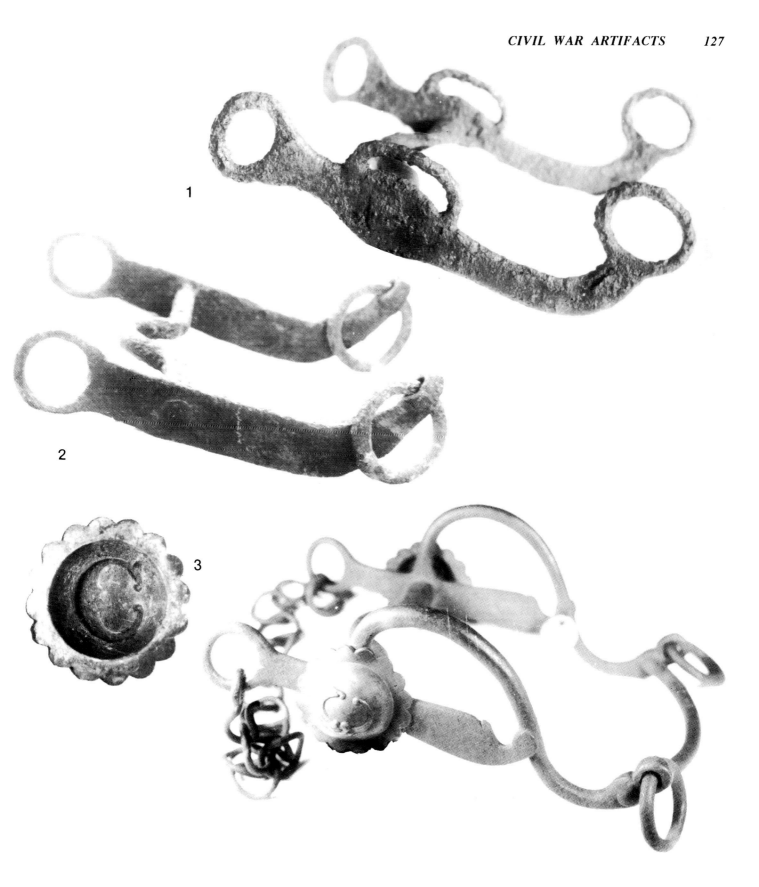

1. A well made curb bit of unknown usage but showing signs of CS design and manufacture. **2**. The standard and widely used CS trooper's bit forged of iron. Many variations in size and workmanship are seen. Likely procured by the CS government on contract from numerous manufacturers. **3**. Finely made iron bit of pre-war manufacture. Evidence exists that these are English imports and were used by some units of Virginia Militia Cavalry. The rather large bosses are high domed brass stampings and were solder affixed.

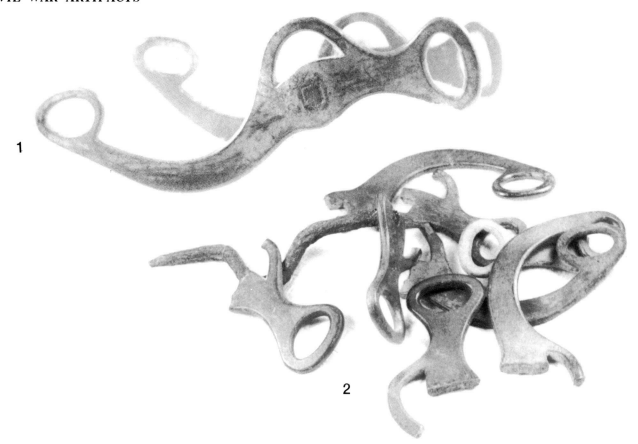

1. A CS officer's bit of brass with iron port bar. Material and finish are similar to the Richmond spurs. These appeared in Virginia in the mid-war period. Intact specimens are very rare but broken pieces are seen in CS cavalry camps. Not a durable design, they were intentionally destroyed. This seems to have been the only CS attempt to manufacture a distinctive "officer's quality" bit. Note the grouping shown in **No. 2.** **3.** A Civilian type curb bit from CS cavalry camp. **4.** Iron curb bit chain of a characteristic "weave" and length, as used on the standard US bit. **5.** Brass curb chains.

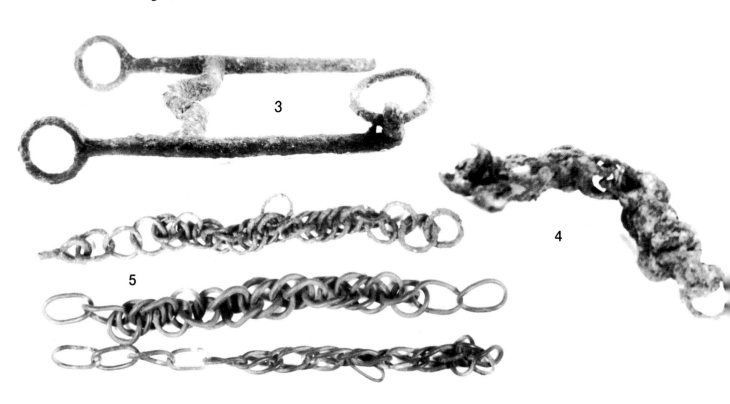

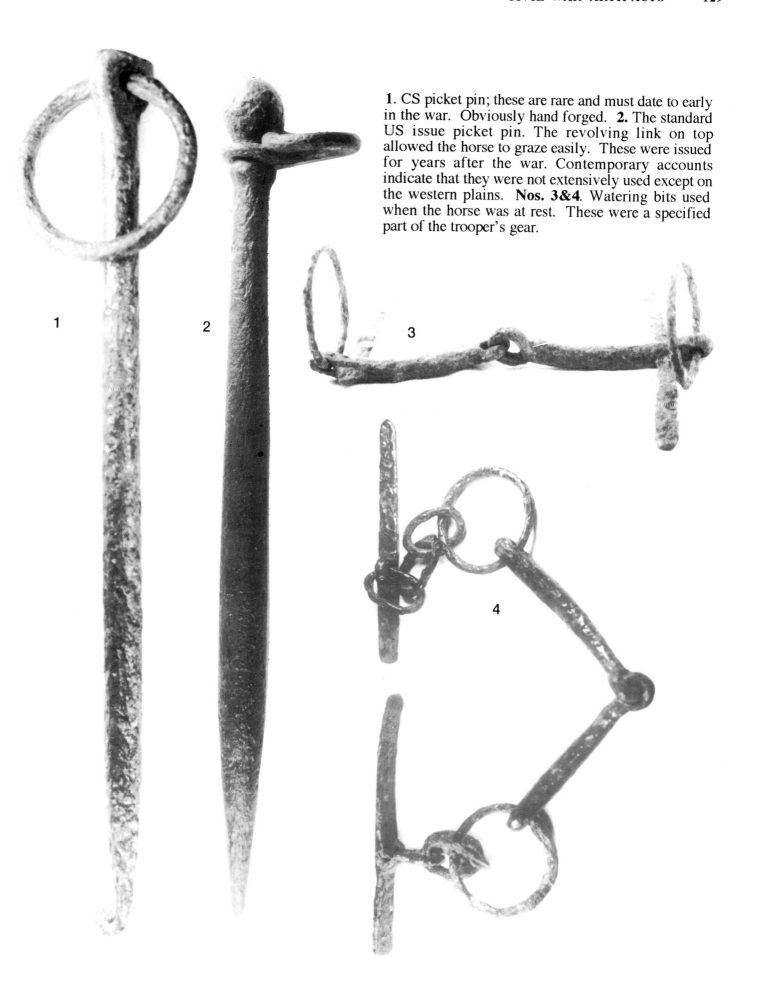

1. CS picket pin; these are rare and must date to early in the war. Obviously hand forged. **2.** The standard US issue picket pin. The revolving link on top allowed the horse to graze easily. These were issued for years after the war. Contemporary accounts indicate that they were not extensively used except on the western plains. **Nos. 3&4**. Watering bits used when the horse was at rest. These were a specified part of the trooper's gear.

Bit bosses. **Nos. 1&2.** Pre-war US Cavalry issue, denoting lettered troops in the 2nd Regiment of Cavalry.   **3.** A rare specimen denoting the US Cavalry.   **4**. Troop I, 2nd US Dragoons.   **5**. Ohio Volunteer Militia.   **Nos. 6,7&8**. War time standard US Cavalry bosses.   **9**. A rare and unknown specimen, factory-made without marking.   **10**. The shield device on this specimen may denote the US Topographical Engineers.   **11.** Portion of US spur with replacement rowel made of a US bit boss.   **12.** Plain brass martingale. These were worn on the front of the horse's harness in the center of the chest.

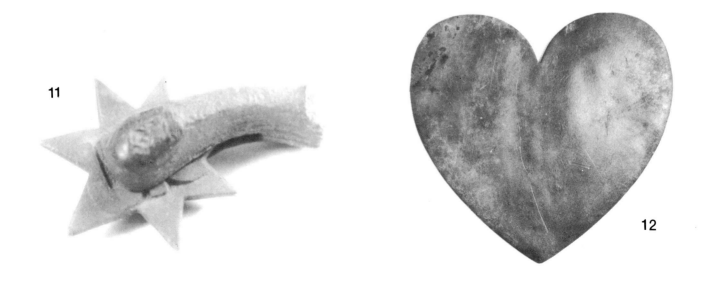

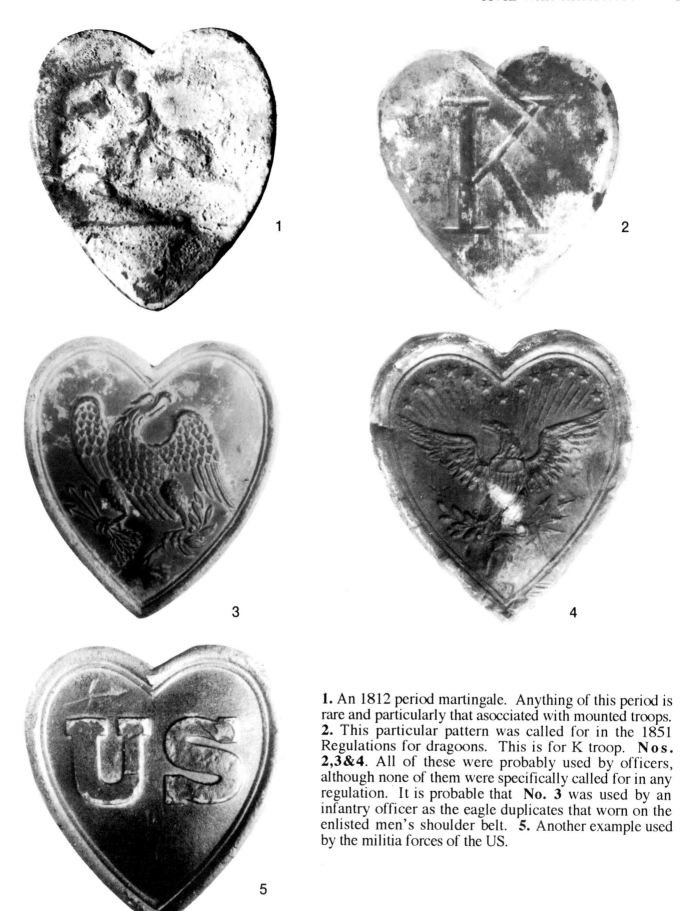

1. An 1812 period martingale. Anything of this period is rare and particularly that asocciated with mounted troops. **2.** This particular pattern was called for in the 1851 Regulations for dragoons. This is for K troop. **Nos. 2,3&4**. All of these were probably used by officers, although none of them were specifically called for in any regulation. It is probable that **No. 3** was used by an infantry officer as the eagle duplicates that worn on the enlisted men's shoulder belt. **5.** Another example used by the militia forces of the US.

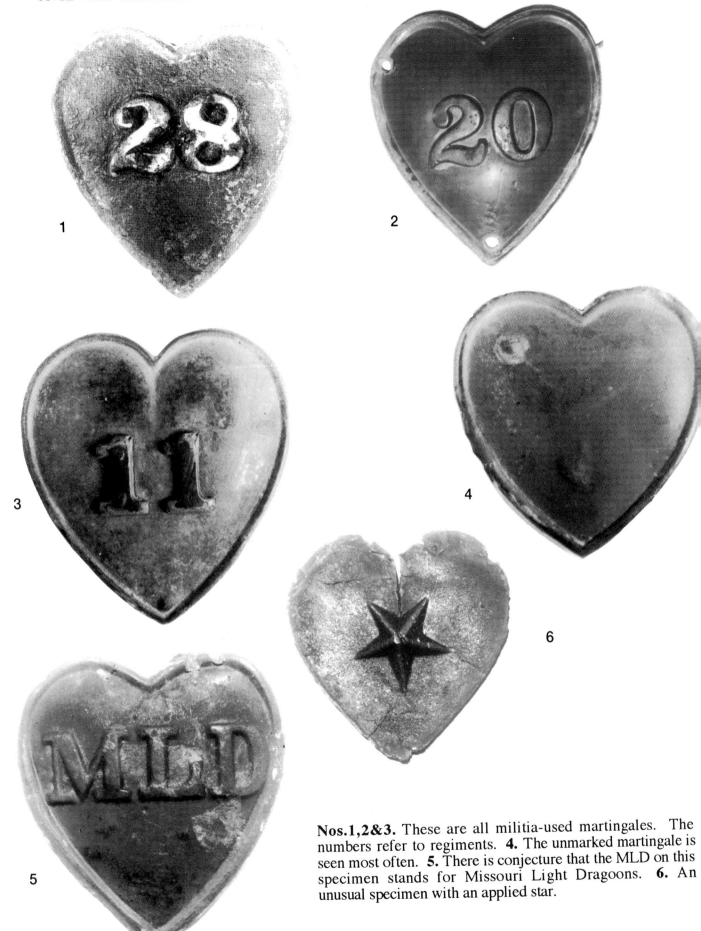

Nos.1,2&3. These are all militia-used martingales. The numbers refer to regiments. **4.** The unmarked martingale is seen most often. **5.** There is conjecture that the MLD on this specimen stands for Missouri Light Dragoons. **6.** An unusual specimen with an applied star.

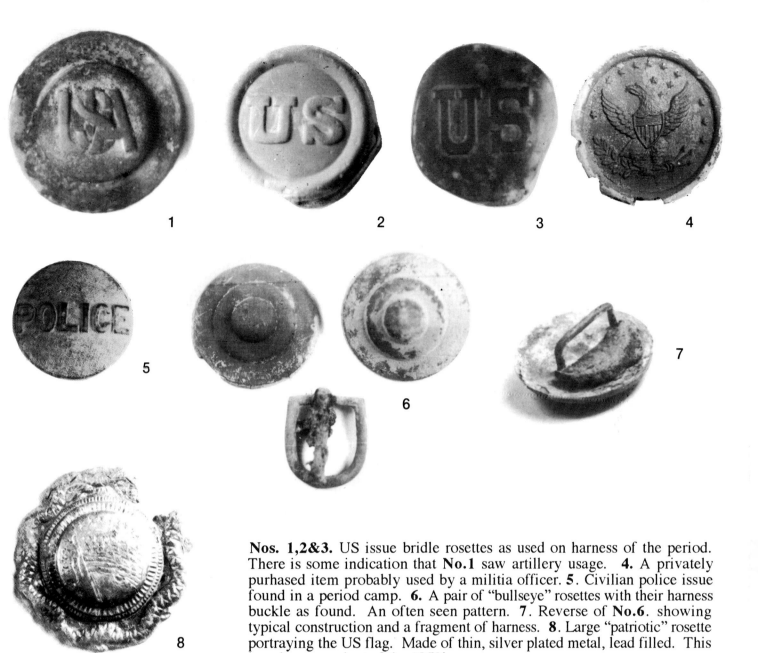

Nos. 1,2&3. US issue bridle rosettes as used on harness of the period. There is some indication that **No.1** saw artillery usage.   **4.** A privately purhased item probably used by a militia officer. **5**. Civilian police issue found in a period camp. **6.** A pair of "bullseye" rosettes with their harness buckle as found. An often seen pattern. **7**. Reverse of **No.6**. showing typical construction and a fragment of harness. **8**. Large "patriotic" rosette portraying the US flag. Made of thin, silver plated metal, lead filled. This is a showy product of the 1850's.

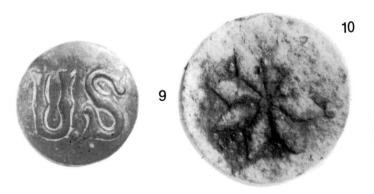

Nos. 9&10. Two rosettes probably of the post-war period. Although **No. 9.** was once military issue, for years surplus gear of all periods has been used by (and lost) from farm animals. **10.** Carrying an iron face and back, this specimen is about 2" across.

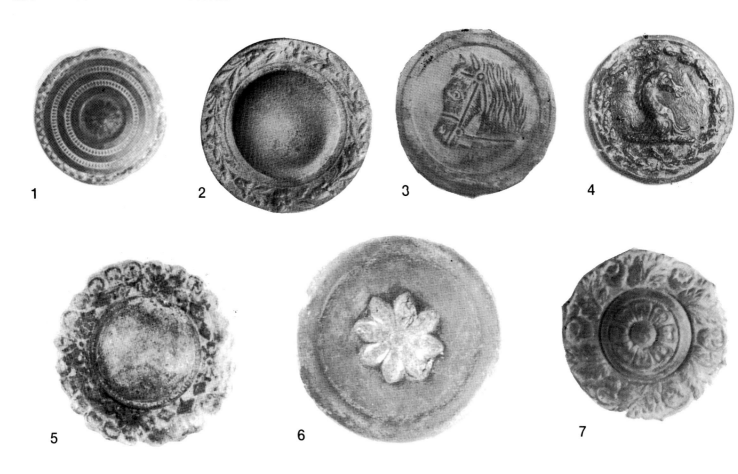

1. Brass rosette of the 18th century. Specimens of this period are generally of fine workmanship (possibly English) and are somewhat smaller than later specimens. They are often not lead filled. **2**. Typical civilian rosette of the Civil War period, of brass with a lead filler. **Nos. 3&4**. "Sporting design" rosettes. **Nos. 5,6&7** are civilian rosettes. **6**. Has attached silvered star. **8**. A simple design often found in CS cavalry camps. **9**. Civilian rosette bearing a shock of wheat, plow and farm design. Possibly emblematic of the farmer's "Grange" organization and which may post date the war. **10**. This specimen bears the Masonic seal and is of a large silvered design.

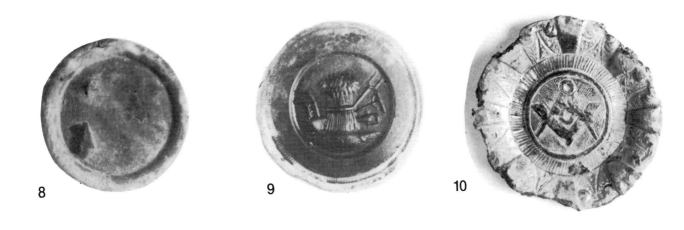

1. An unusual and rare rosette of lead filled stamped brass. There is some evidence of possible CS usage by the Texas Rangers. It has also been reported that this piece may have been one of four such devices used to decorate the corners of a heavy saddle blanket. 2. Found in a Texas camp area at Dumfries, Va., this specimen bears the same flattened star design as the rare Texas "local" waistbelt plate. 3. This item bears an applied brass star. 4. A strange rosette or bridle ornament bearing a horse's head flanked by two alligators. 5. Constructed of thin silvered white metal, lead filled, this specimen is of the "sporting" design and bears a boar's head. Found in the 1st Virginia Infantry camp at Centreville, Va. 6. This rosette may be associated with Maryland as it bears that state's cross.

7. Engraved "W.H.Connor", this rosette was found in a Mississippi Cavalry camp. 8. A finely made item displaying an eagle surrounded by 13 stars. Nos. 9&10. These specimens bearing the star device may have a Mississippi or Texas association.

Above: A well turned out Union officer and his mount. His saddle is of the English sporting type generally carried into war by the newly enlisted CS cavalryman. **1.** A heavy iron stirrup, commonly dug in the Virginia theatre of war. **2.** Solid cast brass and finished like many of the Richmond Arsenal products, this rare specimen may have been a CS officer's item. **3.** A patent breakaway stirrup. The outside frame of this model would open up on the rider's fall to preclude his being dragged. **4.** Another brass stirrup, probably issued with a pre-war saddle. **Inset**: A private purchase officer's saddle from a military outfitter's catalog.

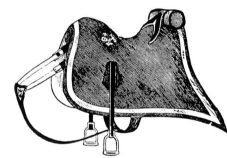

No. 223.
Saddle, Holsters, Valise, Saddle-cloth, Stirrup and Collar, for General Staff Officers.

1   2   3   4

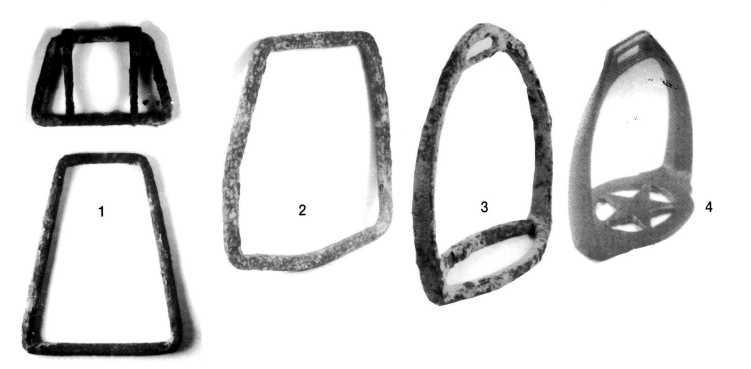

1. Unbelievably crude blacksmith-made stirrup and strap buckle found together. 2. Another crude, simple "last ditch" CS stirrup. 3. The standard issue stirrup that was affixed to the CS copy of the McClellan saddle. They were simply made and sturdy, manufactured by forging a circle then splitting and opening the top and bottom. 4. A fairly small item bearing a star device. 5. US artillery design of heavy cast brass marked "WATERVLIET ARSENAL NY". Nos. 6&7. Two simple forged iron specimens, probably issued under the same circumstances as item No. 3. All three of the latter are found frequently in CS cavalry maneuver areas and camps. Note that there is no common Union stirrup found: the McClellan saddle utilized wooden stirrups.

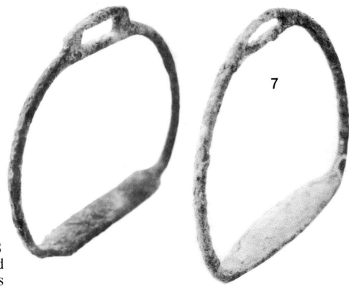

Note: According to regulation, newly mustered CS cavalrymen could furnish their own horses and equipment. They were then paid for these articles according to their quality and condition. This accounts for the wide diversity of such items on CS sites.

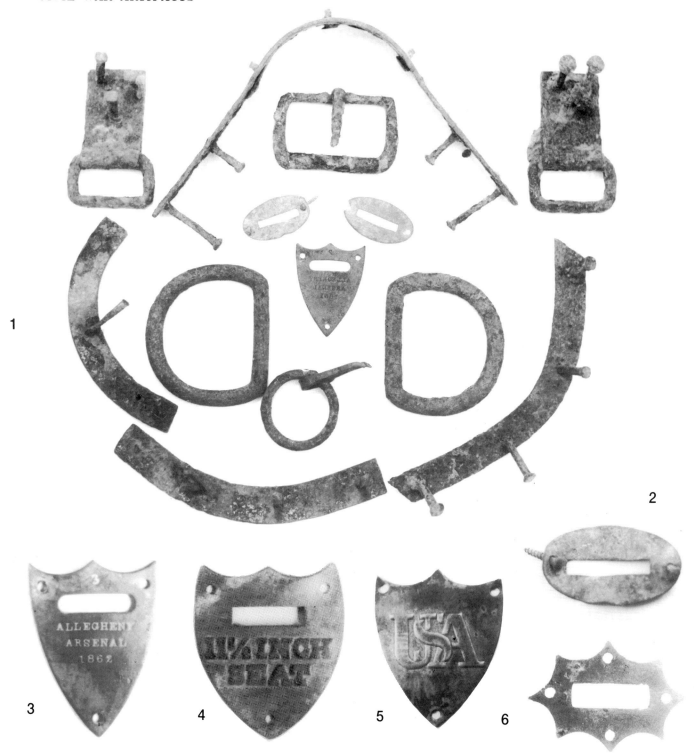

1. Most of the metal portions of a McClellan saddle dug together in a CS cavalry camp. This saddle was preferred by the Southern troopers ; this one must have had a broken tree and was left behind. **2.** Guard plate of sheet brass. These were affixed around the rear rim of the saddle to allow tie down thongs to pass through. **3.** Pommel ornament as found on the Allegheny Arsenal saddle. The "3" at top is a size code for the length of seat. (Seats came in sizes 1,2&3). **Nos. 4&5.** Variants of the same item. **6.** Guard plate used on an unknown saddle. **7.** Die struck brass saddle plate, gilted, and marked "E Waters-Maker- Troy, NY".

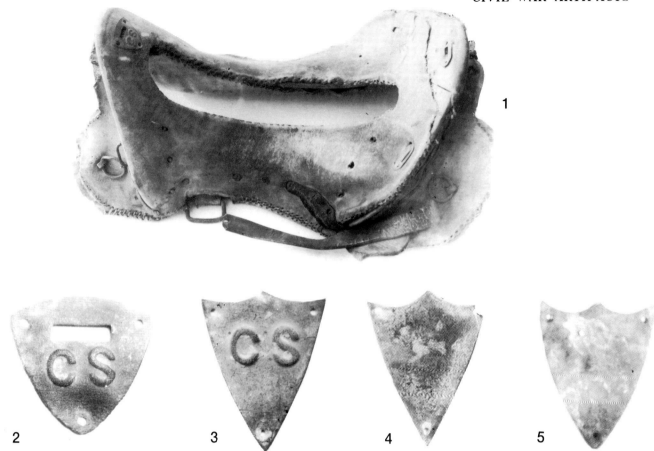

1. Crude CS copy of the US McClellan saddle. Though produced by the thousands, only a few survive 2. Shield as affixed to the front of this model saddle. Of brass, here they are occasionally seen in pewter. **3.** A variant of the preceding. On all specimens noted, the same "CS" die is used. **Nos. 4&5.** Unmarked shields. **6.** Guard plate of hand trimmed brass. **7.** Another, of sheet pewter. **8.** Crude tin version with original square nails.

9. This corner iron originally was punched for a screw at each end and was a brace between two wooden parts of the tree. **10.** Compare the single heavy girth strap ring from a US saddle with the pair of rough and much lighter CS counterparts, found together. Note the two different shapes of the CS items.

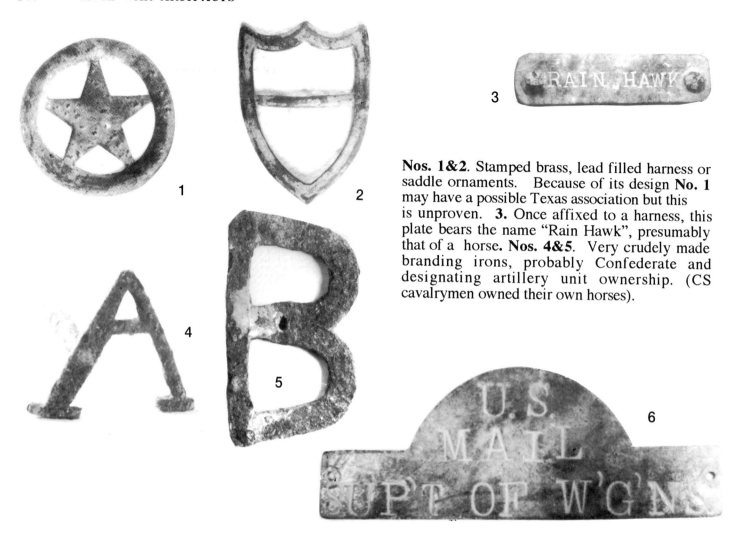

Nos. 1&2. Stamped brass, lead filled harness or saddle ornaments. Because of its design No. 1 may have a possible Texas association but this is unproven. 3. Once affixed to a harness, this plate bears the name "Rain Hawk", presumably that of a horse. Nos. 4&5. Very crudely made branding irons, probably Confederate and designating artillery unit ownership. (CS cavalrymen owned their own horses).

6. Heavy brass tag from mail wagon.   7. Front and rear of decorative brass tips that were affixed to leather harness straps. Found in various sizes and occasionally silver plated. They look like and are often mistaken for personal insignia.   8. Decorative brass ornament as used on horse collars of the period. Nos. 9&10. Cast brass guide rings fitted to horse harness allowing the reins to pass through.

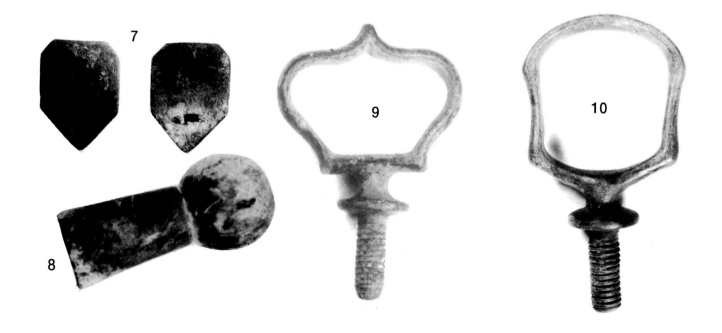

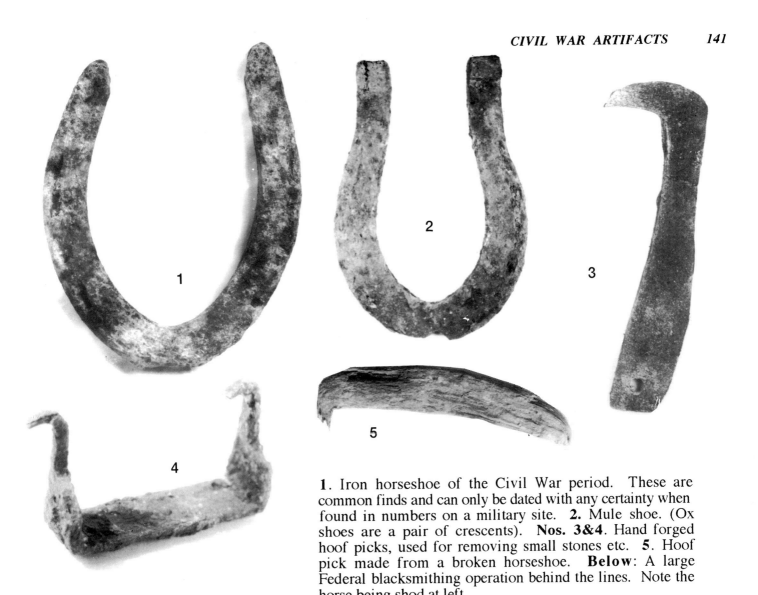

1. Iron horseshoe of the Civil War period. These are common finds and can only be dated with any certainty when found in numbers on a military site. **2**. Mule shoe. (Ox shoes are a pair of crescents). **Nos. 3&4**. Hand forged hoof picks, used for removing small stones etc. **5**. Hoof pick made from a broken horseshoe. **Below**: A large Federal blacksmithing operation behind the lines. Note the horse being shod at left.

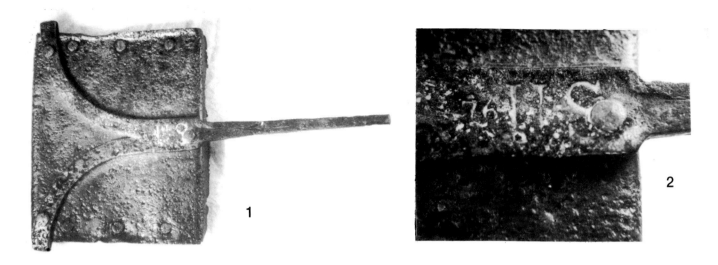

1. Iron curry comb of typical Civil War period design, missing its turned wood handle. **2.** Inset showing markings on this specimen. This is probably a pre-war issue item with "US" markings and the "76" issue number. A rare piece. **Nos. 3&4.** Top and bottom of a curry comb from an early CS camp. Note the usual maker's disc on the top. **5.** Detail view of disc showing its model number.

6. Another brass maker's disc, this one with a horse and rider. The maker's name is not readable. **7.** This curry comb has a perched eagle trademark and a brass handle ferrule.

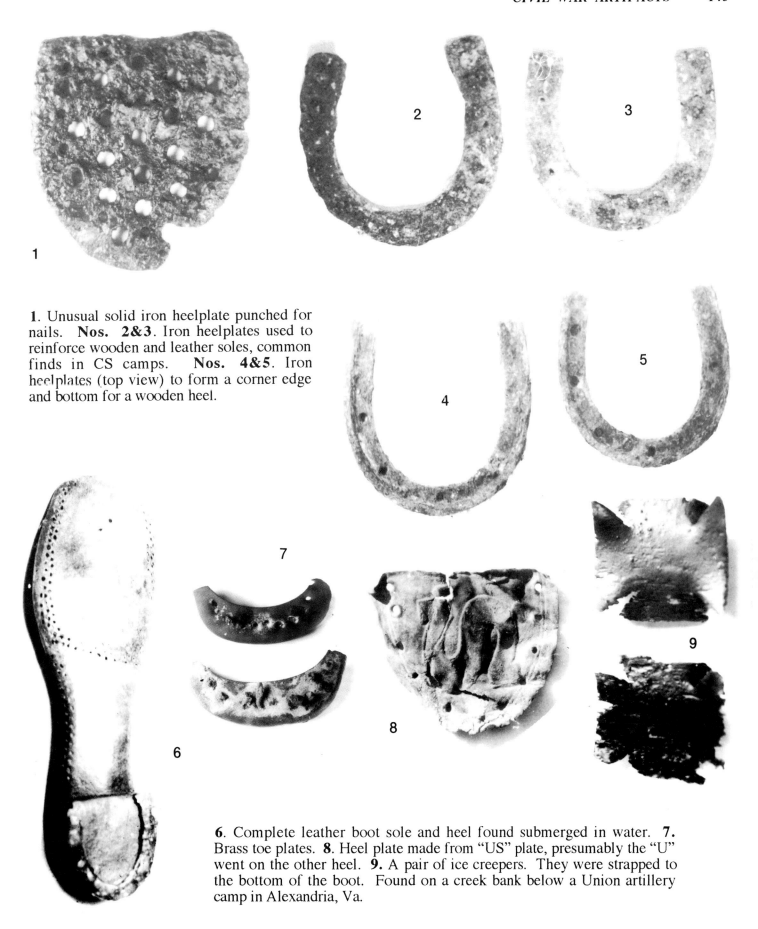

1. Unusual solid iron heelplate punched for nails. **Nos. 2&3**. Iron heelplates used to reinforce wooden and leather soles, common finds in CS camps. **Nos. 4&5**. Iron heelplates (top view) to form a corner edge and bottom for a wooden heel.

6. Complete leather boot sole and heel found submerged in water. **7.** Brass toe plates. **8.** Heel plate made from "US" plate, presumably the "U" went on the other heel. **9.** A pair of ice creepers. They were strapped to the bottom of the boot. Found on a creek bank below a Union artillery camp in Alexandria, Va.

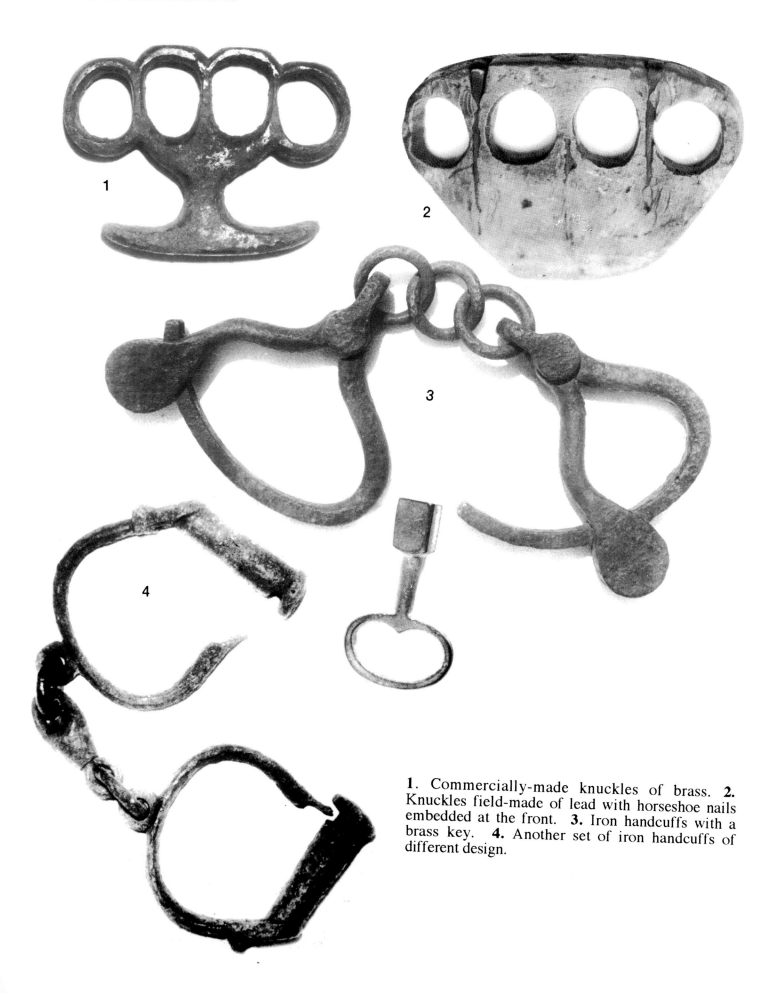

1. Commercially-made knuckles of brass. 2. Knuckles field-made of lead with horseshoe nails embedded at the front. 3. Iron handcuffs with a brass key. 4. Another set of iron handcuffs of different design.

Right: The old sergeant wears the standard Federal oilcloth knapsack and blanket roll. Though huge quantities were produced during the wartime years, many troops on active campaign did not carry them after the first year of war.

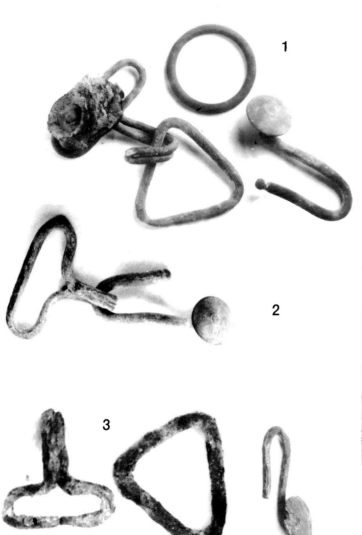

1. Brass parts to Federal knapsacks. **2.** Odd variant made of iron with a brass "button". **3.** Crude iron pack parts, probably CS made.

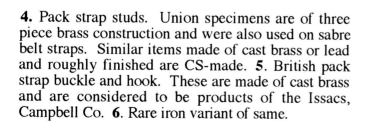

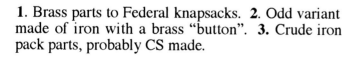

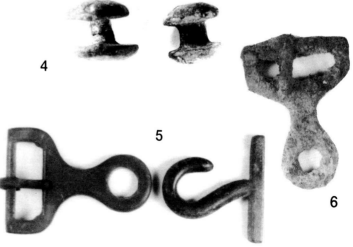

4. Pack strap studs. Union specimens are of three piece brass construction and were also used on sabre belt straps. Similar items made of cast brass or lead and roughly finished are CS-made. **5.** British pack strap buckle and hook. These are made of cast brass and are considered to be products of the Issacs, Campbell Co. **6.** Rare iron variant of same.

1. The US Model 1858 canteen. This was the Civil War standard and was utilized into the next century. It was made of two pressed steel sides, soldered together and fitted with a pewter spout and three tin sling guides. They were covered with cloth and carried on a cotton sling. 2. A modification of the former canteen called the "bullseye". For added strength, a series of rings were impressed on each side. The one shown still carries portions of its cloth cover. 3. A double spout model with an internal divider, possibly Confederate. 4. A smaller, non standard model used either by the Confederates or militia.

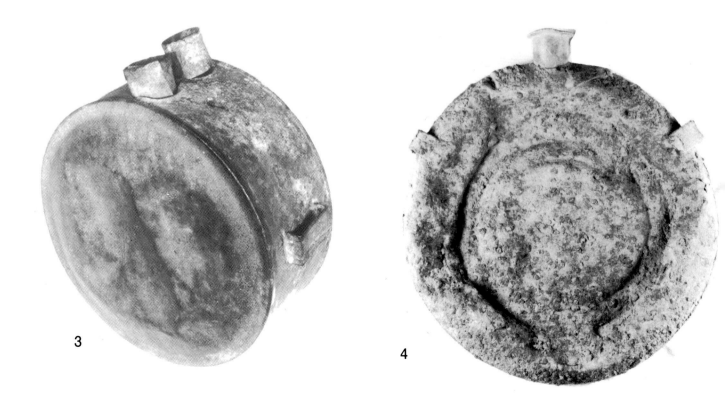

1. A tin plated CS drum canteen with impressed rings. The plating was good enough to keep it water tight through its years in the ground. From an 1861 camp in Fairfax Co., Va. 2. Found near Ft. Donelson, Tenn. this is another CS specimen. 3. An unusual find; this CS drum was run over by a wagon. 4. A small drum canteen, this one made from sheet pewter.

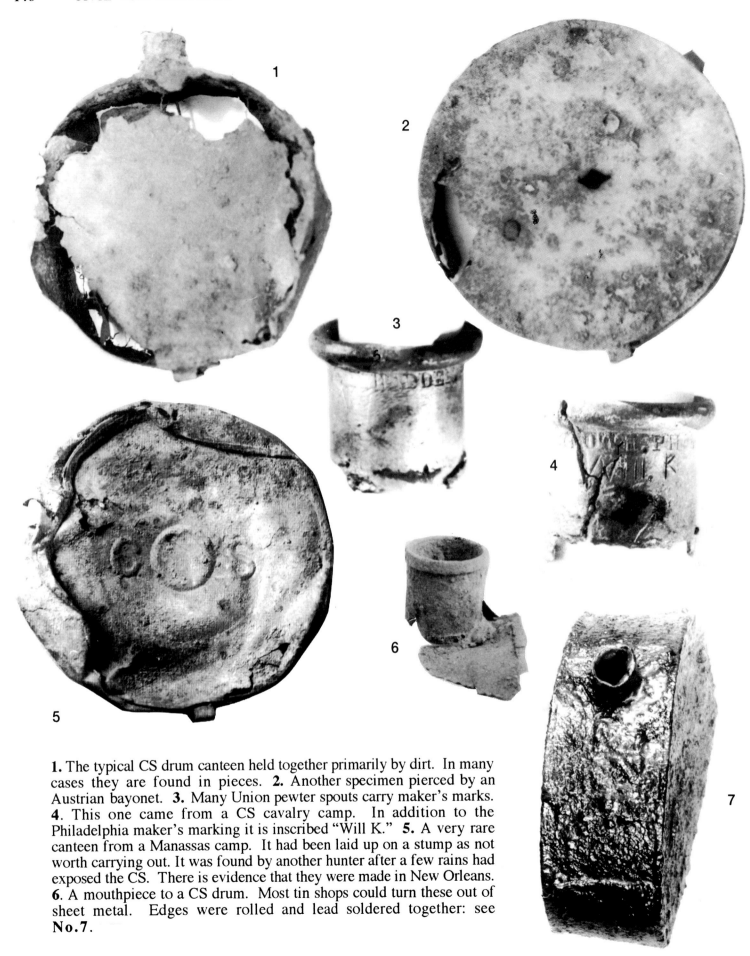

1. The typical CS drum canteen held together primarily by dirt. In many cases they are found in pieces. 2. Another specimen pierced by an Austrian bayonet. 3. Many Union pewter spouts carry maker's marks. 4. This one came from a CS cavalry camp. In addition to the Philadelphia maker's marking it is inscribed "Will K." 5. A very rare canteen from a Manassas camp. It had been laid up on a stump as not worth carrying out. It was found by another hunter after a few rains had exposed the CS. There is evidence that they were made in New Orleans. 6. A mouthpiece to a CS drum. Most tin shops could turn these out of sheet metal. Edges were rolled and lead soldered together: see No.7.

4. *UNIFORM ITEMS*

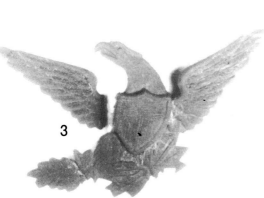

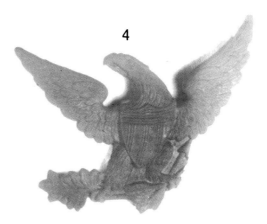

The use of the eagle as a hat device was widespread. **Top**: Here the eagle is worn on the artillery shako. **1**. The specific use of this specimen is not known although the direction the head is facing identifies it as a militia item. Further, the fact that the arrows point inwards dates it to the early 1830's. It is most likely for a chapeau. **Nos. 2,3&4.** These are die variations of regulation cap eagles. The design originated as the 1821 cockade eagle. Those shown here date to the 1850 period.

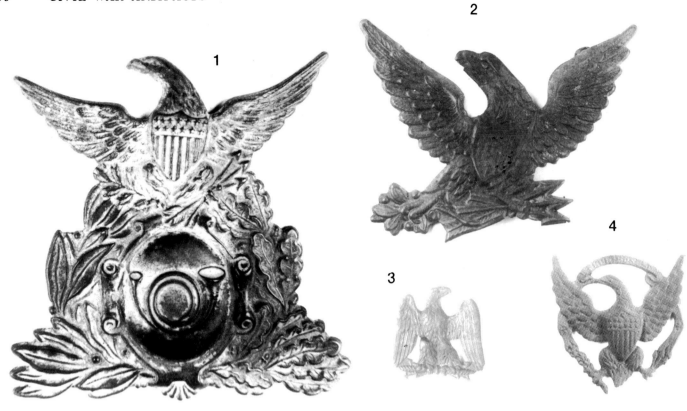

1. A large hat plate from the French "Chasseur de Vincennes" uniform that at one point was issued to the 18th Massachusetts and the 83rd Pennsylvania. 2. A die struck brass hat eagle of the 1830's. 3. An unknown eagle device. 4. An eagle pin of a style that was in use for many years. This design was later used on the 1872 US helmet plate. 5. A dragoon helmet plate of ca. 1812. It is known that the Virginia dragoons later used this plate also. 6. The US 1833 dragoon helmet plate displaying a Napoleonic eagle.

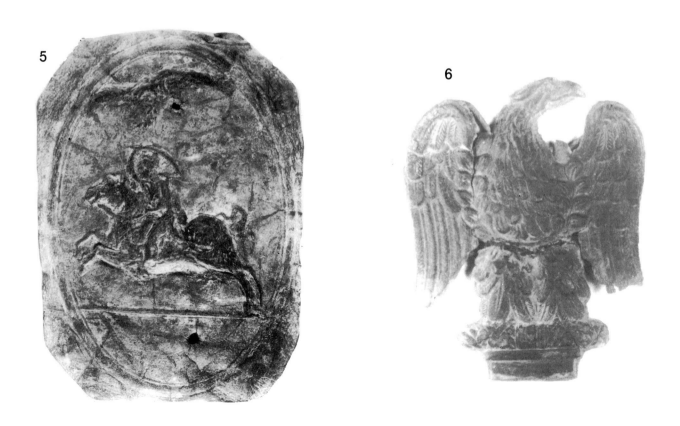

1

2

3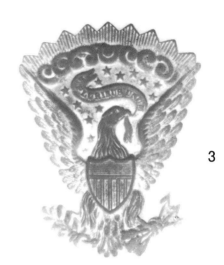

Nos. 1,2&3. Various examples of the Model 1851 "eagle" hat ornament. **No. 3** is very unusual in that it is gilted and the eagle's head faces left. At first these devices were worn at the base of the pompon on the enlisted men's shako. Later they were worn to pin up the side of the enlisted man's and officer's hat. (In 1858 a new, large, felt brimmed hat was authorized for most Army personnel. It is sometimes called the Hardee hat or the Jeff Davis hat, after the then Secretary of War.) Because of this, the eagle hat ornament is often called the "Jeff Davis" hat eagle.

Nos. 4,5&6. Cut-out examples of the "Jeff Davis" hat eagle. To judge from surviving examples this was a popular field conversion. This work was undoubtedly done with a pocket knife.

From a period newspaper, this cut shows a group of Union artillerymen at a halt. Note the hat ornament in wear. The usage of this particular device was probably very rare on the front lines.

4

5

6

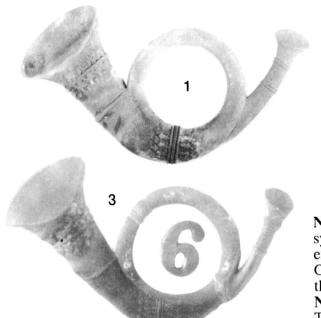

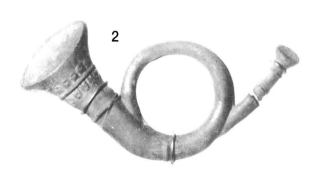

Nos. 1, 2 & 3. The classic "hunting horn" of the infantry, a symbol dating back to the earlier part of the century. These examples were worn on the enlisted man's headgear of the Civil War period and many die variations are known. Note the differences in ornamentation between **Nos. 1** and **2**. **No. 3** as found, carries the regimental number in the center. The company letter was worn above the bend.

4. Small size infantry horn, somewhat unusual being of the small officer's size but in a plain finish. **Nos. 5, 6 & 7.** False embroidered officer's hat insignia. They are finely made and gilted. **8.** A variant die design in silver from a camp of Kentucky troops. **9.** Horn device, hung from a small chain on the front of the 1830's period infantry shako. **10.** Another variant of unusual pattern as worn by some Virginia Militia troops in the pre-war period.

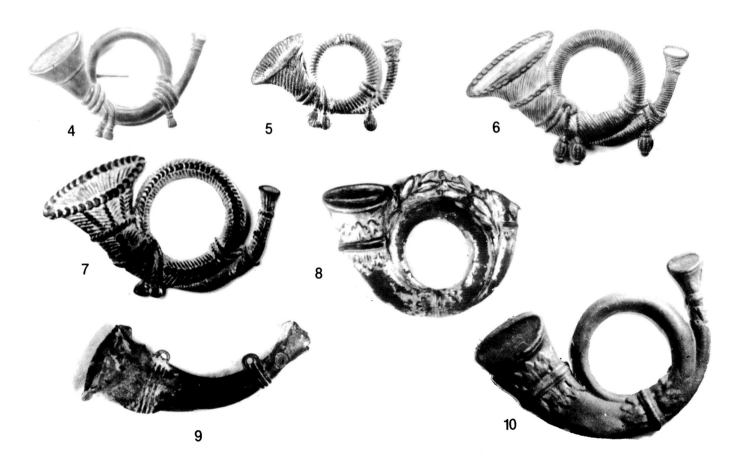

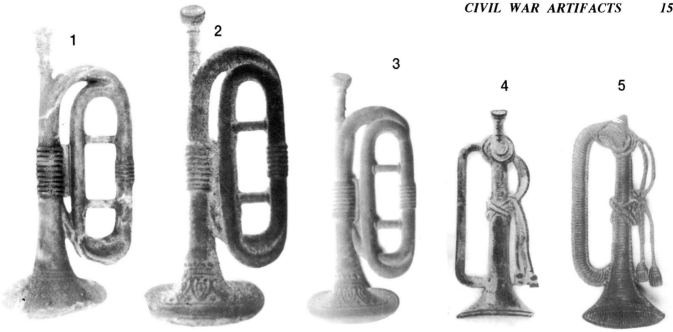

Above: The various bugle hat devices as specified for the Regiments of Mounted Riflemen in 1851. These heavily armed troops rode into action where they were to dismount and fight as infantry. **Nos. 1 & 2.** Enlisted men's bugles, first model. **3.** Smaller second model. **4.** A somewhat unusual variant which may have been used by the militia. **5.** Officer's version, false embroidered. All bugles were worn upright as shown. Riflemen's bugles are far scarcer than the commonly seen infantry horn device.

6. A group of military items found in the northeastern part of Florida. They all date from the 1836-1840 period and are associated with the 2nd Dragoons. Shown here: A hat eagle, various buttons, three pompon holders, and two dimes on a sheet brass buckle.

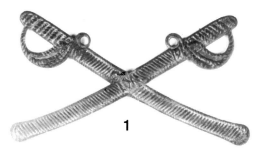

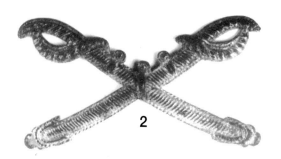

One of the most attractive of all military insignia of the Civil War period is the crossed sabre device which was first authorized in 1851 for officers of the US Dragoons. When the new US Cavalry Regiments were formed in 1855 they too were authorized to wear them. Various changes in the Regulations placed the sabre edges up or down in different years but by the Civil War they were being worn edges up on the front of the kepi with the regimental number above and the troop letter below.

Nos. 1&2. Small size officer's sabres of gilted stamped brass in the false embroidered pattern. **3.** An unusual large pattern of same. All of the above are fairly rare finds. **Nos. 4&5.** Enlisted men's versions of thin stamped brass. Many variants are known. **No. 5** bears its original brass wire attachment hooks. In many cases these sabres are found broken at the center. **Right:** A pre-war Virginia cavalryman wears the sabre device on his kepi.

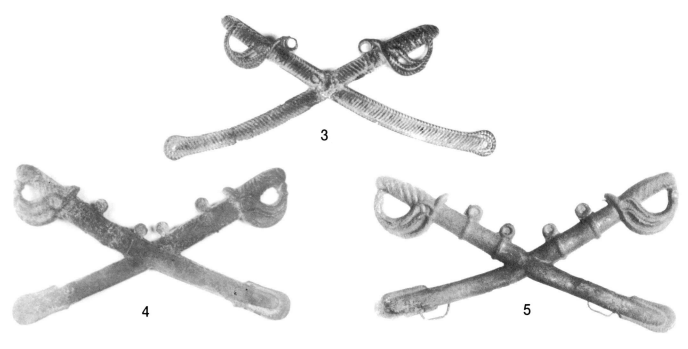

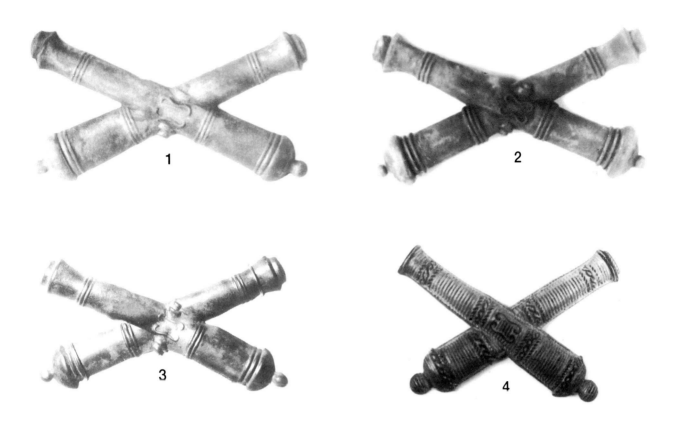

Nos. **1,2&3**. Crossed cannons hat ornaments of stamped brass. These are the large enlisted men's size. As will be noted, these are found in numerous die variations. **4**. An officer's model in the false embroidered design. **Nos. 5,6&7**. Smaller officer's models, all plated. This device originated in the US Regulations of 1834. Specimen **No. 6** was found in Washington, D.C. which was surrounded by extensive fortifications, all manned by artillerymen. Note that some of the rare early versions are very large and are pressed of extremely heavy brass.

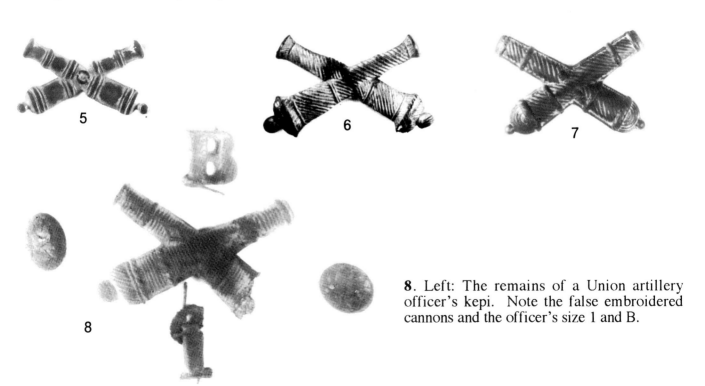

8. Left: The remains of a Union artillery officer's kepi. Note the false embroidered cannons and the officer's size 1 and B.

Nos.   1,2&3. "Turreted Castle" hat devices of the Army Corps of Engineers. Like most other insignia of the period, these were specified in the 1851 regulations. It should be noted that this device was much used by various military schools. **4.** Shield device of the Topographical Engineers. **5.** Device of the Ordnance Corps, worn on the hat and uniform. It portrays a flaming bomb. **6.** Unknown stamped brass star ornament, probably a militia item. **7.** Fancy silver plated kepi buckle.

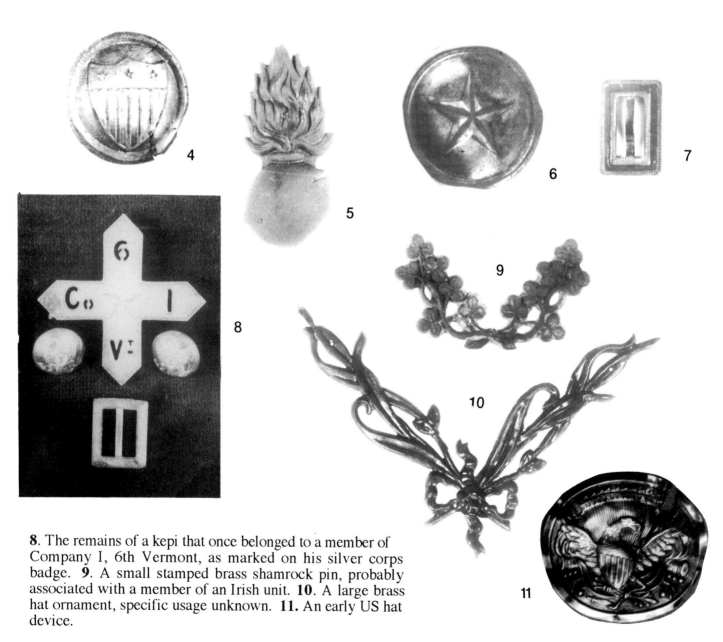

8. The remains of a kepi that once belonged to a member of Company I, 6th Vermont, as marked on his silver corps badge. **9**. A small stamped brass shamrock pin, probably associated with a member of an Irish unit. **10**. A large brass hat ornament, specific usage unknown. **11**. An early US hat device.

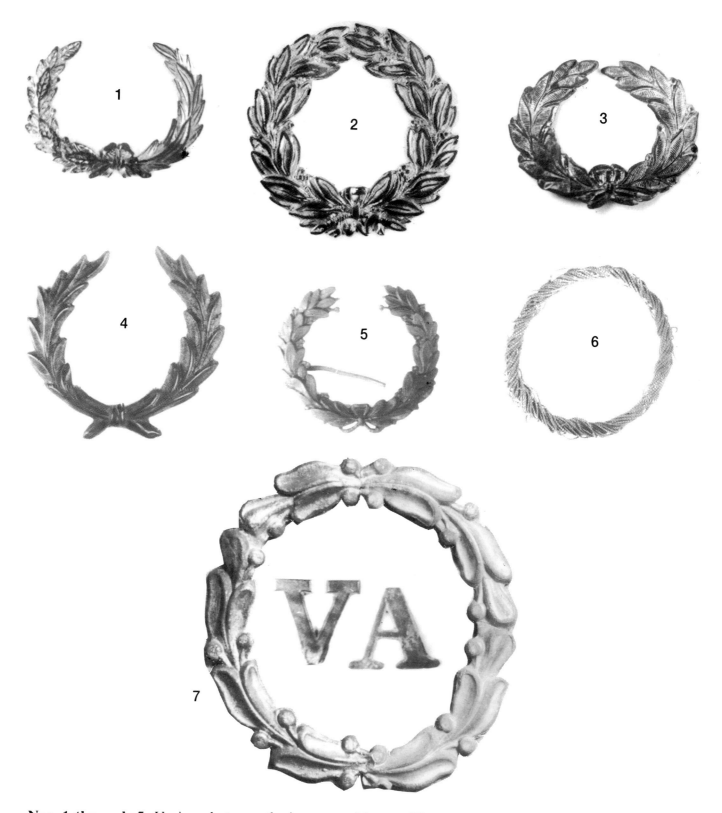

Nos. 1 through 5. Various hat wreaths in stamped brass. There are numerous variants of the above, nearly all silvered or gilted. Specific sizes and even types of leaves were spelled out in the US Regulations. The militia used both these and some of the odder types. **6.** This very unusual specimen is made of twisted brass wire. **7.** This wreath was worn by a specific unit of the 1st Regiment of Virginia Volunteers. It will be noted that hat wreaths are infrequent finds and in many cases are recovered in a broken state.

CS hat ornaments. **Nos.1&2**. From South Carolina, both of these stamped brass pins were made in some quantity. **3.** A quite rare item and silver plated. **4.** Shako device bearing the Georgia seal. **5.** Virginia hat pin, factory supplied and cut from a buckle die strike. Note that some are found field-cut from buckles. These were popular among pre-war troops. **6.** Cut-out brass heart. These were frequently embellished with a cloth center and were worn on the hat or uniform by members of Virginia's Laurel Brigade of cavalry.

7. A very finely detailed Georgia hat device of the pre-war period. Made of stamped brass and gilted. **8.** From one of their battery positions, this set of hand cut letters denotes the Washington Artillery of New Orleans. **9.** A Louisiana hat ornament of stamped brass. **10.** A similar item but this being cut from the rectangular lead filled state buckle. **11.** Again cut from one of the state plates, this specimen bears small punched thread holes.

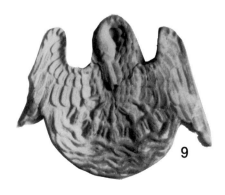

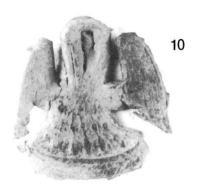

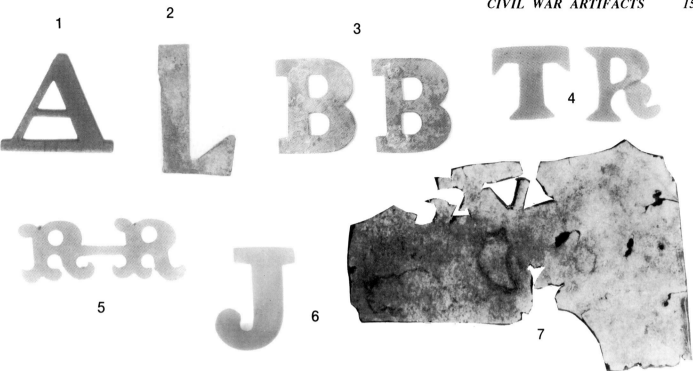

Shown above are non regulation letters of brass; most were probably made by the local tinsmith or jeweler with varying degrees of skill. All are rarely seen and show up almost always on CS sites. **4.** Possibly a Tiger Rifles (La.) set. **5.** Another unknown "Rifles" set. **6.** Sheet brass "J". **7.** A large sheet of zinc-like material from which the letters "VA" and some unknown numbers have been cut. From a camp of Gen. Early's troops at Manassas. **8.** Thin brass die struck company letters originally carrying soldered-on iron wire attachments. They are found through the letter "M" and occasionally higher as other designations with no company letter J used. **9.** Numbers of the same pattern. **10.** These are the smaller officer's size characters and are much rarer than the former.

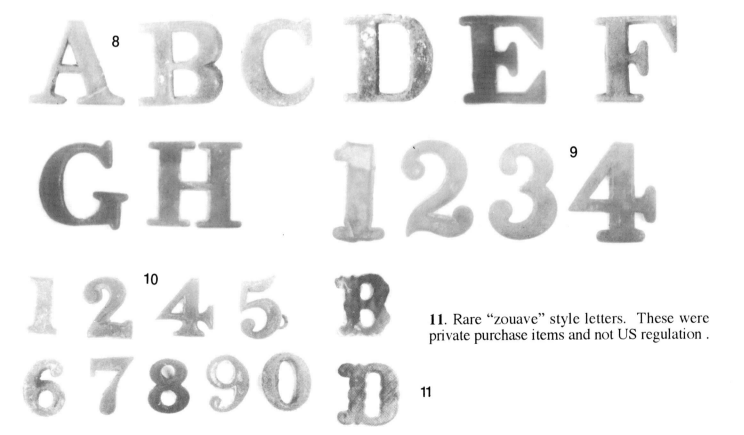

11. Rare "zouave" style letters. These were private purchase items and not US regulation.

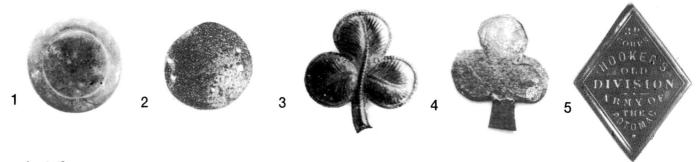

1. A factory-made First Corps badge of brass with a pin back. **2.** Another, but field-made. **3.** The Second Corps used the cloverleaf as its symbol. This specimen is silver plated. **4.** A field-made example. This type of fabrication was very popular in the Army of the Potomac. **5.** A die struck pin marked "3d Corps, Hooker's Old Division, Army of the Potomac."

Corps Badges: Early in the war, the large Union infantry organization had no distinctive insignia to designate any of the different commands. In March of 1862, President Lincoln directed General McClellan "to organize that part of the amry under his direct command into five army corps to be commanded according to his seniority." Later, in May of the same year, General Kearny directed that his men wear a small square of red cloth on their hats. Thus was born the corps badge concept. Corps badges were field- and factory-made. Note that by the war's end some 25 corps had been organized. Only the more common badges are shown here.

Left: A Union officer wears a Third Corps badge on his hat. **6.** A factory-made Third Corps badge of die-stamped brass. **7.** The same, but made in the field of sheet brass and punched with two holes.

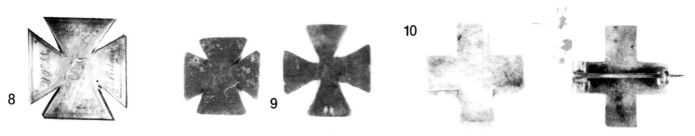

8. The Maltese cross of the Fifth Corps. This one is also an ID pin, a combination that was very popular. **9.** Two field made-badges of sheet lead. These are frequently seen as they could be produced from a flattened bullet trimmed out with a pocketknife. **10.** A sheet silver Sixth Corps badge. Note the typical fastener on the back.

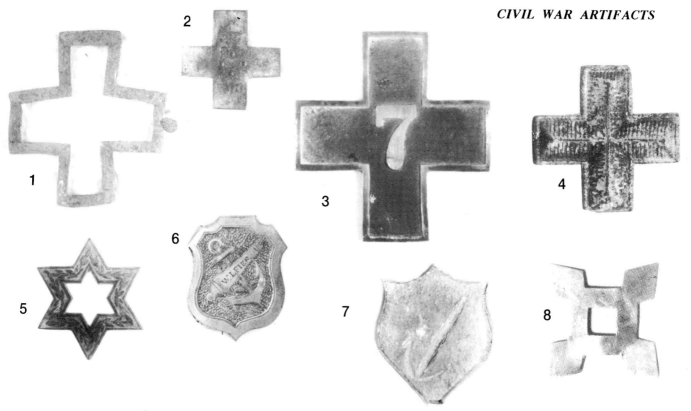

1. The silhouette type Sixth Corps badge. Red, white or blue cloth was used in the center to designate divisions. 2. A field-made version of sheet brass. 3. This large ornate example was found in the yard of an old headquarters site near Culpeper, Va. The border and regimental 7 are of silver. 4. A factory-made badge of silvered brass. 5. This engraved pin may be an Eighth Corps badge which was to be " A star with six rays". 6. The anchor and cannon Ninth Corps badge, this one a silver ID pin. 7. A soldier-made model displaying only the anchor. 8. A silver four-bastioned fort, the emblem of the Tenth Corps.

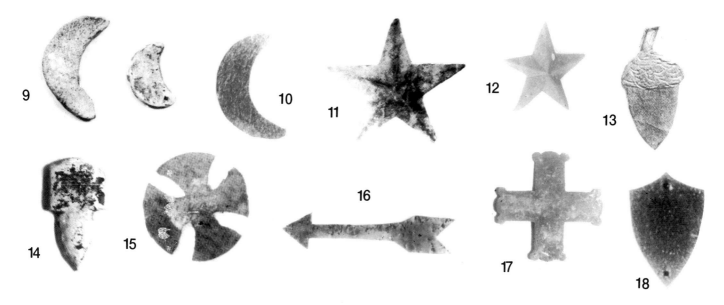

9. The Eleventh Corps used a crescent as its symbol. These two badges are field made of lead. 10. This specimen is cut from sheet brass. Note that the crescent device was also occasionally used by Louisiana troops. (New Orleans was called the "Crescent City".) Nos. 11&12. Two raised star pins. The Twelfth Corps used the star as its emblem. Nos. 13&14. Field-made badges displaying the acorn symbol of the Fourteenth Corps. 15. A field-made Sixteenth Corps badge, "a circle with four Minie balls cut out". 16. An arrow badge, emblematic of the Seventeenth Corps. 17. "A cross with foliate sides" was specified for the Eighteenth Corps. 18. The shield of the Twenty -third Corps.

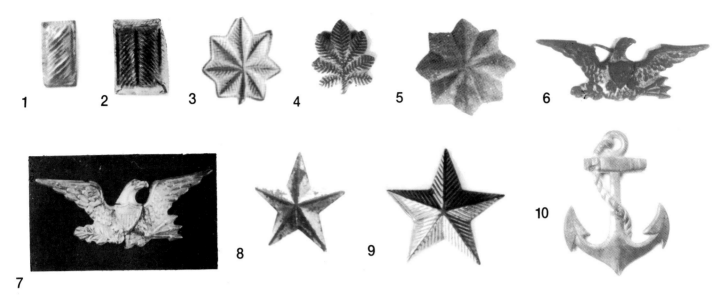

1 2 3 4 5 6

7 8 9 10

1. A silver plated 1st Lt's. bar found at Brandy Station. Note that 2nd Lts. of this period wore no bar. 2. A pair of silvered Captain's bars. **Nos. 3,4&5.** Major's and Lt. Colonel's oak leaves. **No.6.** A colonel's eagle of silver plated stamped brass. 7. Another, but made of solid silver. 8. A raised star. 9. The lined raised star. The star of course is a General's insignia but these devices were used in many applications and some are impossible to classify with certainty. The Uniform Regulations however, were quite specific and this would be an identification guide. 10. A naval device probably worn on the hat.

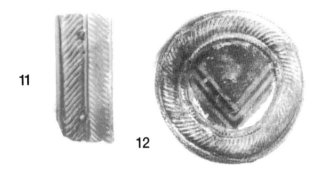

11 12

11. A most interesting piece of insignia of probable CS usage. A broken portion of metal shoulder strap has been punched for wear as a Lt's. bar. **12.** Another unique piece. A First Corps badge has had a set of chevrons painted in blue over a gray background. It came from a CS camp.

13. A ring bearing the legend "W. S. Baird Co. L 6th Pa. Cav.". Made of silver, ID rings such as these are not often seen, and then only made for Union soldiers. **14.** A plated patriotic ring marked "Love your Country". **15.** This gold and bloodstone seal ring carries the letters "CTC" on the face and is engraved "Charles Thomas Campbell" February 17, 1860. Campbell was a Colonel in command of the 57th Pa. whose position was overrun at Fredericksburg where he was left for dead. He lived and later became a General in the western theater. His ring was found only about a mile away in what was a post battle CS camp area. Though it spent 128 years in the ground, its condition is perfect.

13 14

15

Nos. 1&2. Patriotic pins; the lower one bears much original red, white and blue paint. **Left:** A Union soldier wears a patriotic pin similar to those two just described.

The wearing of patriotic pins was quite popular in the Union army. They were heavily advertised in periodicals of the time, chiefly by New York City firms. **3.** A shield bearing the legend "Union". **4.** A patriotic shield. **5.** An eagle surmounting a flag, in silver plated brass. **6.** Flag pin marked "It shall wave". **7.** Shield pin marked "Union". **8.** Pin of the National Union League. **9.** This pin displays the faces of Johnson and Lincoln.

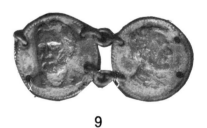

10. Cannon and flag pin of stamped brass. **11.** This plated pin carries a bust of George Washington. **12.** A small gilted shield pin. **13.** Another National Union League pin. **14.** An often seen eagle and flag pin.

With the coming of war, numerous Northern fire companies enlisted en masse, many as Zouave units. **1.** A pin from an unknown company. **Nos. 2&3.** New York City companies. **4.** Stoneham (Mass.) Hook and Ladder. **5.** From the Brooklyn Fire Dept. **6.** A large pin from a New York Hose Co. and so marked. **7.** A rare pin from Duryea's 5th New York Zouaves. This specimen came from the Gaines Mill, Va. area where the unit fought. **8.** A pin from an unknown unit. **Below:** Drawn up in front of their camp is the 114th Pa. Regiment. They were called the "Zouaves De Afrique of the Pennsylvania Volunteers". **9.** This small brass oval was worn by their members as a pin and often as a boxplate.

1. A thistle badge which was probably worn by one of the New York "Highlander" regiments such as the 79th. **2.** A badge of the US Army's Provost Guard, the equivalent to todays MPs and a rare find. **3.** This hand engraved, solid silver badge reads "C.S. DETECTIVE". Shown here enlarged, this is an extraordinarily rare piece which was recently found outside of Richmond. One other is known in a state historical society collection.

Nos. 4&5. These two pins represent the 55th New York Regiment. The same unit used a two-piece buckle bearing the same number. **6.** An unknown pin. **8.** This pin probably had a cloth surround. It bears the profile of the Italian General Garibaldi. **Nos. 9&10.** The arm and sword are components of the Massachusetts seal. **Nos. 7&11.** Unknown horse head pins. **No. 12.** Veteran's pins as used in the Union western theater armies. **13.** A fine solid silver jeweler-made pin about 1&1/4" high. Probably from the 8th Louisiana, which was camped in the vicinity. **14.** The Kearny "patch" of stamped brass. Other numbers are seen.

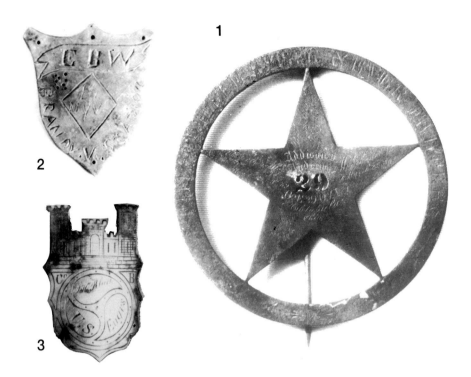

1. A Union 12th Corps badge recovered from the Tennessee River at Bridgeport, Alabama. The star is engraved "ADDISON ANDREWS / ASHTABULA, OHIO / 29 O.V.I. Co. E." The ring is engraved "THE WHITE STAR NEVER FALTERS." The star points carry the names of various Virginia battles. 2. Field-made lead badge marked "E.B.W. 40th. N.Y.V. Brandy Station, Virginia." 3. A solid silver pin engraved " J.H. Black, Co. B US Engrs." The quality of engraving is superb. Found in Fairfax, Va.

Note: The use of personal ID pins or badges became more widespread in the Union army as the war progressed. It would be many years before the government would issue any sort of ID or "dog tag." There are accounts of troops writing their names on slips of paper and putting them into pockets before a charge so they could be identified if killed. As will be noted the various papers of the times advertised many different pins for sale. All of the engraving of this time was hand done and was an art form unto itself. Nearly all of the firms were in New York City. ID badges were all but unknown in the CS service but it will be noted that most CS canteens will have at least a set of initials scratched or carved-on. It is probable that they felt that this would serve the purpose.

4. Co. H of the 73rd New York Infantry was made up of pre-war firemen. A Captain Jackson organized the unit and gave each member one of these silver pins. They were engraved with the owner's name and dated 1862. This one belonged to Robert McKnight of Long Island. It was found in Stafford Co., Va. in one of the many camps that the Army of the Potomac occupied in the winter of 1862-63.

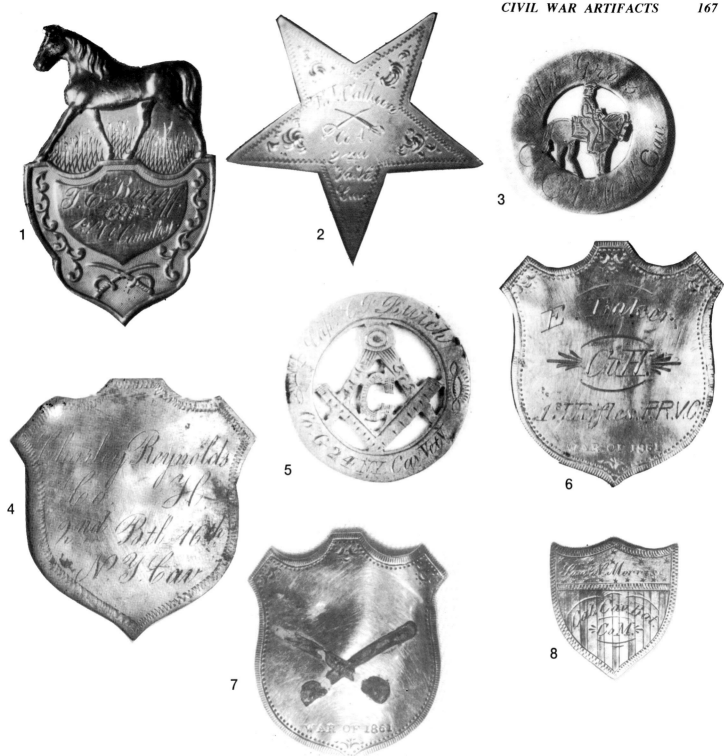

Union cavalry pins, all engraved on silver. They typically measure about 1&1/4" high. **1.** "Thomas E. Bartley Co. F 1st Vermont Cav." The pin was a stock stamping but is rarely seen. **2.** This star belonged to "E.J. Calhoun Co. A. 2nd. Va. Vt." (Veteran). This was a Northern unit. At least two identical pins are known ascribed to members of this organization. **3.** "Peter Gross 4th Mich. Cav." **4.** A shield that belonged to "Charley Reynolds Co. H. 2nd. Btl. 16th. N.Y. Cav." **5.** A Masonic pin engraved "Capt C.J. Burch Co. G 24th N.Y. Cav. Vet. Vol." **6.** "E. Fraley Co. H. 1st. Rifles P.R.V.C." **7.** An unengraved pin. **8.** This unit traveled all of the way across the country to fight for the Union. "Sam N. Morris Cal. Cav. Bat. Co M."

1. Edward Whiley proudly had "Iron Brigade" engraved on his ID pin.   2. This pin was found about 14" down in a pine woods just outside of Washington D.C. Apparently it was a large staging area for the Union cavalry of a number of different states and was heavily used. The pin belonged to "C. Taylor Co. H 1st NJVC."   3. "H.O. Dodge 8th Ill", the E is a company designation.

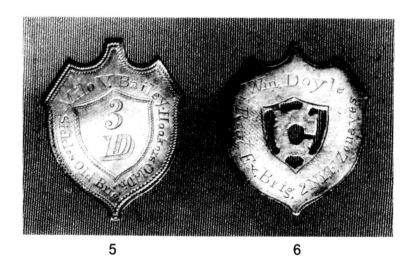

4. The quality of engraving and artistry on some of these pins is very high; note this one. Cpl. Carlough enlisted at Patterson, N.J. in 1861. He was wounded on the Wilderness Battlefield but survived the war. The following pins were found in a central Virginia cow pasture. Years ago it had been the winter camp of the New York Excelsior Brigade. 5. Milo V. Bailey was a farmer from Wayne Co. New York. He was wounded at the Wilderness, recovered and later reenlisted. 6. William Doyle was a trim carpenter from New York City. After joining the army he became a wagoner and then a cook.

1. "C.B. Kenney Co H 1st D.C. Cav."   Any District of Columbia marked item is rare. 2. "A. Howell Co M 2nd U.S. Cav." Regular Army marked items are unusual. 3. "M.T. Kenney Co. D 10th Regt. Mass. Inf. 4. Engraved on the reverse "A.R. Pope Co. G." Augustus R. Pope lost this pin in a camp north of Richmond and would not see Massachusetts again. He was captured and sent to Andersonville where he later died. 5. The pin of "Fred. N. Fox Co. H 14th. C V." (Connecticut Volunteers). Note the pin arrangement on the reverse which is typical of the period.

6. This shield pin belonged to "John Hunt Siege Batt. 1st Conn Art." 7. An unusual pin denoting the 9th New York State Militia. This engraver was well trained in script but the "9th" is a little rougher.

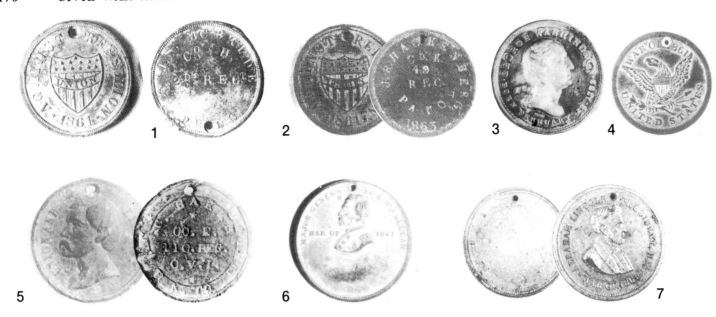

ID Discs: Often called "dog tags", these items were purchased from sutlers or other merchants who stamped them to order. Typically they carry the owner's name, unit, the year and often his hometown. The fronts display a patriotic motif and most are of brass. Note that all of these discs are scarce and silver and gilt finishes are seen. **1.** The "Against Rebellion-1861" type. **2.** Another. **3.** This type bears the bust of George Washington. **4.** The "War of 1861" type. **5.** A pewter disc bearing the bust of McClellan. **6.** Another McClellan type. **7.** Some are found unstamped like this one bearing a bust of Lincoln.

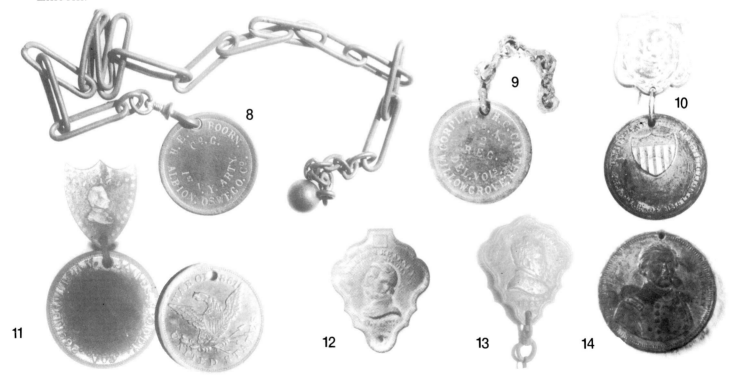

8. Most were worn on a simple thong but this one was used as a watch fob. **9.** An unusual specimen once owned by "Corporal J.H.C. Carter, Co. A, 2 Reg. Del (Delaware) Vols." **10.** Some were worn suspended from a pin device. This one bears a bust of McClellan. **11.** The reverse of another type pin with a McClellan motif. The face is of the "eagle" type. It belonged to James Roddy of the 26th Michigan and was found in Auburn, Va. **12.** This specimen shows the bust of Gen. Kearny. **13.** Gen. Joe Hooker. **14.** This one bears the face of McClellan who was enormously popular with the troops.

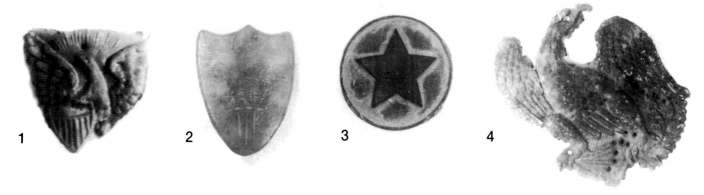

1. A soldier-made badge or hat ornament. This device is probably cut from a powder flask. **2.** A fleur-de-lis badge from a Louisiana camp. This is a popular French symbol. **3.** These stamped brass star devices are found in the western theater. They were probably hat ornaments and are associated with Texas troops. **4.** A field-made device cut from the US eagle plate.

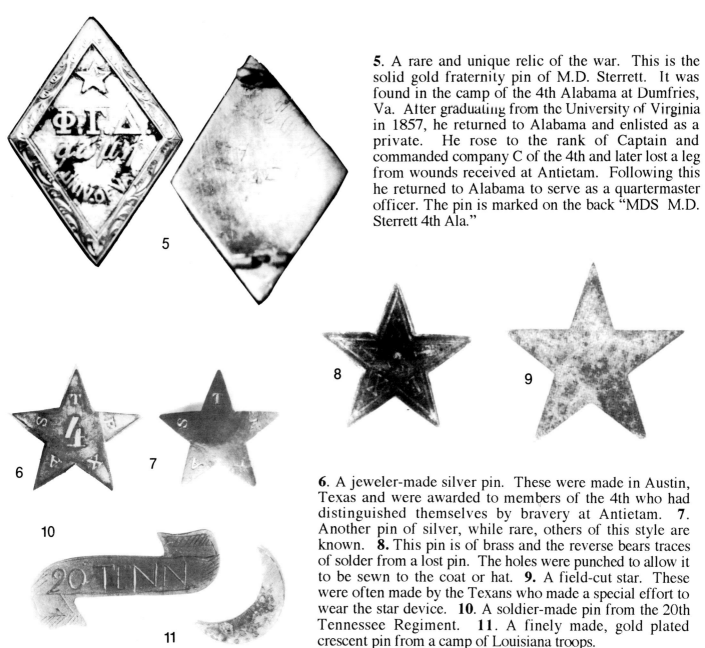

5. A rare and unique relic of the war. This is the solid gold fraternity pin of M.D. Sterrett. It was found in the camp of the 4th Alabama at Dumfries, Va. After graduating from the University of Virginia in 1857, he returned to Alabama and enlisted as a private. He rose to the rank of Captain and commanded company C of the 4th and later lost a leg from wounds received at Antietam. Following this he returned to Alabama to serve as a quartermaster officer. The pin is marked on the back "MDS M.D. Sterrett 4th Ala."

6. A jeweler-made silver pin. These were made in Austin, Texas and were awarded to members of the 4th who had distinguished themselves by bravery at Antietam. **7.** Another pin of silver, while rare, others of this style are known. **8.** This pin is of brass and the reverse bears traces of solder from a lost pin. The holes were punched to allow it to be sewn to the coat or hat. **9.** A field-cut star. These were often made by the Texans who made a special effort to wear the star device. **10.** A soldier-made pin from the 20th Tennessee Regiment. **11**. A finely made, gold plated crescent pin from a camp of Louisiana troops.

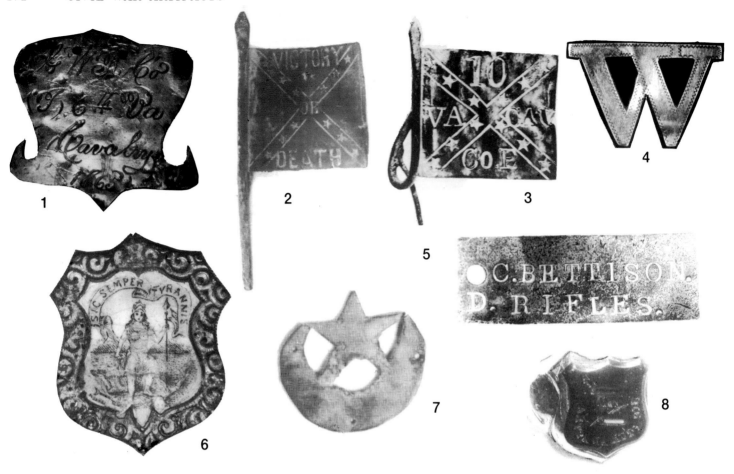

Above: Identification or patriotic pins that are associated with the Confederacy are extremely rare. **1**. This small sheet silver pin belonged to a member of the 6th Virginia Cavalry and is dated 1865. **Nos. 2&3**. This pattern of silver pin has been ascribed to a Richmond jeweler who advertised in a city paper that he was making "flag pins".   **4**. Silver "Virginia Volunteers" pin. **5**. This tag was was located in a CS camp.   **6**. An enameled pin measuring 1&1/8" high and bearing the Virginia seal.   **7**. Lead star and crescent badge associated with Louisiana troops. **8**. An 1859 VMI class ring that belonged to Maj. C.J. Green of the 47th Va.Vols.

9. A scroll badge of silvered pewter engraved "I go for the Union The Constitution and Enforcement of the Law".   **10.** The National Battle Pin as sold by sutlers in varying patterns. A general's photo appeared in the center and different battles around it. **11.** The rare Kearny Cross with top bar. Awarded for valor to members of deceased Gen. Phil Kearny's old First Division, of the Third Corps. Authorized by Gen. Orders No. 48, May 16, 1863.

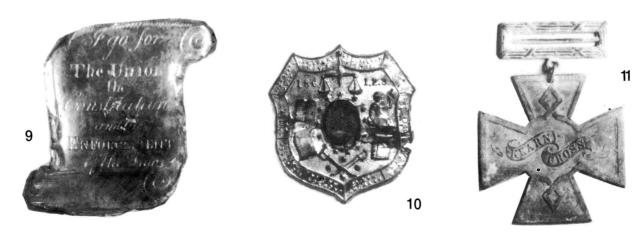

The items shown on this page are cape pins and they are uncommon finds. They were not issue items but were obtained from the sutlers. The Union soldier could pick one representing his branch or a famous leader. **1.** An unknown general. **2.** General McClellan. **3.** The Ordnance bomb. **4.** This subject is unknown but may be Col.Elmer Ellsworth. **5.** For the cavalry. **6.**A Star. **7.** A variant.

8. A very crude star. **9.** This pin is made from two cuff sized eagle buttons. **10.** Star and crescent. **11.** A single turret modification of the engineer's castle and presumably for those troops. **12.** For the artilleryman. **13.** For the ambulance driver. Most cape pins are brass castings.

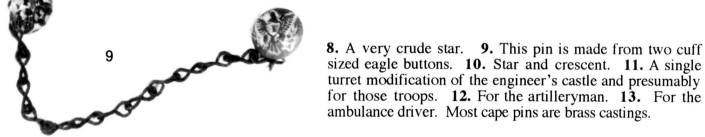

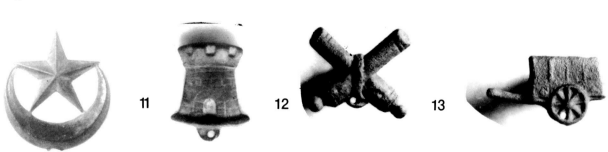

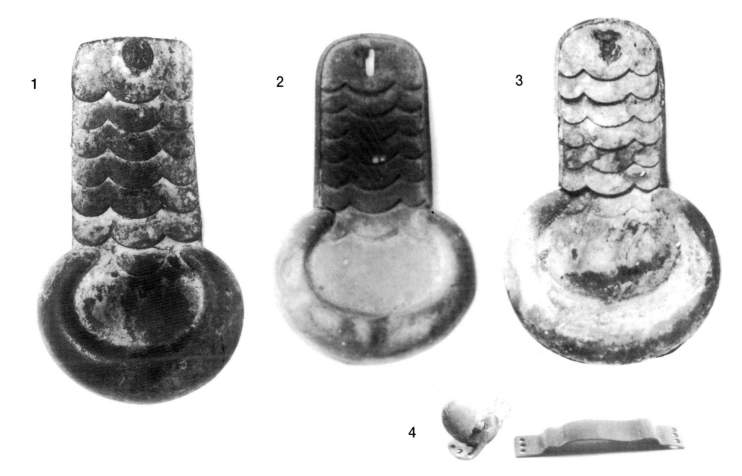

1. An unusual shoulder scale apparently made without the normal rim. 2. The standard US issue shoulder scale as worn by enlisted men. These were supposed to protect the top of the shoulders from sabre cuts but in the field they were quickly discarded. It is not hard to imagine the target these two bright brass mirrors would have made. **Nos.3&5.** Two views of the rarely seen sergeant's model scale. It is larger than the corporal and private's model and has a bottom "pan". Note the sergeant at left. Another very rare model of the sergeant's scale is occasionally seen bearing raised studs on the top. These were worn by staff NCOs. 4. Close up of the attachment system used with the above. These pieces were sewn to the coat. The flat piece accepted a bar on the back of the scale and the turn key device went into the end slot. 6. The bottom bar, often found seperately.

1   2   3

Officer's shoulder straps came in different versions, principally one, two and three-row. Further, with the addition of contrasting ribbing they were "Extra Rich". The Schuyler, Hartley and Graham catalog shows that apparently, with a given dress uniform, these different straps were interchangeable up and down in ranks.

1. A single-row of plated brass. **2.** Extra Rich double-row as found with two Lt's. bars. **3.** Single-row with uniform fragments. **4.** This specimen had an added center of metallic weave. **5.** Double-row type made of woven metallic thread.

4   5

1

2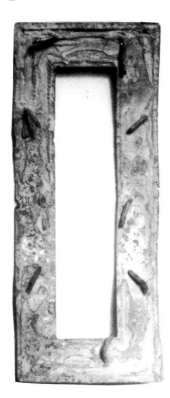

3

1. A heavily plated double-row type.   2. The reverse showing the turned over wire that held it to the uniform. This specimen is solder filled but many are not. 3. A double-row type.   4. The seldom seen triple-row type. **Above:** A Union officer showing the shoulder straps as worn.

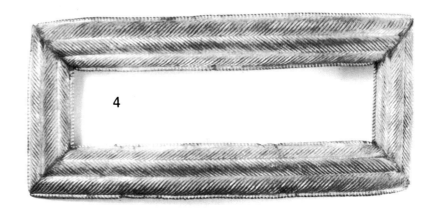

4

Buttons: Military and Civilian

American military buttons of the 19th Century offer the historian not only a wide glimpse into this country's martial development but its manufacturing progress as well. Many of these buttons are works of art in design, and their detail is a tribute to the die sinker's art. The basic designs and sub variations are nearly endless, in both the US and CS service. When found in the field, they can, in many cases, establish the identity of the occupying troops.

During this period it was common for each state to display its seal on buttons: some with variations for the separate combat arms, officer and enlisted, with chronological changes in style, construction, plating etc. In doing so the state militia organizations were loosely emulating the US service. Further, company and regimental units, military schools and other organizations all could have distinctive buttons. When the Civil War came many were worn into service. On the CS side, in addition to all of the above, "letter" buttons (for branch) were authorized. They bought these from abroad and manufactured their own, (called locals). State "seals" were made locally and many civilian buttons were worn.

Note that the chief reference book in this field is the invaluable *Record of American Uniform and Historical Buttons, Bicentennial Edition* by Alphaeus H. Albert. It uses a specific code and numbering system that is standard among collectors. Our purpose here is to show only the various design types and a selection of representative specimens and thus this system is not used.

Button Types: Note that most military buttons will be found in the 19-23 mm size range with a corresponding smaller cuff size. **1.** The early flat button, made like a coin with a brazed-on shank. **2.** The one-piece convex; ca. 1810-1840. **3.** The typical two-piece 1850-1865 button. The back displays the maker's markings in a depressed channel around a raised middle. Backmarks, when present, are an important key to the dating of a given button.

4. A high quality British-made specimen with a flat back. Run through the blockade by the South. Note the cuff button for relative size. **5.** A US staff officer's button. This type of button has a separate rim and is called a three-piece. The standard New York buttons are so made. Made from ca. 1840 on.

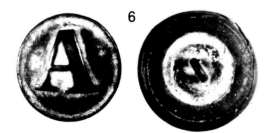

6. A local CS-made artillery button. A less-than-perfectly cut die mated to an unmarked back. The shank was cut-out and drilled. Note that a number of CS makers did use backmarks. There is a large variety of CS locals, made with varying degrees of workmanship. Tinned iron backs were often used and when plating is present it is often thinly done.

Northern Buttons: It is important to note that within the last few years, the collecting of buttons has seen a large increase along with their value. The latter is pronounced with regard to CS specimens. In the case of Union buttons, rarity does not necessarily mean value as is the case with CS buttons. This is particularly true of the Northern regimentals.

Rarity: The following is a very general overview, and certain early specimens may be much rarer. Condition and plating are important. Plain shield eagles are common with the I's a little less so. A's and C's show up less often followed by R's and D's. The V is scarce. Ordnance and Navy's are scarce, the Marine Corps more so. General staffs are often seen but the two Engineers are not.

States: From the common to the rarest they would be NY, CT, MA, RI, MG, ME, WI, VT, NH, PA, NJ. This list is for the normally encountered buttons of that state.

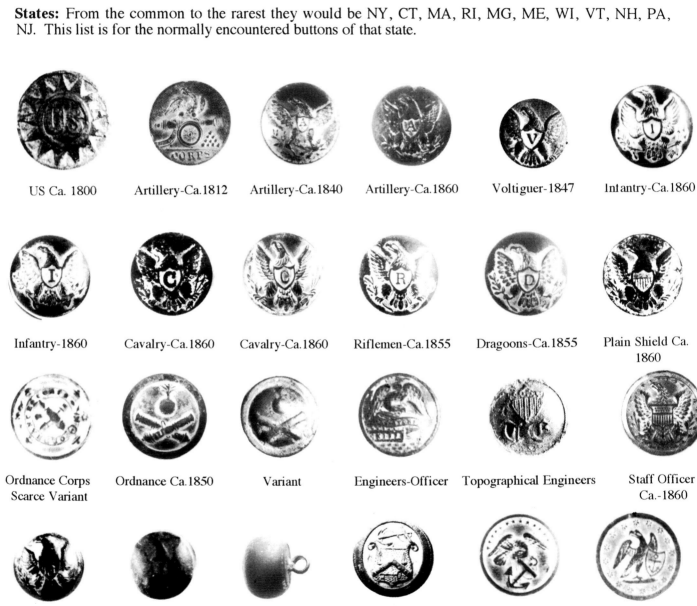

| US Ca. 1800 | Artillery-Ca.1812 | Artillery-Ca.1840 | Artillery-Ca.1860 | Voltiguer-1847 | Infantry-Ca.1860 |

| Infantry-1860 | Cavalry-Ca.1860 | Cavalry-Ca.1860 | Riflemen-Ca.1855 | Dragoons-Ca.1855 | Plain Shield Ca. 1860 |

| Ordnance Corps Scarce Variant | Ordnance Ca.1850 | Variant | Engineers-Officer | Topographical Engineers | Staff Officer Ca.-1860 |

| Hard Rubber-CW | Variant | Zouave-"ball button" | Revenue Cutter Service | Marines | Navy-Ca.1812 |

Navy-Ca.1830

Navy Ca.-1860

Left: A rare hard rubber Navy, backmarked "New York Novelty Rubber Co."

Connecticut   Maine   Massachusetts   Michigan   New Hampshire   New Jersey

New Jersey Militia   New Jersey Rifle Corps   New York   N.Y.-Variant   N.Y. Cuff   Ulster Guard

12th N.Y. Regt.   13th N.Y. Regt.   Pennsylvania   83rd Pa.-Pewter   Pa. National Guard   Rhode Island

Vermont   Vermont Cuff

Wisconsin

No. 188.   1   No. 189.
Shield Button.

1. The commonest button found on Civil War sites, the war-time eagle. They were produced by the hundreds of thousands and were used for years after the war. A wide range in detail and quality will be noted. **Right:** A Union shell jacket.

Southern Buttons: Read all of the notes on Military and Civilian Buttons, but note that as a class CS buttons are much rarer.

General Service: This includes locals and imports. Lettered buttons from the common to the rarest would be I, A, C, R, E. Staffs are scarce with CSA's and Navy's more so. Note that certain buttons in all of these categories are very seldom encountered. Some, like the "Jeb Stuart" button or the block M are extremely rare. The only ones that could be called common would be the Richmond-made block I or A.

States: CS state buttons include all of the pre-war militias, locals and imports. In general, by state from the common to the rarest, they would be NC, SC, VA, GA, LA, MS, AL, TX, MD, KY, TN, MO, AK, FL. Within these of course are some very scarce types that are seldom seen. Note that this would include any specimen from the last five states.

Schools: Military schools were popular in the pre-war era and especially so in the South. Most had their own uniform buttons and many of these were worn in the conflict. All are scarce but the VMI, NCMI, and Hillsborough are seen most often. Some of the school buttons are very rare.

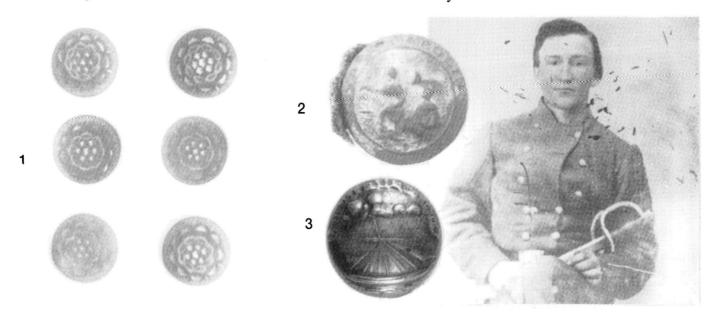

1. A grouping of "flower" buttons as found together in a CS camp. A small amount of plating is left in the low spots. Many of these civilian buttons were worn on CS coats. **2.** A common North Carolina with a piece of the coat still attached as dug. **3.** The very rare Tennessee. Both were produced during the war. **Right:** A Confederate cavalryman.

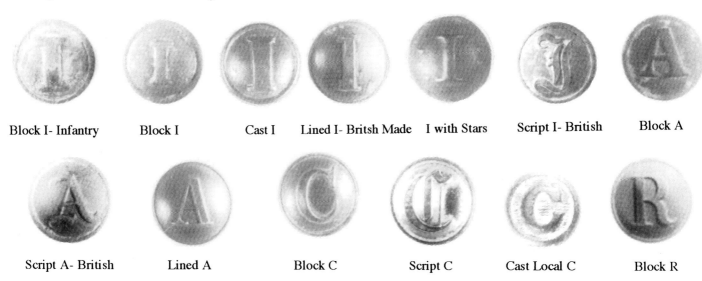

| Block I- Infantry | Block I | Cast I | Lined I- Britsh Made | I with Stars | Script I- British | Block A |
| Script A- British | Lined A | Block C | Script C | Cast Local C | Block R |

Script E-Engineers

1 Pc. CS Staff

CS Staff-British

Local Staff

Local Staff

Local Staff

Local Staff

Local Staff

Local Staff

Staff- British

CS Artillery

Solid Cast CS

"Jeb Stuart"

Hard Rubber CS
Navy

CS Navy

CS Navy "Ship"

CSA-British

Columbus, Ga. Mkd.

Alabama
"Map on Tree"

Alabama Volunteer
Corps

"Wings Up" AVC

Mobile Volunteer
Corps

Arkansas-Staff

Florida

Georgia-Pre-war

Georgia Local

Lamar Mounted
Rifles 1861

Kentucky Pre-war

Louisiana Pre-war

La. Pre-war

LA. Pre-war

Local Louisiana

"Puff Back" to former

Local Louisiana

Pre-war Maryland

Baltimore City
Police

Mississippi I   Mississippi A   Mississippi C   Local Mississippi   Local Mississippi   Missouri

N.C. staff   N.C Standing Shepherd   N.C. Sunburst   Sunburst cuff   N.C. Palmetto   N.C. Local Seal

Hornet's Nest Rifle Corps-N.C.   South Carolina 2-Pc. Pre-war   Variant Pre-war   Variant Pre-war   Variant Pre-war   Scarce Variant

Tennessee   Republic of Texas I   Republic Staff   Republic Dragoons   Republic Navy   Texas Artillery

Waco Guards   Texas Militia-C.W.   Virginia 1-Piece   Virginia 2-Piece   Virginia Staff   Local 2-Piece Staf

Va. Military Institute   Nansemond M. I.   Episcopal H.S.-Va.   Western M. I.-Ky.   Variant W.M.I.   Georgia M. I.

| G.M.I. | Alabama Cadet Corps | North Carolina M.I. | Hillsborough M.I.-N.C. | Kentucky M.I. | Hampton M.A.-Va. |

1. These South Carolina buttons were strung on a piece of iron wire. Lost in the Wilderness. **2.** These are cast white metal buttons, rare but apparently a CS shop-produced item of issue. These specimens were found in Mississippi. **3.** Button made from a coin and a button with a modified back for sewing to the coat.

4. A cuff size flat button bearing the Issacs Campbell name and its full London street address. **5.** A field-cast pewter South Carolina with two sprues from the same hole. **6.** A typical CS jacket, this one with turned wood buttons. <u>Many</u> thousands of these buttons were produced.

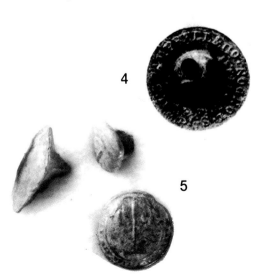
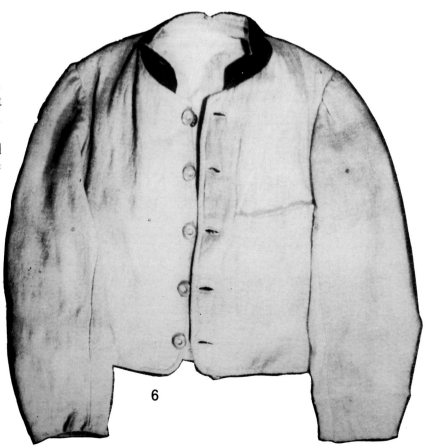

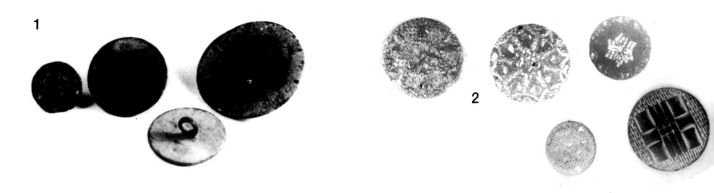

Civilian Buttons: 1. A group of flat or coin type buttons. These are found in all types of sites and were the common civilian button in America for centuries. They are generally of brass, plated or unplated and sometimes of pewter. They are found with and without engraved faces and backmarks. Quite a few are English-made. Many are found in Confederate camps. **2.** Collectors refer to these as "flower" buttons though many will have geometric or other designs. These are two-piece buttons and come in different sizes, many with plating. They date from about 1840 on and are common finds in camps. Some CS jackets were originally equipped with these buttons. **3.** This "coat" of buttons was found in a Louisiana camp; they are English products and heavily gilted. **4.** Porcelain buttons were commonly used on underwear.

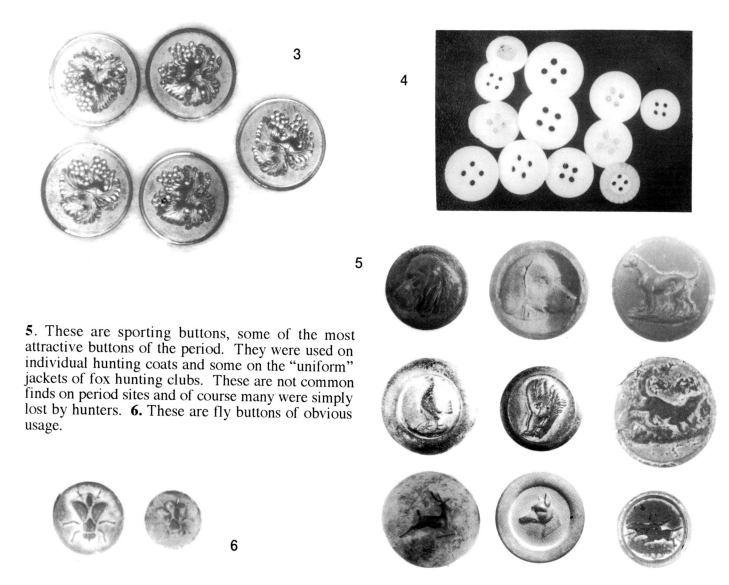

5. These are sporting buttons, some of the most attractive buttons of the period. They were used on individual hunting coats and some on the "uniform" jackets of fox hunting clubs. These are not common finds on period sites and of course many were simply lost by hunters. **6.** These are fly buttons of obvious usage.

5 *ACCOUTREMENT PLATES*

ACCOUTREMENT PLATES

Without question, the most prized of all field recoveries are some of the rarer accoutrement plates. (The term accoutrement is French, meaning equippage or accessories. In the American military the term plates could refer to any decorative and/or functional brass or white metal device worn on the sword or bayonet belt or cartridge box.)

There are numerous reasons for the great interest in such items: They trace their origin to ancient times, when the Vikings wore highly decorated and prized sword belt plates and the medieval knights displayed their heraldic devices on buckles and shields. Additionally, many of these plates are masterpieces of the die sinker's art. Because of their great rarity, some varieties of CS plates are quite valuable.

During the early 1800's the US Army equipped its different units with plates bearing both the heraldic symbols of the country and of the specific arm. The state militias did likewise with many of the states displaying their own state seal or state initials.

Boxplates and breastplates were among the most superfluous items ever to burden the modern soldier and most were promptly "lost" after a few days campaigning. The various US troop staging areas in the East were once almost loaded with discarded specimens. The Southern militias made some use of these items also but their comparatively few numbers makes recoveries rare. (War-time CS production of either is minuscule).

Waistbelt plates served a completely functional purpose and were of course retained, but still many will be recovered in the field. In some instances the rear fastener was broken and the item discarded, in other cases a belt might be lost in the snow or leaves. Often, when CS troops gleaned US equipment from the field, they would strip and discard the plates from cartridge boxes and belts. The careful field researcher will know what type of belt fittings go with a given plate and pay close attention when such parts are initially found.

Common terminology of course describes waistbelt plates as belt buckles. Decorative or functional shoulder belt plates worn on the chest are called breastplates, and cartridge box plates are simply called boxplates. Note that a heavy frame type buckle, even fastening a sword belt is still properly called a buckle.

There are two basic types of plate construction. First are those cast of solid brass from a pattern piece, generally in sand molds with integral hooks. Second are those struck of thin sheet brass in a female die and filled with lead, embedding the fasteners. The latter technique was highly developed in the North and many different items were so made. Frequent mention will be made of the large Massachusetts firm of E. Gaylord who produced many pre-war Southern plates. Some are marked but others are identified to the company by style and workmanship. Gaylord also supplied many sets of cavalry and infantry equipments to the Federal government and individual states on a contract basis.

When the war came arsenals both North and South began producing plates by the thousands. Contracts were also let to private firms for thousands more. The different "US" plates alone show almost endless die variations and during the war many rare and obscure CS plates appeared. Will Gavin, in his pioneering book *Accoutrement Plates, North and South 1861-1865*, was the first person to take on the task of identifying and documenting this important subject, the work first appearing in 1963. Since that time other comprehensive books have come out on the subject.

Because of the popularity and value of the originals <u>many</u> reproduction plates exist. In the early 1900's the Bannerman firm was reproducing the rectangular CSA buckle and by the 1960's many other types were being made for reenactors and skirmishers. Nearly all original cast types have been copied and many new dies have been fabricated to make the stamped varieties.

1

2

A grouping of early plates of the type that were occasionally carried into the Civil War. In general this would apply to the early-war, poorly equipped CS forces. **1.** Regiment of Riflemen enlisted belt plate of the War of 1812 period. **2.** Ca. 1819 enlisted shoulder belt plate. This one was apparently issued with musket equipments at the very outset of the war and is seen more frequently. All were US Regulation.

3

Plates of this type show up with even more regularity and again, in the same context. All are militia items. **3.** Ca. 1820, this one bears traces of silver plating. **4.** From the same time frame, this one is gilted. (Note that period terminology usually uses the term "gilted" in place of gilded, the latter referring to a non-plating process used on furniture or other wood.) **5.** An artillery version, this one is called the star of stars plate. Nearly all of these types are stamped of comparatively thick brass with well soldered hooks and belt loops.

4

5

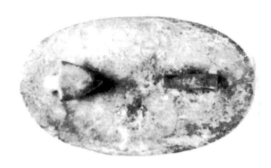

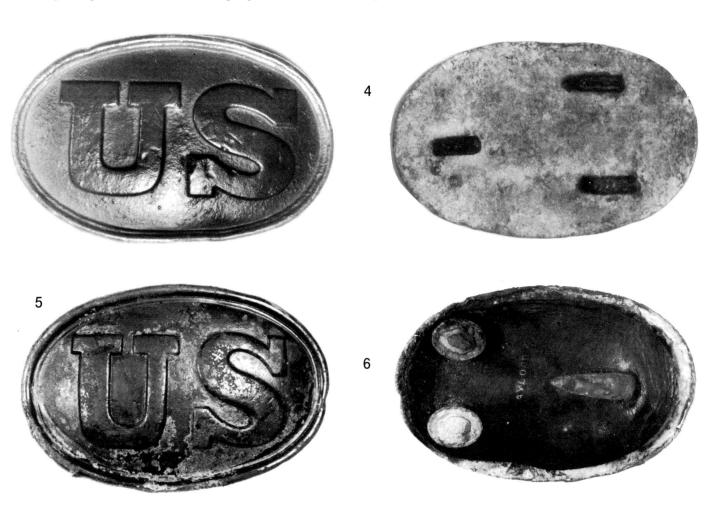

1839 saw the introduction of the oval US plate and in coming years it saw enormous usage. Originally the infantry wore a small one as a buckle and a large one as a boxplate. The cavalry, because of the heavier load, wore a large one on the sword belt. By the Civil War period the large size was being worn by the infantry in both roles.

1. A belt end retainer, issued during the wartime period. **2.** An early pattern small US buckle. **3.** Another; this is a boxplate. These were used on the smaller cartridge boxes in service such as the rifleman's or cavalry. **4.** A pre-war buckle with iron wire hooks. These would prove to be unserviceable. **5.** An early war buckle with stud hooks. These hooks were sturdy castings and in some cases were silver plated to protect the uniform. **6.** The seldom found leather shield on the back of this Gaylord plate served the same purpose. This series of plates served until 1872.

1. W. H. Smith of Brooklyn was a prolific maker of US plates and this marking is often seen. **2.** The Hunter marking is very rare. **3.** These are the arrowhead hooks that are common on mid to late war buckles. **4.** Many die variants of the large US plate are seen.

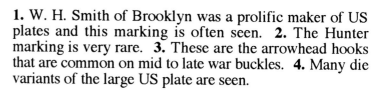

Nos. 5&6. Shown here are the front and back of the uncommon medium sized US buckle. They are also made as boxplates. There is no mention of this plate in the US Regulations and there is no record of any specific contractor having produced them. **7.** This is a die variant.

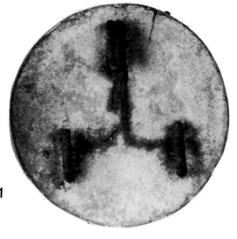

1

2

3

1. This plate originated in the late 1820's as a clasp for the bayonet shoulder belt. It was first formally described in the US Regulations of 1834. This specimen has iron wire hooks and dates to the 1830's. In 1842 it became a non-functioning ornament for the cartridge box strap although NCOs still wore it on the sword sling. It was made in many die variations and hook arrangements. **2.** Made by E. Gaylord, this is an early war plate. **3.** Some are contractor-marked like this J.I. Pittman model. This one has the iron wire eyes intact. **4.** The smaller "Burnside" model as issued to some elements of his command. No reason has been found for this variation. The real mystery concerning the huge usage of the breastplate is why they were issued at all. In the field they made a perfect target in the center of the chest. The troops were no fools and "lost" them quickly by the many thousands.

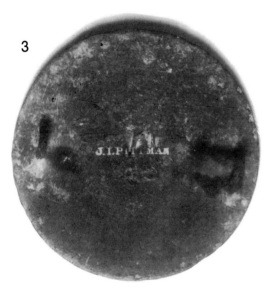

4

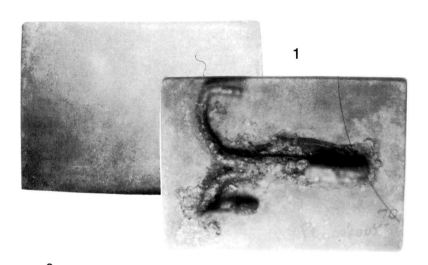

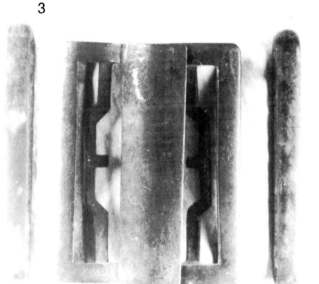

1. A plain brass buckle of medium thickness which first appeared with the US Regulations of 1832. These have slightly beveled edges. The Confederates produced many also. **2.** A shoulder belt plate with two "pipes" for drumsticks. Called the "drummer boy's buckle", they are specified in the 1851 Regulations as the "drum stick carriage" and earlier militia versions are known. **3.** The US rifleman's buckle, made to carry the rifle pouch, cap box and sabre bayonet issued with the Model 1855 Rifle. Originally a French design, the two belt slides had holes at the top for shoulder sling attachment. These often saw CS use.

4. The Model 1839 NCO buckle for all such personnel armed with a sword. These were most often used to carry the short foot artillery sword. The sling stud shown is marked "Storms", a contractor who made many of these belt and buckle sets. **Below:** A Union cavalryman wearing the Model 1851 sword belt plate which replaced all others for carrying all types of swords.

1

2

3

4

These are all specimens of the 1851 sword belt plate, regulation for all troops armed with swords. They were arsenal and contractor-made and many variants exist; most are numbered with matching keeper. **Nos. 1&2.** An Allegheny Arsenal (Pa.) model with both an applied eagle and wreath. (These plates are the only maker-marked 1851's.) **3.** The soldered-on German silver wreath is missing from this specimen, which is typical. **4.** This is a commonly found pattern and was slightly smaller and lighter than most. **5.** This style appeared in 1864 and was used into the 1870's. They are occasionally found in the West. Note that the rays go below the eagle. **6.** A group of belt attachments; see introductory notes.

5

6

1

2

3

No. 43.

Black Enameled Leather,

U. S. Regulation,

with or without Shoulder Strap.

Harness Leather,   do.

Nos. 1,2&3. Model 1851 officers' sword belt plates. These are much more finely made than the enlisted men's version. Note the fine background stippling on these models. All are in gold wash with silvered wreaths. Some of these will carry a medium width tongue. These were privately purchased items and are rare in comparison with the enlisted men's 1851 plates. Note the cut from a period military outfitter's catalog. **4.** A variant of this plate. Made of stamped brass, filled with lead. This type of construction is rarely seen and seems to be associated with very finely made officer's full dress belts. **Note:** This eagle device was used on many waist belt plates well into the twentieth century, particularly on those worn by army officers and military school cadets. Post-Civil War plates normally are of stamped brass with no lead fill, have a standing belt loop bar on the reverse and a wide tongue.

4

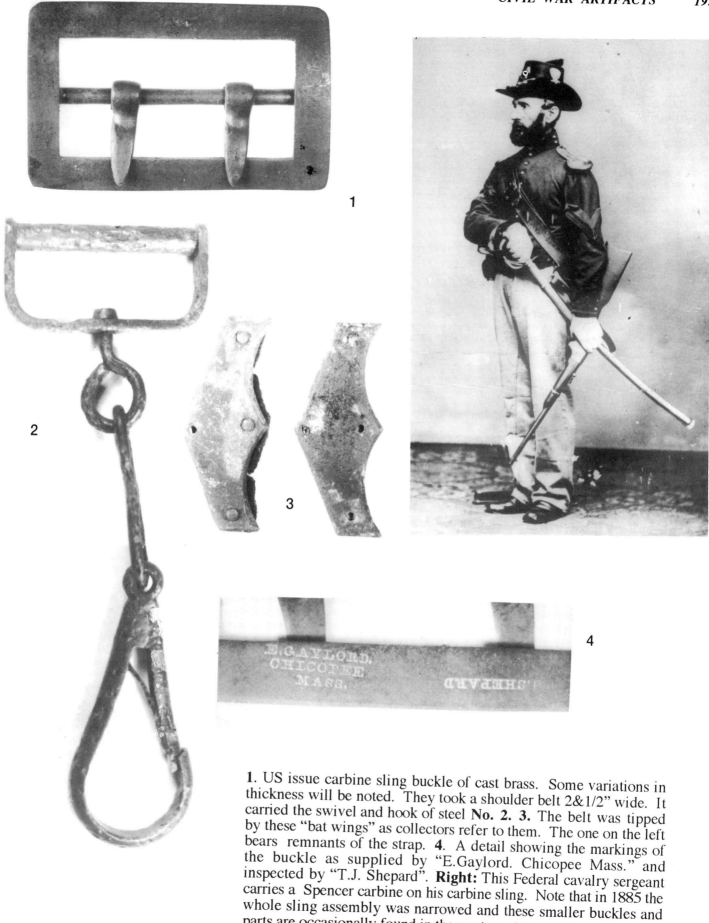

1. US issue carbine sling buckle of cast brass. Some variations in thickness will be noted. They took a shoulder belt 2&1/2" wide. It carried the swivel and hook of steel **No. 2. 3.** The belt was tipped by these "bat wings" as collectors refer to them. The one on the left bears remnants of the strap. **4.** A detail showing the markings of the buckle as supplied by "E.Gaylord. Chicopee Mass." and inspected by "T.J. Shepard". **Right:** This Federal cavalry sergeant carries a Spencer carbine on his carbine sling. Note that in 1885 the whole sling assembly was narrowed and these smaller buckles and parts are occasionally found in the western states.

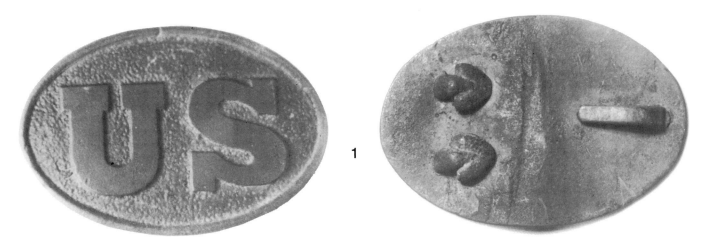

1. An unusual and rarely seen US buckle with a stippled background. The hooks are an integral part of the casting. There is some association of this plate with Ohio troops. Supplies were scarce in the western areas early in the war and this buckle may have been made there. **2.** An unusually crude and rare buckle. Note that there is no inner border on the face. In comparison with the CS products US buckles were made to a standard, making these two plates unusual.

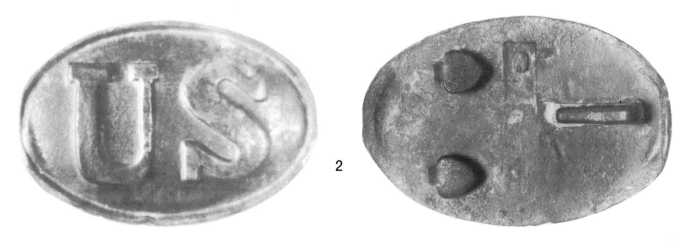

Below: Buckles seem to have been popular targets probably on and off the person. The center plate has been hit with shotgun pellets while the sabre plate was probably hung from the belt loop and fired at with a pistol. The left one has been hit with a Minie ball.

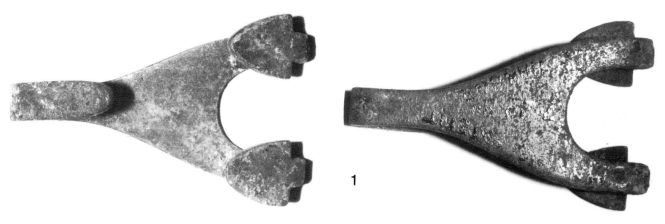

1. A "Mann's Patent" waistbelt buckle, so marked, very well made and finished . This was an attempt to furnish the troops with something lighter and more practical than the oval lead filled buckle. They appeared late in the war but saw little use.

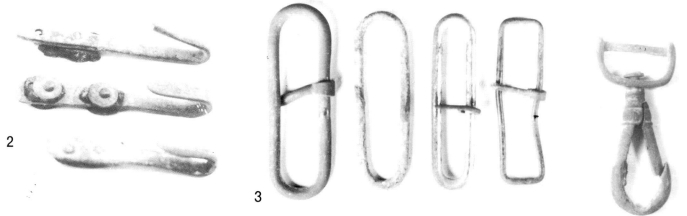

2. Brass belt end hooks as used on Union sabre belts and many others. **3.** Belt end adjusters. These were sewn to the belt end with the other end passing through them. They are often seen on dress belts carrying two-piece buckles. The very flimsy one on the right was probably attached to a thin white web belt. **4.** A sword sling hook. The spring loaded side opened to take the scabbard ring. **5.** A small, thin, brass buckle. **6.** The cast brass stud hook assembly as melted out of a belt buckle. It is conjectured that some CS troops wore these as buckles. **Nos. 7&8.** The Model 1859 detachable sabre hanger device designed and patented by then US cavalry officer Jeb Stuart. The two slots took leather straps. The hook on the one shown has been bent . Note markings.

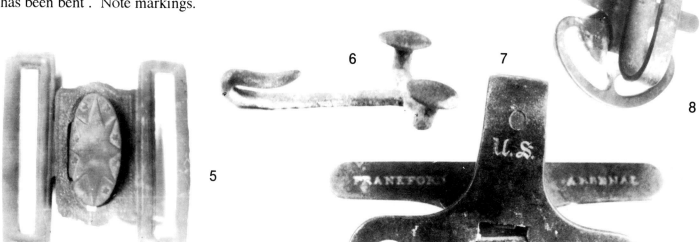

1

2

The first four buckles shown on this page are referred to by collectors as "panel plates" because the main design is displayed on a central panel. This design dates to the 1840's and was very popular with the militia troops. Many designs are known and they are on varying thicknesses of brass, both plated and unplated. They carry a wire belt loop and flat tongue.

1. The popular eagle design. 2. Because of the star this plate may have been associated with Texas or Mississippi. This one is of heavy stock and is silver plated. 3. Another eagle design which is often seen. 4. This specimen is very unusual in that it is a representation of the Illinois seal. This state had no marked plates of other types.

3

4

5. This buckle illustrates an unusual sidelight to American military history. In the pre-war era many German immigrants had their own militia-social organizations. This buckle belonged to Charles Hohmeier, later a member of Co. E of the 58th NY. Engraved at the top is "Bahn Frei" or "Clear the way".

5

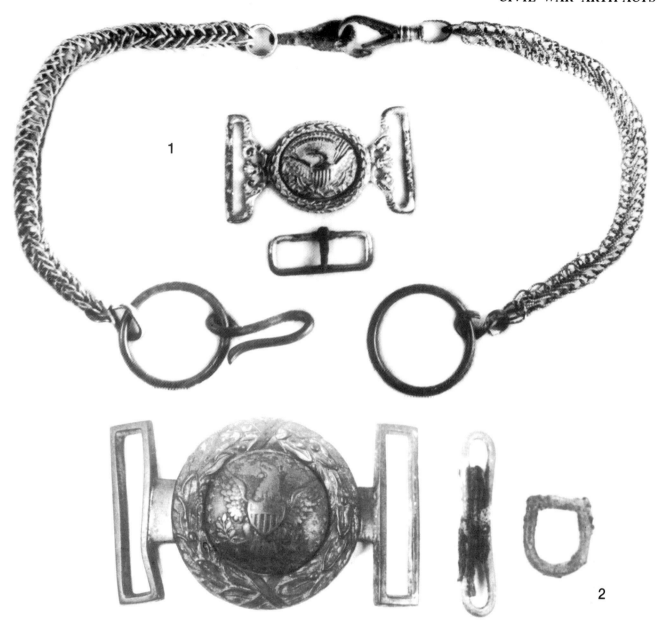

1. A ca. 1825 militia officer's two-piece buckle. It was found with its ornate chain sword hangers and belt fittings. Much original gold and silver plating remains. **2**. An 1840 period "standard" or "stock" pattern militia officer's buckle with belt fittings. It was found with a sword at Wolf Run Shoals, Va. **Note**: Plates such as this can often be dated by the number of stars (for states) in the design. Further, this wreath was used by the Confederates for the "Richmond" CS two piece wreath. **3**. The seldom found US 1833 NCO buckle. While one side is blank others are seen with branch markings. **4**. A portion of another, for the artillery.

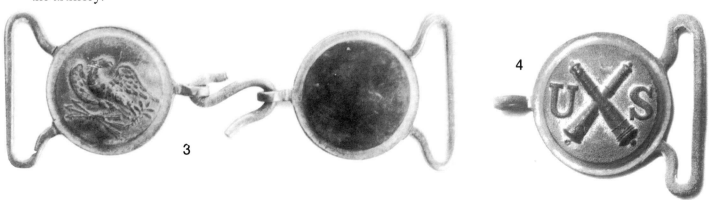

1. The shield shaped breastplate of the 6th Mass. Regiment. This was one of the first units to come south and save Washington. **2**. A plain faced artillery style buckle as used by many state militias. Some of these may have had their US lettering removed by the Confederates. **Nos. 3&4**. Two brass snake buckles. These and many other variants saw much use in the CS armies. Most were British imports and some were also used by the North. **5.** An 1830's period buckle of crude manufacture found in an Alabama camp. **6.** A stock pattern buckle. From the wartime period this one denotes company I.

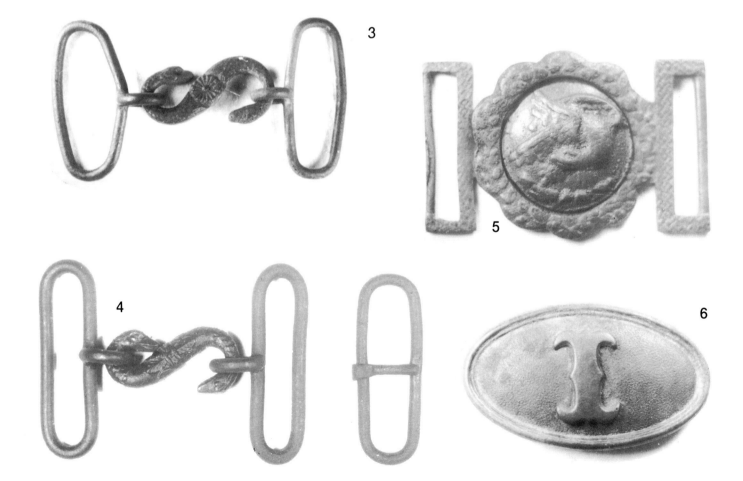

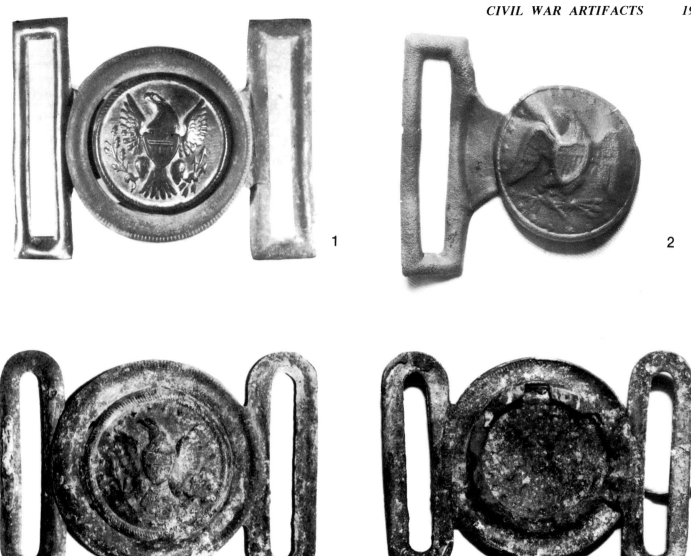

1

2

3

Nos. **1 through 3**. are all so called "sash buckles". In reality, when a sash was worn under a sword belt it was simply wrapped around the body and there was no provision for any sort of buckle. These thin stamped buckles were worn on very light cloth belts and were popular for both civilian and military wear. Many designs exist and they are frequently found bent or broken. Note the thin construction as shown by the back of specimen **No. 3. 4.** A silver plated eagle plate. These were not regulation but were made up as militia items and are unusual.

4

1. The Massachusetts two-piece buckle, a rare item. They are seen only occasionally and seem to be the only plate from this state seeing any field usage **Nos.2&3**. The Washington Grays and National Cadets, along with other units, were numbered regiments in the New York State Militia. The buckles shown here are typical of those units. The engraved letter in the center designates the company. They were worn with white web belts. Note the back of the Cadets plate showing the fastening system used with web belting.

4. The buckle of the 9th New York Zouaves. This is a very rare hand engraved specimen from their 1862-3 camp in Stafford Co., Va. **Left:** The Brooklyn Fire Zouaves charge at First Manassas.

Shown above are examples of the SNY plate (State of New York). These are normally seen as buckles and occasionally as boxplates. New York went to great efforts to furnish its troops with state marked equipment. In addition to many already issued, they placed an order for thirty-three thousand more in 1861. **Nos. 1&2** are commonly seen while **No. 3** is much rarer. **4.** The small size version dates to well before the war and is uncommon.

5. New York was a prosperous state with a large militia organization. In most cases they quickly copied the new US patterns. This is their version of the 1851; it was specified for all those armed with a sword. Many variants are known and in general those in plain brass were for enlisted men and those that are gilted with a silvered wreath and letters were for officers. **6.** A variant. All of these plates are scarce.

6

Plates of the Ohio Volunteer Militia. This was a well populated state when the war began and its troops fought heavily in both theaters of the war. **1.** The "flat letter" style, seen as both a stud hook buckle and a boxplate. This variety is rare and dates to the mid 1850's. **2.** Appearing early in the war, this variety also was made in boxplates and buckles. **3.** The rare Ohio shoulder belt plate. These are the counterpart of the US eagle plate but display the state seal. **4.** This is an occasionally seen field modification. A portion of the M has been flattened leaving an I, making the plate signify the "Ohio Volunteer Infantry".

5. The front and back of the medium size OVM buckle. These appear to have been contracted for and issued in the pre-war period.

1. Existing as both buckle and boxplate, this is the plate of the Philadelphia Home Guard. They are rare.
2. Displaying the Pennsylvania state seal, this is the buckle of the Reserve Brigade. It has arrowhead hooks and was also made as a boxplate. The brigade never actively fought as such, but some members later went into other units. This specimen was found many years ago in the Wilderness in the position of the 119th Pa.

The state of Maine was able to field 10 regiments of infantry in the opening days of the war and they were equipped with the plates shown here. Note that they followed the US system of a small belt buckle and a large boxplate. **3.** The front and back of the boxplate. By regulation standards they are somewhat crude; there is no inner border in the design and some are seen without lead filling. **4.** The buckle front and back. Almost certainly by the same maker. All of the previous comments apply here.

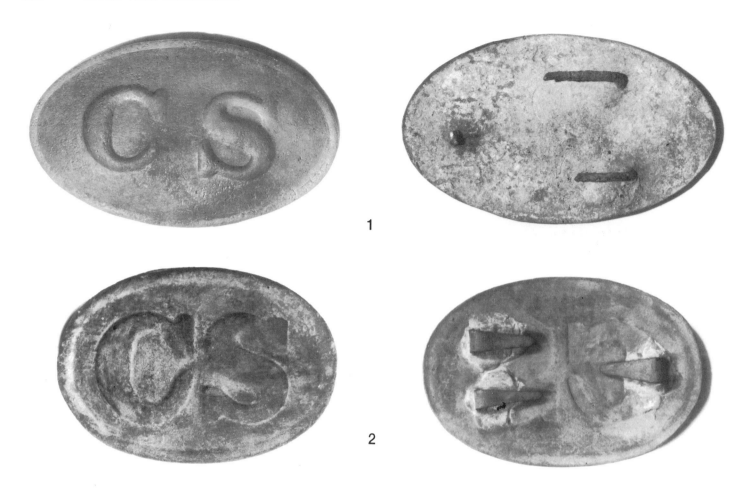

1. This oval lead filled buckle is called the "Virginia " style. The hooks are made of iron wire. 2. The "Breckinridge" plate shown here was so named because originally they were found in areas occupied by that CS General's command. The hooks are made of scrap sheet brass. 3. This is the "rope border" style. Notice the small inner border on the face. 4. The design of this buckle follows the CS regulations closely and so it is called the "Regulation Style". Like the others it has sheet brass hooks. All of these CS ovals were made in fairly large quantities.

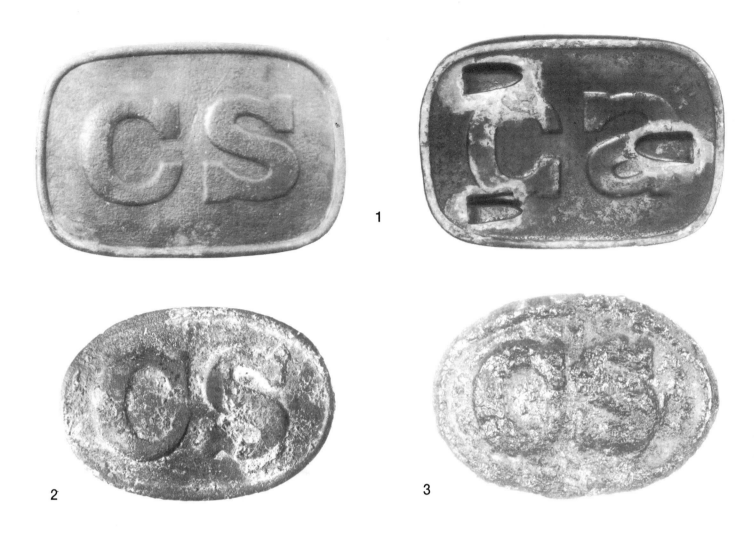

1. The so-called sardine can CS (from its shape). This is the Virginia style as it is occasionally found there. A western theater variant exists. Both are rare. 2. A solid cast plate using a stamped Breckinridge oval as a pattern. It has integral hooks, and few examples are known. 3. A sheet iron CS that was probably struck from the die that was used for the Breckinridge plate. 4. This rare cast plate is only found in the western theater. There is one star for each of the Confederate states. 5. Another very rare buckle. These are lead-filled stampings with iron wire hooks.

1. The solid cast CS buckle that saw much use in the western theater. These were strong and sturdy pieces of equipment. Variants are seen. 2. Many of these buckles have hooks that were finished out with some sort of spinning trimmer device. 3. The "line in hooks" style solid cast CS, so called because of the small cast-in lines evident on the hooks, note **No. 4**. This variant has a much thinner border and different letters. Many were delivered with the background of the face painted in black enamel to highlight the letters. 5. A rare CS oval of lead filled, sheet brass stamped from a simple die. This variety has arrowhead hooks made of copper.

1

2   3

Shown above is the most common marked Confederate buckle, and many variants exist. These are the two basic types. **1.** The large letter or Atlanta Arsenal style. Collectors believe that most of this type were made by this facility or were contracted for by them. In general, the hook pattern is common to all. **2.** The small letter or Virginia style. Many of these are also found in Tennessee. **3.** The cast pewter CSA, a less than sturdy buckle with iron wire hooks. Collectors feel that they were made in Rome, Ga. They are much rarer than the cast brass versions. **4.** The distinctive Richmond Arsenal two-piece. These feature a spoon-type tongue, and distinctive letters with a raised ring around them. **5.** The belt attachments associated with the Richmond buckle. These were all castings.

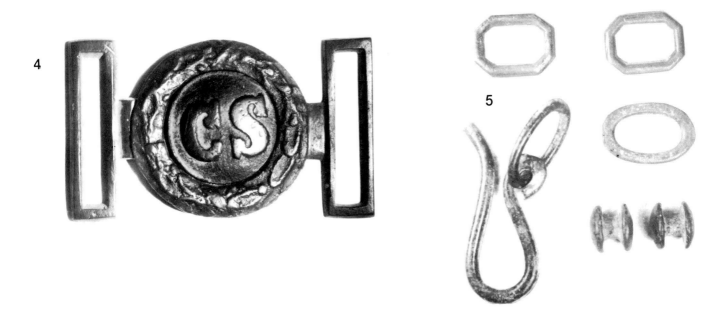

4

5

1. The "bar type" CS two-piece buckle, found in quantity and in the same areas as the Richmond type. These were the products of a fairly large Virginia manufacturer. **2.** The "serif" style buckle. This is another Virginia product and it is found with both guttered and flat back wreaths. **3.** This buckle is rare and was probably a product of the Virginia Armory and made for officers. **4.** The very rare artillery style buckle as found in Virginia. On the few known the letter position differs slightly. These items are large and heavy. **5.** An attractive buckle of fine detail and workmanship, these are attributed to the L. Haiman Co. of Columbus, Ga. **6.** This is the "coin" style buckle as used by the Army of Tennessee. Variations exist.

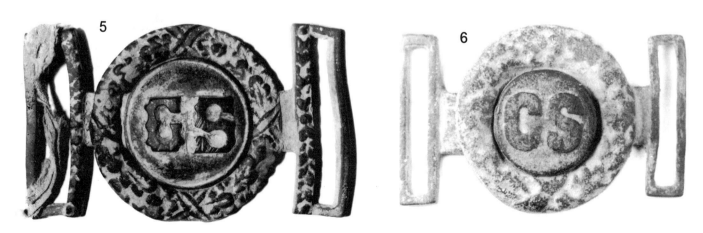

1. A very rare CS two-piece made by Leech and Rigdon (Memphis Novelty Works) to accompany some of their swords. Few of these are known and they are somewhat crudely made. **2**. Another rare piece is this left handed tongue, occasionally found in Arkansas, Missouri and Mississippi. They take a plain ring wreath.

3. This large, heavy, well made tongue was found at Brandy Station It is not normally seen in Virginia and must have belonged to a transferred trooper. **4.** By working from a hole in the back, an industrious Texan converted a small US buckle to a CS. **5.** Here the US artillery buckle has had its letters ground off and the letters "WA" engraved in their place. These were used by the Washington Artillery of New Orleans and a number of like specimens have been noted. **6.** This an extremely rare buckle and the few known were used in the Western theater.

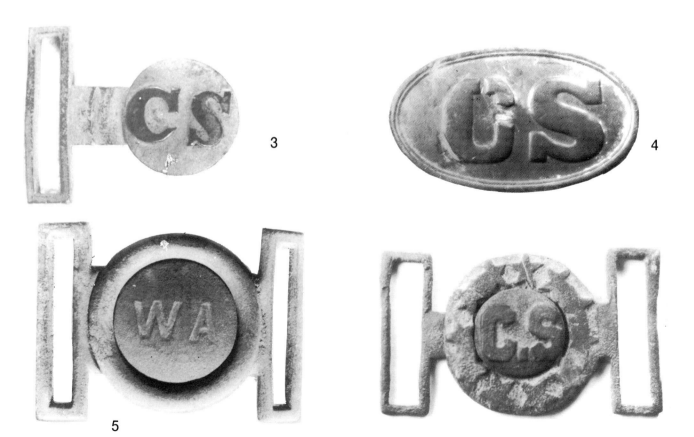

1. Belt buckle of the Alabama Volunteer Corps, the statewide militia unit formed immediately prior to the war. Of lead filled, stamped brass with stud hooks. 2. Matching cartridge box plate of similar construction. One other die variation has been noted. 3. Cast sabre belt plate bearing the state seal. Probably made by E. Gaylord, (see introduction). 4. Tongue portion of a two-piece buckle, brass with traces of gilt. 5. The rare and desirable "map on tree oval". This attractive lead filled buckle was made up in the pre-war period and few specimens are known. This one was recovered in Northern Virginia at a picket post guarding an important river ford. 6. The rarest of all southern state seal plates is this Arkansas. Of lead filled stamped brass and bearing a detailed rendition of the seal, the few noted are all belt buckles.

1. Belt buckle as issued to the Georgia militia in fairly large quantities. Stamped brass, lead filled with stud hooks. Also commonly seen as boxplates. Occasionally the latter are found arsenal-converted to buckles with wire hooks. Both are probable Gaylord products from the same die. **2**. "Georgia Militia" lead filled boxplate. These are quite uncommon and must have seen very limited usage. **3**. Shoulder belt plate of the Georgia Military Institute. Stamped brass, with pin on reverse and a rare plate. **4**. A finely made belt buckle displaying the state seal. Probably the pre-war product of a northern firm, it carries a brass belt loop and tongue on the reverse.

5. This is one of the numerous varieties of two-piece Georgia buckles known. It features a cast brass construction and a stamped center disc. Other specimens are solid cast, particularly those made during war time. **6**. Solid cast two-piece Kentucky plate bearing the state seal. This is a copy of an earlier version which was made with a stamped center disc. This style is the only known "seal plate" to originate from this state and they are rare.

1

2

1. A somewhat crude die struck plate of the Kentucky Military Institute and excavated at that site. This specimen is a belt buckle and a similar boxplate exists. **2.** A war time Louisiana state seal plate of cast brass. These two-piece plates are rare and were worn on sword belts of the pre-war era. Others will be noted of varying design and method of manufacture. **3.** This state's military organization was a large one in the pre-war era. Most of these troops were equipped with this plate, if one can judge by the number of surviving specimens. Constructed of lead filled, die struck brass with sheet brass hooks, as shown. Slight die variations will be noted in these plates.

3

A LOUISIANA "PELICAN"

Above: A Louisiana "Pelican" wearing a version of plate **No. 3.** He is well equipped with a sword, gaiters and is smoking a cigarette.

1

2

3

4

1. One of two similar die variants, this stamped brass Louisiana was not lead filled. While originally equipped with a belt loop and tongue, the soldier has field repaired this one to tie it to a belt. **2.** Of similar construction, this plate bears the initials "NO" at the bottom of the oval, designating a New Orleans unit. Another version of this buckle carries the wording "We defend our rights". **3.** The very rare "Pelican with rays " plate. Die stamped of brass without lead filling. **4.** A very rare plate with a crude rendition of the state seal. One of two specimens known. **5.** The Maryland sabre plate by Gaylord with all of that firm's design features. **6.** For the infantry, the same company also made lead filled buckles and boxplates.

5

6

Above: Men of the 9th Mississippi Regiment at Pensacola, Florida in 1861. While having no uniforms to speak of, they are well equipped with the Model 1841 rifle and standard infantry accoutrements. Two of the men are wearing state seal buckles. **1**. Oval belt buckle of the familiar Gaylord type. This fine specimen shows little use and was found at Shiloh. Also made as a boxplate. **2**. Mississippi sabre plate by the aforementioned maker, serially numbered and issued with matching numbered belt keeper. All of this state's plates are considered rare.

1   2

1. Sheet brass buckle with seamed top and bottom edges (for reinforcement), with applied pewter star. Probably worn by a pre-war Mississippi unit. **2.** The very rare, lead filled brass North Carolina buckle. These plates carry stud hooks on the reverse. **3.** The famous 6th North Carolina buckle. Cast of solid brass, it featured fragile, soldered-on belt hooks that frequently pulled loose. Supposedly they were cast in the railroad shops at Raleigh, N.C. It is the only CS regimental plate. **4.** Two-piece North Carolina buckle. These are made like the more common CS two-piece and were affixed to the same type of sword belt but are very rare.

5. Large oval South Carolina buckle. Conventionally made of stamped brass with a lead fill and stud hooks. **6.** Small oval SC buckle made as the former but with single "arrowhead" hook. A similar medium size buckle is also known. Some boxplates of the large pattern exist. All of the foregoing items were issued to the state's large militia organization.

1. Shoulder belt plate displaying the South Carolina seal. They are also seen with buckle hooks. Issued to the pre-war militia in some quantity. **2**. Stamped brass buckle displaying a fairly crude die design. **3**. Large "panel" plate, These buckles saw widespread use and many die variations will be noted. This foliate bordered design dates back to the 1840's and was popular with designers of military plates. **4**. Two-piece of cast brass with stamped center disc, heavily gilted. Many variations exist of these plates. **5**. Another two-piece as found with belt adjuster and remains of belt. **6**. An extremely rare buckle, the "Southern Confederacy" two-piece. Nothing is known of this plate; it is included here because of the palmetto motif. One non dug specimen was noted years ago. The one shown was recently excavated in central Virginia.

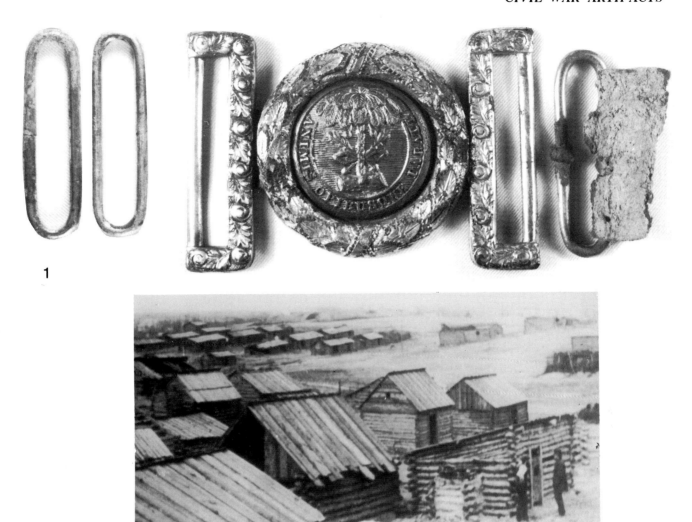

1. One of the most impressive finds in recent years is the buckle shown above.   This is a South Carolina two-piece of the 1840's and is heavily silvered.   Shown as found with belt attachments, adjuster and leather remnants.   It was no doubt the property of a Colonel or General Officer, and was found at Centreville, Va. Nearly this whole area, once the sight of extensive camps and well preserved fortifications, was bulldozed in the late 1980's for shopping centers and townhouses.   The above piece was taken just ahead of the heavy equipment.   **Center:** The famous Brady photograph of the Confederate winter huts at Centreville, taken just after the Union troops occupied the area in March of 1862.

2. The sheet brass "V S" buckle.   These are attributed to Tennessee, the "Volunteer State".   They were made in an unusual way, indicative of a small shop production.   Each letter was hand struck from the reverse and letter registration differs from plate to plate.   They are very rare and no other marked plate is associated with that state.

1

2

Two rare plates and a rare image. This young Texas private wears a waistbelt fastened by a plate bearing a lone star. **1**. A true Texas buckle, this specimen is struck in brass from an extremely crude die. It is lead filled with hooks of heavy iron wire. These are found in Texas camps and were probably fabricated in that state in the early days of the war. **2**. "Lined star" buckle of stamped brass with brass hooks. Another plate seeing genuine Texas usage, and there is some indication that they date back to the Mexican war.

1

2

1. Cast brass Virginia sabre belt plate displaying the state seal on a lined field. They are probably products of the famous Gaylord firm dating to about 1858 or 1859. They are serially numbered on the back with a matching keeper. Used by the Virginia Cavalry throughout the war. Most in existence are excavated, indicating the hard war time use that they were put to. 2. The "Virginia in arc" plate of cast brass. It carries a medium width tongue on the back and most are marked with a one or two digit serial number. At least two different design variations are noted. The specific usage of these plates is unknown.

3

4

3. Large, ornate, stamped brass two-piece buckle. It is of sturdy construction: the various pieces are soldered together and silver plated. Its ornate design dates it to the 1830's. 4. A war-time, solid cast brass two-piece. Many variations of the two-piece plate were used by the state. **Inset:** Two soldiers, probably brothers. The man on left wears a two-piece Virginia plate.

Note: All of the plates on this page were utilized with the showy white web belting of the pre Civil War period. They are all of thin stamped brass with belt attachments soft soldered to the reverse. As such they were not suited to field service.   **1**. The very rare round breastplate displaying the Virginia seal. This is one of two die variants known, both having a pin on the reverse. One lead filled waistbelt plate has been noted.   **2.** The "thick" style buckle. Some few of these were made as boxplates. **3.** The widely used "thin" buckle made by James S. Smith and Sons, New York and so marked on the tongue.   **Nos. 4&5**. Needing a large number of plates quickly, the state turned to the use of these plain brass belt and shoulder beltplates respectively. The buckle **No. 4** is the most commonly seen Confederate used plate and saw some use with states other than Virginia. They are commonly called "sheet brass buckles" or "clipped corners".

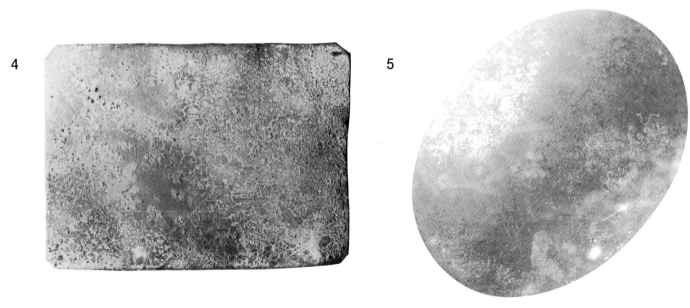

Nos. 1&2. The "clipped corner" provided a ready surface for the pocket knife or engraving tool. 2. Marked "W.L. Higdon No. 36". 3. Cartridge box plate as used by the Virginia Military Institute. These are rare items that date to the 1840's. Made of stamped brass crimped over an iron back, they are occasionally found in Virginia campsites. 4. The "Mount Vernon Guard" was an Alexandria, Va. militia unit. This plate dates to the 1850's. 5. The cast brass shoulder belt plate of the "1st Regiment of Virginia Vols" a large unit from the Richmond area. 6. The somewhat crude belt buckle of the Young Guard, also of Richmond.

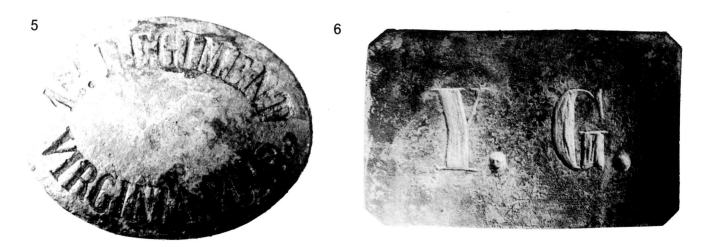

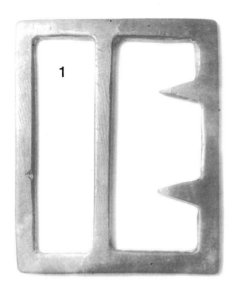
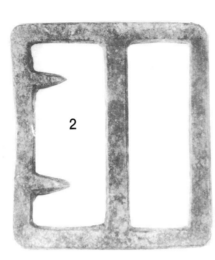
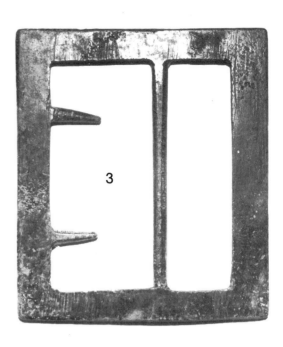

Nos.1,2,3&5. Confederate general issue frame buckles. These belt buckles were supplied with contract sets of infantry equipment by the thousands. There are many variants in style, size and quality.The reverse of some are "guttered out for strength and conservation of metal. **No.1** is the "beveled edge" style and **No.2** is a variant. **No.3** is known as the "standard" style. **No. 5** is the "heavy thick" style. Note that years ago, when these buckles again began seeing the light of day, they were often thought to be some type of harness buckle.

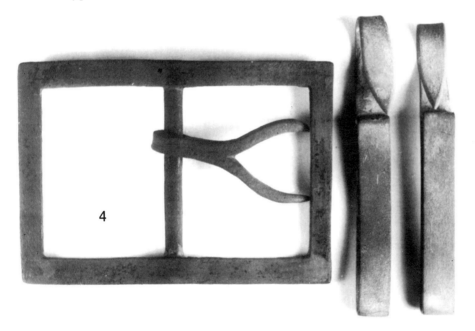
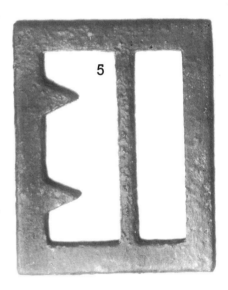

No. 4. The "snake tongue or wishbone" buckle. This combination (found together) is a great rarity. Some unknown Southern contractor furnished a belt with shoulder support straps like the pre-war US Rifleman's belt and buckle assembly. The two hook belt slides flanked the buckle in wear. **6.** A very crude CS roller buckle. It is made of heavy iron wire, painted black with a sheet lead 'roller'. These were issued on a tarred cotton infantry belt with a leather tongue. Showing how hard pressed the Confederates were, this specimen was found in an early 1863 camp.

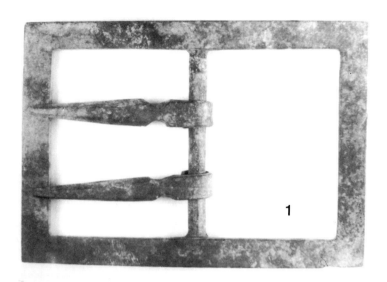

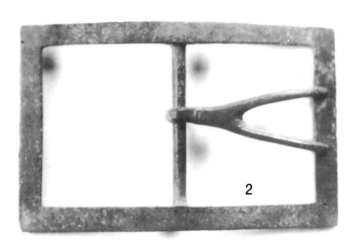

1. The rare double tongued frame buckle. These appear to be the products of one specific maker and are large and well finished. **Nos. 2,3&4**. Fork tongue frame buckles varying in size and quality of finish. These were furnished on contract with sets of infantry equipment. Many thousands of these sets were furnished to the Confederate government.

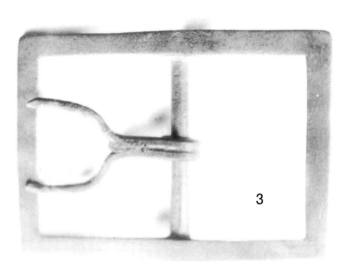

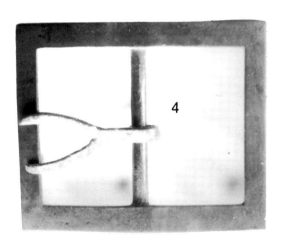

3. This buckle is fitted with an unusual wire tongue that is probably a replacement. **4.** This size buckle is very rare. It is theorized that they were issued with a sword belt and referred to as the "cavalry size". **5.** A CS nondescript buckle, well made of cast brass. These were also general issue and will be noted in period photographs. They were produced in numerous variations.

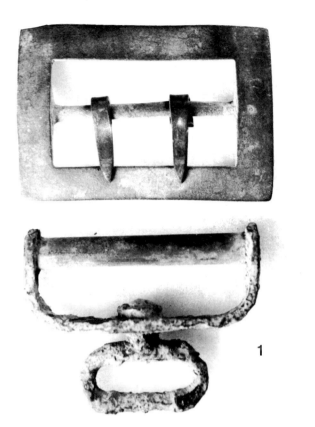

Some of the rarer CS buckles are those shown above. They are carbine sling buckles, modeled loosely after their Union counterparts. **1.** This is the most frequently noted and is a thin casting with hand trimmed sheet brass tongues. Found with it was the strap swivel, again quite a variation from the US article. The small loop took an iron hook. **2.** A heavy thick casting, quite crude in finish, it was dug at Mine Run, Va. **3.** An unusual variant roughly finished on the reverse but smooth on the face. It was found near Harrisonburg Va. Note that the CS manufacture of carbines utilizing sling bars and rings was minimal.

Right: A Confederate cavalryman, by artist Allen C. Redwood

1

2

1. Almost nothing substantive is known about this plate. The few found have come from CS occupied points and their construction suggests Southern manufacture. **2**. A sheet brass buckle has been mated with the cut out device of a Federal breastplate. Done in the field, it was probably the work of a Southern craftsman.

3

4

3. This is an unusual variant of the "two-piece star" belt buckle. Note the filled in right side of wreath. It is conceded that these sword belt plates were worn by officers of both Texas and Mississippi. **4**. This two-piece sash buckle displays a square rigged ship. Such oddities (for an inland infantry camp) almost always show up on CS sites where all manner of military equipment was pressed into use. **5**. From the Western theater of war, this small belt buckle is attributed to the "Ringgold Militia". **6**. Tongue portion of a US Model 1852 naval officer's two-piece buckle. From a Confederate hutsite, it was another captured or handed-down piece that went to war.

5

6

1. A great example of the die maker's art is this stamped brass lead filled buckle, used by an unknown pre-war militia unit. The few found have come from Confederate camps, primarily in Virginia. **2.** The "oval V" buckle. A medium sized plate with iron wire hooks set in lead, most likely made for the US Voltiguers, a Mexican War unit. Very scarce, but noted with a Virginia troop association. **3.** A plain counterpart of the US "eagle" plate, this specimen was made by the New York firm of R. Dingee. It is so marked on the reverse and was used by the Virginia dragoon units of the pre-war era. **4.** One of a few like specimens, this heavy brass buckle was probably used by the "Hibernia Rifles" of South Carolina. **5.** A plain two-piece buckle found in the Western theater of war. These plates are attributed to the Tennessee firm of Leech and Rigdon. **6.** A field repaired sheet brass buckle, inscribed "C.W. Brooks 13th Tenn".

6 *"EARLY & LATE"*

Colonial: In a number of cases, Civil War sites will overlay an earlier one. All of the above are the typical remnants of colonial housesites as found some two hundred years later. Such sites are common in the eastern US, whether intact and overgrown with woods or lying exposed in a plowed cornfield. **1.** A broken candlestick, a clay pipe stem, two clay marbles, broken shoe buckles and the ever present flat buttons. **2.** The common surface indicators of old habitation: fragments of dishes, crockery and an oyster shell.

3. A European sword of the early colonial period, probably French or Spanish, which no doubt could tell a grim tale. It was found near the site of a period Indian village and may have been taken on one of their raids on an early settlement. **4.** A patriotic button, one of many popular at the time. **Nos. 5&6.** George Washington inaugural buttons. Other varieties exist. **7.** A solid cast pewter navy button. **8.** A very ornate silver plated brass button with a pierced design. **9.** The ever present lead hem weight, a common find.

1

1. The shoulder belt plate of Colonel Joshua Frye who was in command of the Virginia Volunteers during the French and Indian War. He was killed on campaign and George Washington, one of his officers, carved a short eulogy on the tree that marked his grave. This plate was found in a field where Frye's plantation house once stood in Essex Co., Va. The plate was cast with integral hooks to crimp through the leather and the face engraved. This type construction is typical of the 1700's.

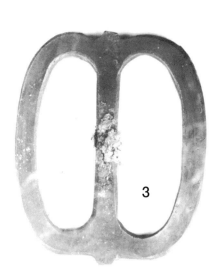

2

3

4

2. A very heavy cast brass sword sling buckle. By their bulk alone the civilian usage of such buckles can be eliminated. **3.** A "figure 8" buckle of cast brass that was often used on the infantry waist and shoulder belts of the Revolutionary War period. **4.** A silver plated civilian shoe buckle. These are frequent finds on period sites.

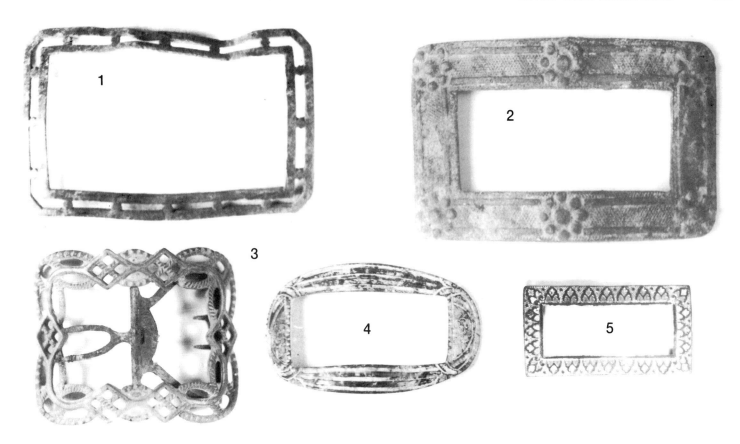

Nos. 1 through 4. These are all shoe buckles. Most often they are made of cast brass but occasionally of pewter. Silver plating is common and there are many varieties. Their double tongue design seems to have been the origin of the later CS wishbone or forked tongue buckle. **5.** This smaller, heavily plated buckle was probably worn at the knee.

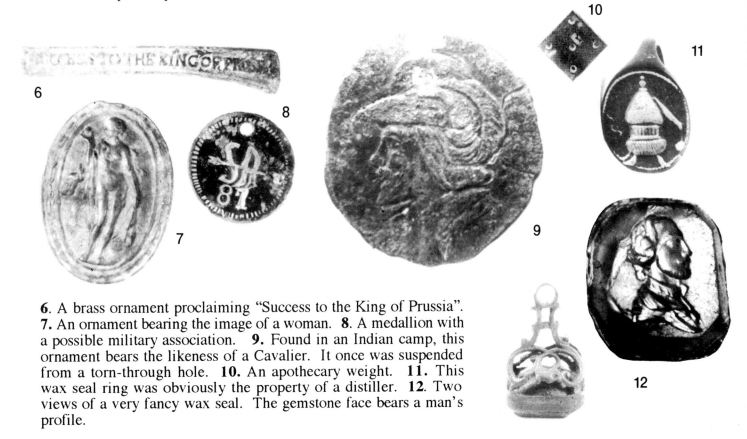

6. A brass ornament proclaiming "Success to the King of Prussia". **7.** An ornament bearing the image of a woman. **8.** A medallion with a possible military association. **9.** Found in an Indian camp, this ornament bears the likeness of a Cavalier. It once was suspended from a torn-through hole. **10.** An apothecary weight. **11.** This wax seal ring was obviously the property of a distiller. **12.** Two views of a very fancy wax seal. The gemstone face bears a man's profile.

Above: A grouping of items found in Revolutionary War period US camps in New York State. Shown are issue screwdrivers, a gun wrench, a pocket knife, a belt axe, two forks, a flintlock hammer and a piece of a bayonet. **1.** Furniture brasses of various types. **2.** A bit boss. **3.** A chunk of iron slag from an early furnace. **4.** A token, probably denoting five cents, found at an old plantation site owned by a family named Anderson.

"Late": -The standard term used to describe anything post-war. Almost anywhere Civil War period items are found there is often an overlay of these items, and often military in nature. 1860's battle and maneuver areas have been used for training by Army and Marine troops right up to the present, and of course Civil War veterans often visited the old camp or battlefield. Troops in the western US, during the Indian Wars, were still using Civil War materiel. By the early 1870's new patterns of equipment were appearing and a mixture of the two would be expected. On some button patterns the backmark is the only way to tell the late specimens.

1. A corn knife found on the Salem Church Battlefield. It is a simple blacksmith-made piece about 18" long. These are often found. **2.** A US Model 1872 Hagner plate, found in a Texas camp area near Dumfries, Va. These occasionally turn up, along with others bearing the state initials instead of the US.

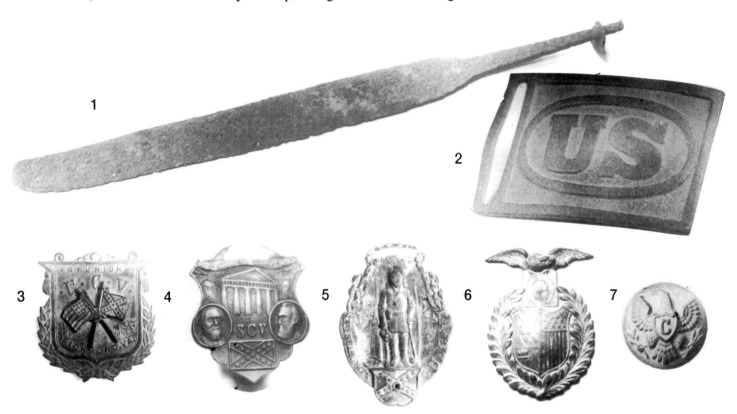

3. A "UCV" (United Confederate Veterans) pin, from a Richmond 1907 Reunion. Found at Mechanicsville, outside of Richmond. **4.** An SCV (Sons of Confederate Veterans) pin, with faces of Jackson and Lee. **5.** CS veteran's pin. **6.** A very well made pin backmarked "Tiffany", displaying the New York state seal. **7.** Post-war button with an <u>applied</u> eagle.

8. A fly button marked "US Army" with stars. WW2 period but little different from the Civil War version. **9.** 1870's period side device as used on helmets. In general the crossed rifle motif was not used until after the Civil War. **10.** The often found 20th century US button. This device is called the "Great Seal" and is used on numerous insignia. This specific design originated in 1902 although the basic design dates to the 1700's. **11.** Model 1872 enlisted crossed sabres, smaller than Civil War period type. **12.** Gold washed officer's collar ornament ca. 1917, found in a Virginia troop camp.

THE PRESERVATION OF ARTIFACTS

The proper preservation of excavated artifacts is of utmost importance to the historian. In some cases the recovered artifact may remain physically stable with minimal attention; in others it may start an immediate degrade. The two critical factors here are the material (or materials) of which the artifact is made and the type and condition of soil the artifact is recovered from.

For example, when found in the typical woods, bronze-brass alloys will have developed a protective patina which varies from brown to green and should not be removed. When this type of artifact has been recovered from a fertilized field, a thicker green encrustation may be present and the underlying surface pitted or eroded.

Lead items suffer time in the ground easily. They will develop a thick white oxidation under almost all conditions. Bullets however, when dumped in quantities of loaded cartridges will often be eroded by the action of the decaying powder. Pewter, a varying alloy of lead and tin does not usually hold up as well. In many cases such artifacts will be in a rough, porous, and brittle state.

Ferrous artifacts will of course be in a rusted condition. In some cases this rust may be thin, hard and the underlying metal in a stable condition. When found in a low lying wet area the rust may be far more advanced, and when in a coastal salt water situation the artifact may be in an advanced state of degrade.

Note that the following preservation techniques must be viewed in light of the condition of the newly excavated specimen. Some fragile 'field' buttons may only survive the most minimal cleaning. A Bowie knife may be so heavily rusted that only a slight amount of core steel remains. Further note that the over cleaning of any coin, button, plate, ID tag etc. can result in a great loss of value!

Brass: These artifacts should be soaked in a water diluted solution of soapy ammonia (five parts water to one ammonia) for a few minutes and cleaned with a toothbrush. This will bring out any gilt or silver but note that too long a soaking may start to lift it off. Diluted lemon juice is even stronger and should be used with care and frequently checked. Field items with a heavy green crust can be soaked in diluted vegetable oil and ammonia, then brushed. All items should be given a thorough final cleaning in warm water to completely flush away all traces of cleaning solution.

Lead and pewter: Lead items need only the first water-ammonia treatment. Pewter is treated the same way but with far more close attention and minimal brushing. Note that delicate items like pewter buttons should be handled with care in all situations.

Ferrous items: Rust may be carefully cleaned away with a hand held wire brush and chipped out of cavities with an ice pick. The item is then cleaned with solvent and wiped down with a satin finish varnish. This basic technique will apply only to sound relics from "dry" ground. Note that the stabilization of iron items is a science within itself, particularly with regard to shells, and any items from salt water conditions. Here the electrolysis process is often used to completely neutralize the rust. It is fully described in the book *Field Artillery Projectiles of the American Civil War*, by Thomas S. Dickey and Peter C. George.

Silver: Coins and silverware are often untouched by ground action and need only to be cleaned in soap and water. Such items should never be brushed or dry rubbed in the field as the dirt will scratch them. Note that some coins are quite valuable, and the former practice will greatly lessen their value.

Glass: A careful soaking in soapy water and a thorough brushing is indicated here. This subject is well covered in *The Collector's Guide to Civil War Period Bottles and Jars*, by Mike Russell.

Leather, Wood and Water Recoveries: In most cases the two former items can be cleaned and preserved as they would be in a non-dug condition. For a complete overview of the preservation techniques used in underwater recovery the following book is invaluable; *The Blockade Runner Modern Greece and Her Cargo*, by Leslie S. Bright of the North Carolina Department of Cultural Resources.

BIBLIOGRAPHY

Albaugh, William A., III, and Edward N. Simmons, "Confederate Arms," the Stackpole Company, Harrisburg, Pa., 1957.

Albert, Alphaeus H., "Record of American Uniforms and Historical Buttons with Supplement, 1775-1973," Alphaeus H. Albert, Hightstown, N. J., 1973.

Bazelon, Bruce S. and William F. McGuinn, "A Directory of American Military Goods, Dealers and Makers, 1785-1885," REF Typesetting and Publishing, Inc., Manassas, Va., 1987.

Bright, Leslie S., "The Blockade Runner, Modern Greece," Archeology Section, Division of Archives and History, North Carolina Department of Cultural Resources, Raleigh, N.C., June 1977.

Campbell, J. Duncan and Edgar M. Howell, "American Military Insignia 1800-1851," Museum of History and Technology, Smithsonian Institution, Washington, D. C., 1963.

Coates, Earl J. and Dean S. Thomas, "An Introduction to Civil War Small Arms," Thomas Publications, Gettysburg, Pa., 1990.

Crouch, Howard R., "Relic Hunter, The Field Account of Civil War Sites, Artifacts and Hunting," SCS Publications, Third Printing, 1988.

Dammann, Dr. Gordon, "Pictorial Encyclopedia of Civil War Medical Instruments and Equipment," Pictorial Histories Publishing Co., Missoula, Montana, 1983.

Dickey, Thomas S. and Peter C. George, "Field Artillery Projectiles of the American Civil War, Revised and Supplemented 1993 Edition," Arsenal Publications II, Mechanicsville, Va.

Edwards, William B., "Civil War Guns, The Complete Story of Federal and Confederate Small Arms: design, manufacture, identification, procurement, issue, employment, effectiveness, and postwar disposal," The Stackpole Co., Harrisburg, Pa., 1962.

Flayderman, Norm, "Flayderman's Guide to Antique American Firearms... and Their Values," DBI Books, Inc., Northfield, Illinois, 1977.

Gavin, William G., "Accoutrement Plates, North and South, 1861-1865," Riling and Lentz, Philadelphia, Pa., 1963.

Hardin, Albert N., Jr., "The American Bayonet, 1776-1964," Albert H. Hardin, Jr., Pennsauken, N. J., 1964.

Harris, Charles S., "Civil War Relics of the Western Campaigns, 1861-1865," Rapidan Press, Mechanicsville, Va., 1987.

Kerksis, Sydney C., "Plates and Buckles of the American Military 1795-1874," The Gilgal Press, Kennesaw, Georgia, 1974

Melton, Jack W. and Lawrence E. Pawl, Introduction to Field Artillery of the Civil War, 1861-1865 Kennesaw Mountain Press, Kennesaw, Ga. 1994

McKee, W. Reid and M. E. Mason, Jr., "Civil War Projectiles II, Small Arms and Field Artillery with Supplement," Moss Publications.

Mullinax, Steve E., "Confederate Belt Buckles and Plates," O'Donnell Publications, Alexandria, Va., 1991.

North South Trader Magazine, P.O. Drawer 631, Orange, Va., various volumes.

Peterson, Harold L., "The American Sword 1775-1945," Ray Riling Arms Books Co., Philadelphia, Pa., 1970.

Phillips, Stanley S., "Civil War Corps Badges and Other Related Awards, Badges, Medals of the Period," S. S. Phillips, Lanham, Md., 1982.

Russell, Mike, "The Collector's Guide to Civil War Period Bottles and Jars," Russell Publications, Herndon, Va. 1988.

Shaffer, James B., Lee Rutledge, R. Stephen Dorsey, "Gun Tools, Their History and Identification," Collectors' Library, Eugene, Ore., 1992.

Steffan, Randy, "The Horse Soldier 1776-1943, The United States Cavalryman: His Uniforms, Arms, Accoutrements and Equipments, Vol. I, The Revolution, the War of 1812, the Early Frontier 1776-1850." University of Oklahoma Press, Norman and London.

Steffan, Randy, "The Horse Soldier 1776-1943, The United States Cavalryman: His Uniforms, Arms, Accoutrements and Equipments, Vol. II, The Frontier, the Mexican War, the Civil War, the Indian Wars 1851-1880," University of Oklahoma Press, Norman, 1979.

Sylvia, Stephan W. and Michael J. O'Donnell, "Civil War Canteens," Moss Publications, Orange, Va. 1990.

Todd, Frederick P., "American Military Equipage 1851-1872, Vol. I," The Company of Military Historians, Providence, R. I., 1974.

STATE SEAL IDENTIFICATION GUIDE

SEALS SHOWN ARE THOSE USED DURING THE CIVIL WAR PERIOD

ALABAMA   ARKANSAS   CONNECTICUT   FLORIDA

GEORGIA   KENTUCKY   LOUISIANA   MAINE

MARYLAND   MASSACHUSETTS   MICHIGAN   MISSISSIPPI

MISSOURI   NEW HAMPSHIRE   NEW JERSEY   NEW YORK

NORTH CAROLINA   PENNSYLVANIA   RHODE ISLAND   SOUTH CAROLINA

TENNESSEE   TEXAS   VERMONT   VIRGINIA

INDEX

Top: Spring 1865. Taken amid the muddy trenches and gun positions of the Petersburg line, this photo shows three of its stalwart Confederate defenders, dead where they fell.

Bottom: Some few years after the war, a child would lose this brass cannon in the trenches outside of the same city. No doubt it once looked out over the same Union positions at one time commanded by Confederate cannon. Found in the late 1980's.